SAT* BIOLOGY E/M
CRASH COURSE™

By Lauren Gross, Ph.D.

Research & Education Association
Visit our website at: www.rea.com

Research & Education Association
61 Ethel Road West
Piscataway, New Jersey 08854
E-mail: info@rea.com

SAT BIOLOGY E/M CRASH COURSE™

Library of Congress Control Number 2012932838

ISBN-13: 978-0-7386-1033-7
ISBN-10: 0-7386-1033-X

SAT BIOLOGY E/M CRASH COURSE™ TABLE OF CONTENTS

PART I **Introduction**

PART II **Cellular and Molecular Biology**

PART III **Ecology**

ABOUT THIS BOOK

REA's *SAT Biology E/M Crash Course* is the first book of its kind for the last-minute studier or any student who wants a quick refresher on the material covered on the test. The book will provide you with an accurate and complete representation of the SAT Biology E/M Subject Test.

Written by a veteran biology teacher, our easy-to-read format gives students a crash course in biology. The targeted review chapters prepare students for the exam by focusing only on the important topics that will be tested on the SAT Biology E/M Subject Test.

Unlike other test preps, REA's *SAT Biology E/M Crash Course* gives you a review specifically focused on what you really need to study in order to ace the exam. The review chapters provide a concise way to learn all the important facts, terms, and key topics before the exam.

The introduction discusses the keys to your success on the test and teaches you strategies to help build your overall score. Also included is an overview of the three different types of questions you will encounter on the SAT Biology E/M Subject Test.

Each review chapter presents the essential information you need to know about biology and includes Test Tips designed to help you attain the highest score on the SAT Biology E/M Subject Test.

To check your test readiness for the Biology-E (Ecological) and Biology-M (Molecular) Subject Tests, either before or after studying this *Crash Course*, take REA's **FREE online practice exam**. To access your free online practice exam, visit *www.rea.com/studycenter* and choose the practice test that reflects the version of the Biology Subject Test you're taking.

Our true-to-format practice test features automatic scoring, and detailed explanations of all answers, which will help you identify your strengths and weaknesses so you'll be ready on exam day!

No matter how or when you prepare for the SAT Biology Subject Test, REA's *Crash Course* will show you how to study efficiently and strategically, so you can boost your score.

Good luck on your SAT Biology E/M Test!

ABOUT OUR AUTHOR

Lauren Gross currently teaches Advanced Placement Biology to homeschooled children in the United States and abroad for Pennsylvania Homeschoolers, where she is also a home education evaluator. Throughout her teaching and research career she has taught a wide range of students from elementary through graduate levels, including preparing students for the SAT Biology Test. As assistant professor at Loyola College in Maryland, she taught General Biology, General Genetics, Molecular Genetics, Cell and Molecular Biology, and Botany. She holds a B.S. in Biology from Dickinson College and a Ph.D. in Plant Physiology from Pennsylvania State University.

ACKNOWLEDGMENTS

In addition to our author, we would like to thank Larry B. Kling, Vice President, Editorial, for his overall guidance, which brought this publication to completion; Pam Weston, Publisher, for setting the quality standards for production integrity and managing the publication to completion; Alice Leonard, Senior Editor, for editorial project management; and Diane Goldschmidt, Managing Editor; and Mel Friedman, Lead Math Editor, for preflight editorial review.

We also extend our special thanks to S4Carlisle Publishing Services for production services.

PART I:
INTRODUCTION

KEYS FOR SUCCESS ON THE ──── SAT BIOLOGY E/M SUBJECT TEST

OVERVIEW OF THE SAT BIOLOGY E/M SUBJECT TEST

WHY DO STUDENTS TAKE THE SAT BIOLOGY E/M SUBJECT TEST?

Some colleges require or recommend that students take the test for admission to the college, or to specific majors and special programs. If you plan to attend college, performing well on the SAT Biology E/M Subject Test can enhance your application by demonstrating your proficiency in biology. The test is highly recommended for any student who wants to strengthen his or her college application, as well as homeschooled and other nontraditional students who wish to independently demonstrate academic achievement.

WHAT COURSE WORK IS RECOMMENDED PRIOR TO TAKING THE TEST?

The test is typically taken after a one-year college-preparatory biology course, preferably with laboratory experience, and a one-year course in algebra. Although prior study in these courses is the essential foundation of your knowledge, intimate familiarity with the testing format, the specific content and skills required, and the types of questions used on the test is essential for a successful outcome.

WHO ADMINISTERS THE TEST AND WHERE IS IT GIVEN?

The SAT Biology E/M Subject Test is produced by the College Board and administered by Educational Testing Service (ETS). Testing sites are located throughout the United States, usually in high schools. Ask your guidance counselor for additional information or visit the College Board website at **sat.collegeboard.org** for test locations, fees, and required preregistration.

WHEN IS IT BEST TO TAKE THE TEST?

Generally it is best to take the SAT Biology E/M Subject Test as soon as possible after you have taken your biology course, and after you have conducted a thorough review and familiarized yourself with the test format by taking a number of practice tests under the same conditions as the actual test. In deciding when to take the test, be aware of the application deadlines of the colleges to which you will apply. Double-check those deadlines and then coordinate a testing date that works best for you by visiting the College Board website at the URL provided earlier.

DO I NEED TO BRING A CALCULATOR TO THE TEST?

No. Calculators are not allowed or necessary to take this test. Units of measure are in the metric system.

·FORMAT OF THE SAT BIOLOGY E/M SUBJECT TEST

WHAT IS THE FORMAT OF THE TEST AND HOW MUCH TIME IS ALLOTTED?

There are two forms of the test for Biology: Ecological (Biology-E) and Molecular (Biology-M). Each test has a common core of 60 multiple-choice questions. The test you choose will then branch off to present 20 additional multiple-choice questions concentrating on the respective specialized subject matter. You may take both of these tests, but NOT on the same day. Each test must be completed in 60 minutes. Because biology is such a broad discipline, the two alternative tests allow you to choose the area in which you have more familiarity. Choose Biology-E if your strengths are in the areas of **ecology** and **evolution & diversity**. Choose Biology-M if your strengths are in the areas of **cellular & molecular biology** and **genetics**. If you are not sure, ask your teacher which area was more emphasized in the biology course you took.

Ecological
20 questions

Common Core: 60 multiple-choice questions

Molecular Biology
20 questions

WHAT TOPICS ARE COVERED ON THE TEST?

The major topics covered on the SAT Biology E/M Subject Test, and the comparative percentages of emphasis on both versions of the test, are shown in the following table. Further details for each major topic can be found in the Table of Contents.

Major Topics Covered on the SAT Biology E/M Subject Test

Major Topic	Biology-E Test Approximate %	Biology-M Test Approximate %
CELLULAR & MOLECULAR BIOLOGY	15%	27%
ECOLOGY	23%	13%
GENETICS	15%	20%
ORGANISMAL BIOLOGY	25%	25%
EVOLUTION & DIVERSITY	22%	15%

WHAT TYPES OF QUESTIONS ARE ON THE TEST?

There are three main types of question on the SAT Biology E/M Subject Test, and they are present in approximately equal numbers. As you complete the practice tests offered by REA, you will become very familiar with each type of question and the different forms they take on the SAT Biology E/M Subject Test.

1. Factual Recall. This type of question asks you to recall a fact. These include matching terms with definitions, matching organisms with characteristics, matching items with their correct descriptions or functions, labeling a figure, etc. A question may use a matching format or an item with five possible answers—only one of which is correct. The content sections of this book will equip you with a valuable store of information to answer these questions.

2. Concept. This type of question asks you to apply a concept in order to answer the question. Examples include working out an inheritance problem in order to determine the ratio of offspring, identifying a similarity or difference between two or more processes, groups, etc., or evaluating the BEST example of a general principle. The clearly explained concepts presented in the content sections of this book will provide you with the background necessary to answer these questions.

3. Analysis. This type of question asks you to analyze and evaluate a set of facts, a situation, a diagram, a set of data, a graph, or an experimental design in order to draw a reasonable conclusion. In these types of questions, you are presented with information and you generally use two main tools to transform that information in some way to reach a sound conclusion: 1) application of the correct concept combined with 2) logical thinking. You often need to be able to read graphs accurately or to construct graphs from raw data. These questions, whether part of a multi-question set, or a single, stand-alone question, take the longest time of all three types to answer because it takes time to read and analyze the information. The skills you will develop and hone by doing a large number of these questions on our practice tests will allow you to approach these types of questions with confidence and arrive at correct conclusions more rapidly.

HOW TO USE THIS BOOK

Step 1: Familiarize yourself with the topics covered on the test. Read through the content-related portions of this book (Chapters 2 to 21) to familiarize yourself with the topics covered on the test. It is not necessary to study the material in depth on your first reading. Your goal should be to refresh your memory of the content you learned in your biology course, and to note any content that may be new to you.

Step 2: Take either the full-length Bio-E or Bio-M practice test provided by REA. You'll have a choice to practice for Biology-E or Biology-M. Biology-E presents more questions on biological communities, populations, and energy flow. Biology-M stresses biochemistry, cellular structure and processes, such as respiration and photosynthesis. Access the practice tests at the online REA Study Center at www.rea.com/studycenter. Find a comfortable, quiet place to work, with no notes or source materials, and allow yourself 60 minutes to take the test.

Step 3: Evaluate topics for further study. Use the answer key to score your test. For each question you did not answer correctly, mark the specific content area to which it relates in the Table of Contents. For additional help identifying the correct topic to which the question refers, read the answer explanation provided with REA's practice tests.

Step 4: Study the topics you have identified. Locate the appropriate content, and study that material in depth using the outline and figures. The answer explanations in our practice tests provide additional help in understanding difficult concepts.

Step 5: Work on analysis skills. Use the "Special Skills for Experiment-Based Questions" (Chapter 22) to review and strengthen your analytical skills.

Step 6: Use your practice test to prepare optimally for the actual test. Follow up your thorough content review by retaking the practice exam at the online REA Study Center. Doing so will allow you to simulate the specific conditions of the SAT Biology E/M Subject Test.

FIRST READ-THROUGH

- Read the first question carefully; read all the answer choices; re-read when necessary for clarification.
- Eliminate all wrong answer choices and cross off their lead-letter (A, B, C, D, or E) with a slash.
- Decide on the right answer choice and then fill in the correct oval for that question.
- If you can't eliminate all the answer choices on this first read-through, write down the question's number on your scrap paper, and skip its space on the answer grid.
- Swiftly, but carefully, work on the rest of the questions in order.
- Periodically check to make sure you are keeping your proper place on the answer grid, and to see how much time you have left.

Second Read-Through

- When you come to the end of the test, do a second read-through. Start from the beginning and work only on the questions you left blank on the first read-through.

Final Read-Through

- If you have completed the test and time remains, check over your work to make sure you haven't made any avoidable errors, such as filling in the wrong oval for any question you answered.

SHOULD I GUESS IF I DON'T KNOW THE ANSWER?

The questions on the SAT Biology E/M Subject Test are ordered so that the questions which are the shortest to read and answer come first. All questions are worth the same: 1 point. Also, you receive 1 point for each correct answer, you lose 1/4 point for each incorrect answer, and you receive no points for each question you leave blank. There are five answer choices for each question. For these reasons, you should definitely do the following:

- Attempt each question in order.
- Take your best guess at any question for which you can eliminate even ONE wrong answer choice.
- Leave any question blank for which you can not eliminate at least one wrong answer choice.

SCORING THE SAT BIOLOGY E/M SUBJECT TEST

The SAT Biology E/M Subject Test, like all SAT Subject Tests, is scored on a 200–800 scale.

HOW DO I SCORE MY PRACTICE TEST?

Your exam is scored by crediting one point for each correct answer and deducting one-fourth of a point for each incorrect answer. There is no deduction for answers that are omitted. Use the worksheet below to calculate your raw score and to record your scores for the practice test you take (Biology-E or Biology-M). To determine your scaled score, you will need to use the score conversion chart for the SAT Biology E/M.

The score conversion chart changes from test to test, but a good estimate for raw score to scaled score ranges is as follows:

Raw Score	Scaled Score
78 to 80	800
61 to 77	700 to 790
47 to 60	600 to 690

(continued)

Raw Score	Scaled Score
30 to 46	500 to 590
14 to 29	400 to 490
−4 to 13	300 to 390
−14 to −5	200 to 290

SCORING WORKSHEET

_____ — (_____ × 1/4) = _____

number correct | number incorrect (do not include unanswered questions) | Raw Score (round to nearest whole point)

	Raw Score	Scaled Score
Test 1 Biology-E	_____	_____
Test 2 Biology-M	_____	_____

WHAT TO DO AS TEST DAY APPROACHES

WHAT SHOULD I DO THE WEEK BEFORE THE TEST?

Briefly re-read the content chapters of this book, paying particular attention to italicized words and phrases, and retake the online practice exam accessible at the REA Study Center. Make sure you know where the test is to be given, and how to get into the building. Make sure you have the materials listed below.

WHAT SHOULD I DO THE DAY BEFORE THE TEST?

Do not study. Exercise. Do something healthy and enjoyable. Don't worry. Get a good night's sleep. Be sure to gather the following materials together:

- Your admission ticket
- An acceptable photo ID (visit the College Board website at www.collegeboard.org for a list of acceptable IDs and get your ID in hand well in advance of your test date)
- Two No. 2 pencils with soft erasers
- A watch without an audible alarm
- A snack
- A map to the test site, if necessary

WHAT SHOULD I DO ON THE DAY OF THE TEST?

Bring the materials listed in the previous section. Arrive at the testing site 15 to 20 minutes early to allow yourself time to settle in and get comfortable before the start of the test. Remain confident and relaxed while taking the test. Do your very best!

PART II:

CELLULAR AND MOLECULAR BIOLOGY

CELL STRUCTURE
AND ORGANIZATION

I. Key Concepts

A. All organisms are made up of one or more cells.

B. The cell is the basic unit of structure and function of organisms.

C. New cells only arise from existing cells by cell reproduction.

D. Cells exchange substances with their environment by transporting these substances in and out of the cell across the plasma membrane.

II. There are two main types of cells that are distinctly different.

A. *Prokaryotic cells* are simpler and more ancient than eukaryotic cells.

   1. Prokaryotic cells have no nucleus or membrane-bound organelles.
   2. Prokaryotic cells are typically smaller than eukaryotic cells.

B. *Eukaryotic cells* are those of protists, fungi, plants, and animals.

   1. Animal cells are generally smaller than plant cells.
   2. Plants have some cellular structures that animals don't have.

i. Plants have rigid cell walls made of the polymer, cellulose.

ii. Plants have chloroplasts where photosynthesis is carried out.

iii. Many plant cells have a large, central vacuole that is absent in animal cells.

iv. Compare the animal cell diagram (Figure 2.1) to that of the plant cell diagram (Figure 2.2).

Figure 2.1 Animal Cell

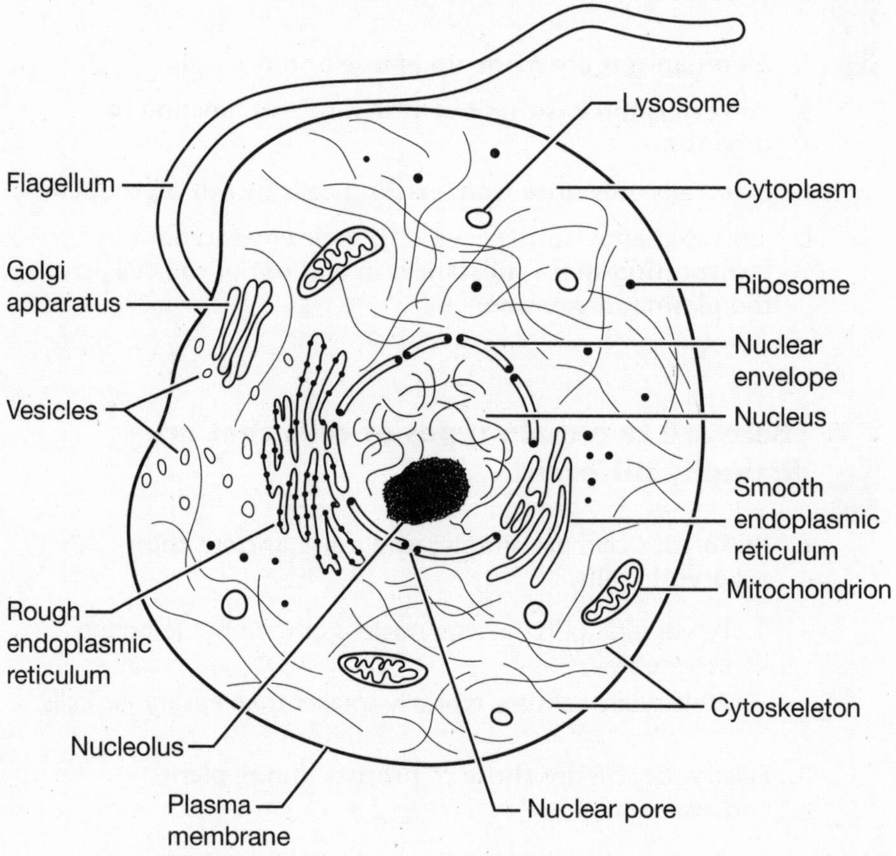

Figure 2.2 Plant Cell

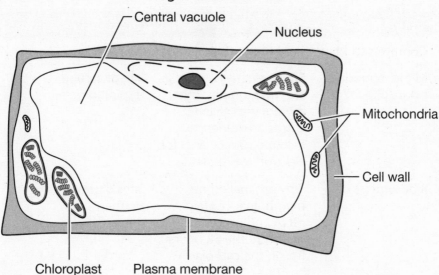

 III. The structures and functions of important cell features and organelles are shown in Table 2.1, with an emphasis on the differences between prokaryotes and eukaryotes, and between plant and animal cells.

Table 2.1 Structures and Functions of Various Cell Types

Feature	Structure	Function
Common to all Cells (Prokaryotes & Eukaryotes)		
Plasma membrane	Lipid bilayer containing proteins for transport and other functions	Barrier; controls the entrance and exit of substances into and out of the cell
Cytoplasm	Gelatin-like aqueous fluid (cytosol) with dissolved substances and organelles	The site of many biological reactions, such as synthesis of protein and glycolysis

(continued)

Table 2.1 (continued)

Feature	Structure	Function
Common to Plant and Animal Cells (Eukaryotes)		
Mitochondrion (-dria, pl.)	Small organelle with two membranes; inner membranes called *cristae* are folded to increase surface area for electron transport	Site of aerobic respiration
Ribosome(s)	Tiny organelles; no membrane; contain rRNA and protein; bound to the ER or float free in the cytoplasm	Sites of protein synthesis
Endoplasmic reticulum (ER)	Rows of flattened, membranous sacs with or without ribosomes attached (rough and smooth ER, respectively)	Sites of protein and membrane synthesis
Golgi apparatus	Rows of flattened, membranous sacs	Modifies and transports proteins, etc., for export from the cell
Vesicle(s)	Small, spherical, numerous; surrounded by one membrane	Move substances from the ER to the Golgi apparatus and from there to the plasma membrane
Lysosome(s)	Small, spherical; surrounded by one membrane	Contains hydrolytic enzymes that digest macromolecules, pathogens, and old organelles
Cytoskeleton	Network of microfilaments and microtubules throughout the cytoplasm	Controls cell shape; causes movement of chromosomes and organelles within the cell

(continued)

Table 2.1 (*continued*)

Feature	Structure	Function
Cilia & flagella (-um, sing.)	Hairlike; cilia are short and flagella are longer; 9+2 arrangement of microtubules	Locomotion of cells; movement of fluid surrounding a cell
Nucleus	Large, round; surrounded by nuclear envelope consisting of two membranes studded with pores	Site of chromosome (DNA) storage and RNA synthesis (transcription)
Nucleolus	Dense, spherical area within the nucleus	Site of rRNA synthesis and ribosome production
Plant Cells Only		
Cell wall	Rigid; contains cellulose	Provides support and protection for cells
Vacuole(s)	Small or large; surrounded by single membrane	Provides turgor pressure for gross plant support; storage of substances
Plastid(s) (chloroplasts, etc.)	Various membrane bound organelles; chloroplast has— double membrane plus thylakoids shaped like stacked coins to increase surface area	Chloroplasts are the site of photosynthesis; other plastids store starch or fats

Test Tip

Know the names, structures and functions of each cellular component and be able to identify each from a figure of a cell.

IV. **Concept: The *plasma membrane* is a barrier protecting a cell from its immediate environment, but it also must allow substances to be transported into and out of the cell.**

A. The plasma membrane is *selectively permeable*, meaning that it allows some substances to pass through it, but not others.

    1. The lipid portion of the membrane is composed mainly of phospholipids.

        i. *Phospholipids* have a *hydrophobic* (water-fearing) tail and a *hydrophilic* (water-loving) head.

        ii. The cytosol and the fluid outside the cell (the extracellular fluid) are both aqueous (watery) environments.

        iii. Therefore, phospholipids form a *bilayer* as shown in Figure 2.3 because the hydrophilic heads associate with the cytoplasm and the extracellular fluid, while the hydrophobic tails associate with each other.

    2. In addition, proteins specialized for transporting molecules across the membrane are embedded in the lipid bilayer.

Figure 2.3 Plasma Membrane Structure

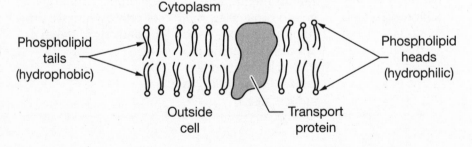

Cytoplasm

Phospholipid tails (hydrophobic)

Phospholipid heads (hydrophilic)

Outside cell

Transport protein

B. There are two main types of *cellular transport:* **passive transport and active transport.**

1. *Passive transport* does not require the cell to use ATP energy.

   i. In *diffusion*, a substance moves down its concentration gradient from an area of higher concentration to an area of lower concentration.

      a) Substances moved are small, uncharged molecules (e.g., carbon dioxide and oxygen).

      b) Substances move directly across the lipid bilayer.

Figure 2.4 Diffusion

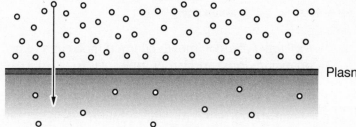

High concentration
of substance

Plasma membrane

Low concentration
of substance

   ii. *Osmosis* causes water to move across the plasma membrane from a hypotonic solution to a hypertonic solution.

      a) A *hypotonic* solution has a lower concentration of solutes (dissolved substances) than a *hypertonic* solution.

      b) If two solutions have equal concentrations of solutes, they are called *isotonic* and there is no net movement of water across the plasma membrane. This is called *dynamic equilibrium.*

      c) In osmosis, the solute molecule is not able to cross the *semipermeable* plasma membrane.

Figure 2.5 Osmosis: Hypertonic, Hypotonic, and Isotonic Cells

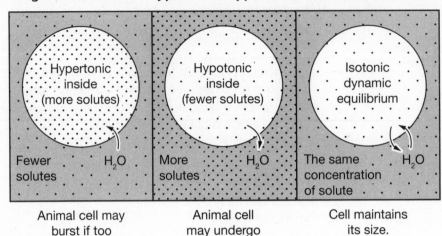

Animal cell may burst if too much water enters.

Animal cell may undergo shrinkage.

Cell maintains its size.

    iii. *Facilitated diffusion* moves charged molecules (e.g., potassium ions) and larger molecules (e.g., glucose) into and out of the cell.

        a) As with diffusion, facilitated diffusion moves a substance down its concentration gradient from an area of higher concentration to an area of lower concentration without the use of ATP.

        b) Unlike diffusion, however, the substance moves with the help of carrier proteins or through a channel protein.

Figure 2.6 Facilitated Diffusion Uses Carrier or Channel Proteins

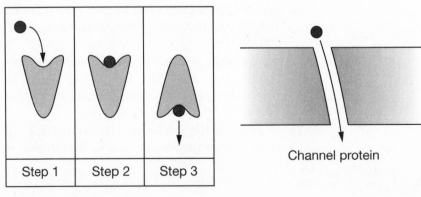

2. *Active transport* requires the cell to use ATP.

   i. The *sodium–potassium pump* is a type of carrier protein called a *cell membrane pump*. A pump requires energy to move substances (in the present case, sodium ions: Na^+ and potassium ions: K^+) against their concentration gradients from areas of low concentration to areas of high concentration.

     a) The Na^+-P^+ pump is important to animal cells, which must maintain a difference in charge across the plasma membrane.

     b) The Na^+–P^+ pump moves 3 Na^+ out of the cell, while at the same time moving 2 K^+ into the cell.

     c) The pump picks up 3 Na^+ on the inside of the cell and then changes shape, causing it to deposit them outside the cell after ATP adds a phosphate to the pump.

     d) By a similar shape change, the pump moves 2 K^+ in the opposite direction as the phosphate group leaves the pump protein.

Figure 2.7 The Sodium–Potassium Pump

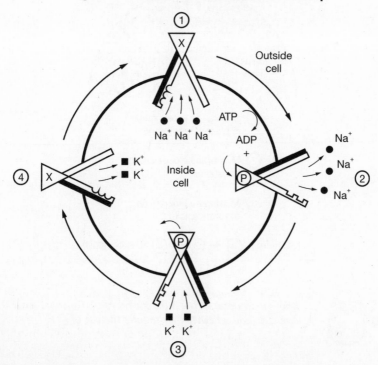

ii. *Exocytosis* and *endocytosis* move large molecules and food particles, etc., across the plasma membrane with the expenditure of ATP.

    a) *Exocytosis* is the process whereby newly synthesized proteins and other molecules to be exported are carried in vesicles from the ER and Golgi apparatus to the plasma membrane.

    b) The membrane of the vesicle then fuses with the plasma membrane, expelling its contents to the exterior of the cell.

    c) In the opposite process—*endocytosis*—substances are taken up by a small in-folding of the plasma membrane and are incorporated into a vesicle.

    d) *Pinocytosis* is the uptake of liquids, while *phagocytosis* is the uptake of solid substances.

Figure 2.8 Endocytosis and Exocytosis

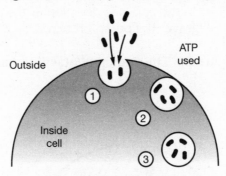

ATP used

Outside

Inside cell

① Substance enters pocket in plasma membrane

② Membrane closes around substance

③ Membrane pinches off to form vesicle

(going from ③ → ② → ① is exocytosis)

Test Tip

Know the names of the different types of transport, how they operate, and whether they require the use of ATP.

MITOSIS

I. Key Concepts

A. The number of chromosomes an organism has in its body cells does not vary from cell to cell, nor does it vary from organism to organism of the same species.

B. The genetic material of all organisms is contained on chromosomes that become especially compact during cell reproduction.

C. The cell cycle is the life cycle of a cell and includes time periods when a cell is not dividing as well as those when it undergoes cell division.

D. Mitosis occurs in eukaryotes and produces cells with nearly identical genetic makeup.

　1. Mitosis is used for the purpose of organismal reproduction in single-celled organisms.

　2. It is used for the purposes of development and cell replacement in the normal growth and maintenance of the bodies of multicellular organisms.

E. Prokaryotes generally reproduce by a process called binary fission.

II. *Chromosomes* **contain the genetic material (DNA), and are found in the nucleus of a eukaryotic cell.**

A. All the cells of animals and plants, except sperm and egg cells, are called *somatic cells*, and each somatic cell has the same number of chromosomes.

B. Each member of a species generally has the same number of chromosomes.

C. Most sexually reproducing organisms have pairs of autosomes and sex chromosomes. For example:

  1. Humans have 46 chromosomes, grouped into 23 pairs.
    i. Humans have 22 pairs of *autosomes*.
      a) Each pair of autosomes is called a *homologous pair*.
      b) For each of these 22 autosomal pairs, one homologue of the pair was inherited from the father and the other homologue was inherited from the mother.
      c) The two chromosomes of a pair are called *homologous* because each has genes for the same set of characteristics in the same locations along their (relatively) equal lengths.
    ii. The other pair of human chromosomes, X and Y, are called the *sex chromosomes*.
      a) A male inherits one X chromosome from his mother and one Y chromosome from his father (XY).
      b) A female inherits two X chromosomes, one from each parent (XX).
      c) The two sex chromosomes are not homologous because they do not contain genes for the same set of characteristics along their entire lengths and are of different sizes.
    iii. A *karyotype* is a photograph of an organism's highly compact chromosomes that have been prepared from cells undergoing mitosis (and are therefore duplicated); the images of the chromosomes are then cut from the photograph and arranged from largest to smallest.

Figure 3.1 Karyotype: Autosomal and Sex Chromosomes of a Human Female

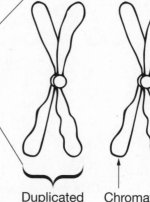

Homologous chromosomes

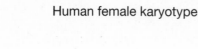

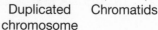

Human female karyotype

Duplicated chromosome

Chromatids

 III. **DNA with associated protein is called *chromatin*, which forms highly condensed chromosomes as it prepares to undergo cell division.**

A. Prokaryotes generally have one circularized chromosome associated with proteins that help it fold into a relatively compact form.

B. Eukaryotic cells have a number of pairs of linear chromosomes associated with histone proteins.

   1. When cells are not dividing, *histones* fold and unfold different parts of the chromosomes to allow access to specific segments of DNA: for RNA transcription and DNA replication.

   2. Before a cell divides, the DNA of all of its chromosomes is copied.

      i. The resulting identical copies of a chromosome are called *chromatids*.

      ii. Each pair of chromatids is joined together at a region called the *centromere*.

3. When a cell prepares to divide, histones aid the packaging of chromosomes into highly condensed units to protect them from damage during their subsequent movements during cell division.

Figure 3.2 Levels of Chromosome Structure

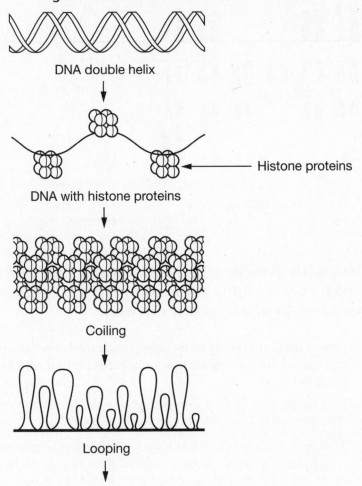

DNA double helix

DNA with histone proteins

Histone proteins

Coiling

Looping

Figure 3.2 (*continued*)

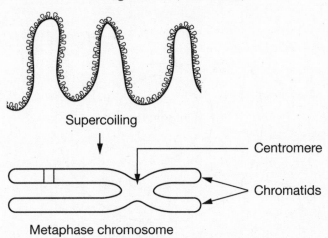

Supercoiling

Centromere

Chromatids

Metaphase chromosome

Test Tip

Don't confuse the paired chromatids (chromosomes that have been duplicated before mitosis and are held together by their centromeres) with homologues that do not pair with each other during mitosis. (Note: The situation in meiosis is different.)

IV. The two main phases of the cell cycle are interphase and cell division.

A. *Interphase*: Cells spend most of their time in interphase.

1. G_1 *phase*: The first phase of interphase is G_1 during which the new cell grows to mature size and may begin to carry out its specific function.

2. *S phase*: If the cell is going to divide again, it copies its chromosomes during the S phase by the process of DNA replication.

3. G_2 *phase*: Once the DNA is replicated, the cell enters G_2 during which it prepares for cell division.

4. G_0 *phase*: Some cells do not divide, or they delay division; these cells enter the G_0 phase sometime during G_1 as shown in Figure 3.3.

Figure 3.3 The Cell Cycle

S

G2

Interphase

G1

Go

mitosis

cytokinesis

cell division

B. The second main phase of the cell cycle is cell division, which includes mitosis and cytokinesis.

 V. *Cell division* occurs in eukaryotic cells and results in the production of two nearly identical cells.

A. *Mitosis* is the division of the nucleus, which leads to the separation of the chromosomes that were previously duplicated in the S phase to produce two chromatids that are attached at their centromeres; it has four main stages.

1. *Prophase*
   i. The chromatids condense.
   ii. The nuclear membrane breaks down and disappears.
   iii. A cytoskeletal structure called the *mitotic spindle* forms, which will be used to pull the chromatids apart to either pole of the cell.

a) Two *centrosomes* are synthesized.

b) In animal cells, the centrosomes contain small cylindrical bodies called *centrioles*.

c) The centrosomes move to opposite sides of the cell.

d) Spindle fibers, made of microtubules, radiate outward from the centrosomes and some, called *kinetochore fibers*, attach to each chromosome at its centromere.

2. *Metaphase*: During metaphase, the chromatids line up across the center of the cell called the *metaphase plate*.

3. *Anaphase*: Chromatids separate from one another during anaphase, at which point each chromatid is now considered to be an individual chromosome.
   i. The centromeres of the chromatids split.
   ii. The kinetochore fibers pull one copy of each chromosome to one pole and the rest to the other side of the cell.

4. *Telophase* is the last stage of mitosis.
   i. The mitotic spindle disassembles.
   ii. The chromosomes unwind from their highly compacted state.
   iii. A new nuclear membrane forms and surrounds each new complete set of chromosomes.

Figure 3.4 The Stages of Mitosis

   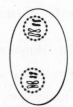

Prophase   Metaphase   Anaphase   Telophase

Test Tip

Some text books divide mitosis into five stages: prophase, pro-metaphase, metaphase, anaphase, and telophase.

B. *Cytokinesis* is the division of the cytoplasm following mitosis whereby the two newly formed nuclei become incorporated into separate cells.

1. In animal cells, a special collection of microfilaments of the cytoskeleton form a *cleavage furrow* in the center of the cell, which causes the cell to be pinched into two cells.

2. In plant cells, vesicles from the Golgi apparatus form a *cell plate* in the center of the cell along which new cell wall material is deposited between the two newly forming plasma membranes.

Figure 3.5 Cytokinesis in Plant and Animal Cells

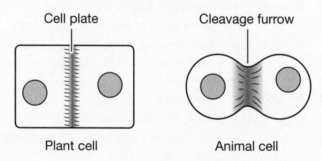

Cell plate   Cleavage furrow

Plant cell   Animal cell

 VI. **Cell division occurs by *binary fission* in prokaryotic cells, resulting in the production of two nearly identical individuals.**

A. The single prokaryotic chromosome is copied.

B. The cell grows in size.

C. Finally, a new cell wall grows between the two new chromosomes, resulting in two individual cells with nearly identical DNA.

Figure 3.6 Binary Fission in Prokaryotes

Chromosome

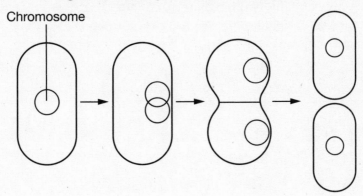

PHOTOSYNTHESIS

I. Key Concepts

A. Photosynthesis occurs in all photosynthetic autotrophs including plants, algae, and photosynthetic prokaryotes.

B. In eukaryotes, photosynthesis occurs in chloroplasts; in prokaryotes, it occurs in the plasma membrane and the cytoplasm.

C. The overall equation for photosynthesis is:

$$6CO_2 + 6H_2O + \text{light energy} \rightarrow C_6H_{12}O_6 + 6O_2$$

D. Photosynthesis is affected by a variety of environmental factors.

E. Where does each step of photosynthesis take place in eukaryotic chloroplasts?

Figure 4.1 Chloroplast and the Steps of Photosynthesis

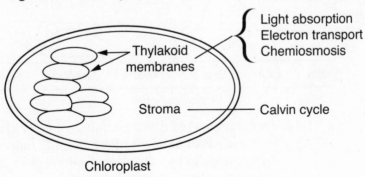

II. *Photosynthesis* **has two main steps: (1) the absorption of light energy and its conversion to the chemical energy of ATP and the reducing power of NADPH, and (2) the use of that ATP and NADPH to convert CO_2 to sugars using the Calvin cycle.**

   A. Absorption and conversion of light energy to ATP and NADPH are often called the *light reactions*

      1. *Light absorption* occurs in the *thylakoid membranes* of chloroplasts in eukaryotes.

         i. *Pigment molecules* collect light energy.

            a) Leaves appear green because their chloroplasts contain pigment molecules that reflect, as opposed to absorb, green light.

            b) *Chlorophyll a* is the main photosynthetic pigment.

            c) *Chlorophyll b* and *carotenoids* are accessory pigments that allow leaves to capture a wider spectrum of visible light than chlorophyll alone.

Figure 4.2 Absorption Spectra of Photosynthetic Pigments

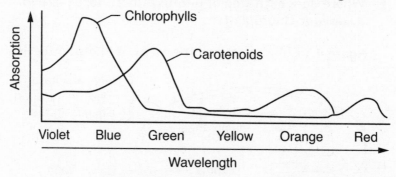

         ii. *Photosystem I (PS I)* and *photosystem II (PS II)* consist of hundreds of pigment molecules that funnel light energy to two chlorophyll *a* molecules at the *reaction center* of each photosystem.

      2. *Electron transport* also occurs in the thylakoid membranes.

         i. The *electron transport chain* is a group of proteins that undergo redox reactions in series.

a) When PS II reaction center chlorophyll *a* molecules receive light energy, they transfer some of their electrons to the primary electron acceptor.

b) The primary electron acceptor passes those electrons to the next electron carriers, until the electrons are donated to PS I.

c) When the chlorophyll *a* molecules of PS I are excited, they send those electrons to the next electron carriers, until the electrons are finally donated to NADP$^+$ to reduce it to NADPH.

ii. To replace the electrons lost by PS II (which is at the beginning of the whole chain), water is split:

$$2H_2O \rightarrow 4H^+ + 4e^- + O_2$$

iii. The resulting increase in H$^+$ (called *protons* or *hydrogen ions*) on the inside of the thylakoid represents potential energy that is used to make ATP by chemiosmosis.

3. *Chemiosmosis*

i. H$^+$ ions move down their concentration gradient from inside the thylakoids to the stroma.

ii. As they do this, they pass through the enzyme, *ATP synthase*, which causes the catalysis of ATP from ADP and P$_i$.

Figure 4.3 Electron Transport and Chemiosmosis of Photosynthesis

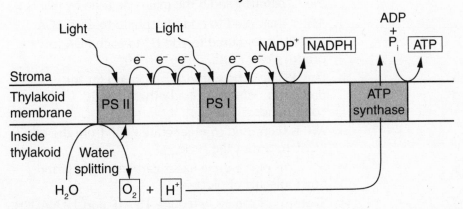

4. Flow summary: Absorption and conversion of light energy to ATP and NADPH

    i. Pigments absorb light energy.

    ii. Light energy sends electrons down the electron transport chain.

    iii. The electrons eventually reduce $NADP^+$ to NADPH.

    iv. Water is split forming e^-, H^+ and O_2.

    v. H^+ concentration builds up inside the thylakoids (the thylakoid space).

    vi. When H^+ move through ATP synthase from the thylakoid space to the stroma, ATP is formed.

    vii. NADPH and ATP are used in the second step of photosynthesis, carbon fixation.

Test Tip

Being able to explain photosynthesis to an interested person (such as a parent) using pencil-and-paper sketches will help you master your understanding of the steps involved and how they are related to each other.

B. **Carbon fixation by the Calvin cycle (C_3) occurs in the stroma of chloroplasts.**

1. The *Calvin cycle* uses ATP and NADPH to fix the carbon of CO_2 into organic molecules.

    i. CO_2 is added to RuBP (a 5-carbon molecule) to produce two molecules of PGA (a 3-carbon molecule) by the action of the enzyme RUBISCO. (This is called the *C_3 pathway* and is the main one used by plants.)

    ii. ATP is then used to add phosphate to each PGA.

    iii. NADPH is also used to add H^+ to each PGA to produce two PGAL.

    iv. One PGAL is the starting compound for the production of sugars, and other organic compounds.

    v. ATP is then used to regenerate RuBP from the other PGAL to restart the cycle.

    vi. Six turns of the cycle fix six carbons, representing one molecule of glucose.

    vii. Six turns of the cycle require 18 ATP and 12 NADPH.

Figure 4.4 The Calvin Cycle

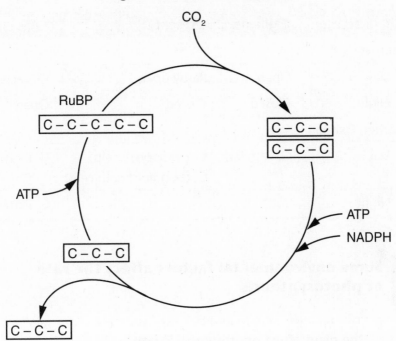

2. C_4 and CAM plants
   i. Why are there alternate ways in which plants fix carbon?
      a) CO_2 for photosynthesis enters the leaves of a plant and O_2 exits by way of pores called *stomata* (sing, *stoma*).
      b) When the stomata are open, water is lost from the plant, but when stomata close, RUBISCO eventually stops fixing CO_2 due to low CO_2 levels.
      c) Some plants in hot, dry climates use alternative ways to carry out carbon fixation while simultaneously reducing water loss.
      d) Some plants temporarily use a special carbon fixation enzyme, *PEP carboxylase*, which works better at low CO_2 concentrations than the C_3 enzyme, RUBISCO.
   ii. *C_4 plants* reduce water loss by separating the locations of C_3 and C_4 pathways.
   iii. *CAM plants* reduce water loss by separating the timing of C_3 and C_4 pathways.

Table 4.1 Comparing C_3, C_4, and CAM Plants

Characteristic	C_3 Plants	C_4 Plants	CAM Plants
Stomata			
Day	Open	Partly open	Closed
Night	Closed	Closed	Open
Carbon Fixation			
Day	C_3 Pathway	C_4 (mesophyll cells) C_3 (bundle-sheath cells)	C_3 Pathway
Night			C_4 Pathway

 Some environmental factors affect the rate of photosynthesis.

A. The *intensity of light* and the *concentration of CO_2* available to the plant affect photosynthetic rate.

   1. As either of these factors increases, so does the photosynthetic rate, but the rate eventually *levels off*.

      i. For light intensity, the photosynthetic rate levels off because the photosystems become saturated and cannot work any faster.

      ii. For CO_2 concentration, the leveling off is due to the fact that the Calvin cycle enzymes are processing CO_2 as fast as possible.

   2. As *temperature* increases, the photosynthetic rate increases to a maximum and then declines as temperatures increase further.

      i. Stomata may close at higher temperatures, thereby decreasing available CO_2.

      ii. Also, all enzymes, including those of the Calvin cycle, have a *temperature optimum* at which they process substrates at the highest possible rate.

Figure 4.5 The Effects of Light Intensity, CO_2 Concentration, and Temperature on Photosynthesis

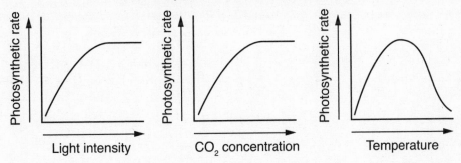

Don't forget to compare the processes of photosynthesis and cellular respiration, as this is commonly tested on the SAT Biology test.

CELLULAR RESPIRATION

I. Key Concepts

A. Cellular respiration is the catalysis (breakdown) of glucose to produce energy (ATP) and organic intermediates used in the synthesis of other important organic molecules (amino acids, lipids, etc.) needed by the cell.

B. Some form of cellular respiration takes place in nearly all organisms.

   1. Glycolysis is virtually universal and takes place in the cytoplasm of cells.
   2. Aerobic respiration—the Krebs cycle, electron transport, and chemiosmosis—takes place in mitochondria in eukaryotes.

C. Refer to the overall equation for cell respiration:

$$C_6H_{12}O_6 + 6O_2 \rightarrow 6CO_2 + 6H_2O + energy$$

Although this equation is almost the reverse of the equation for photosynthesis, the two processes involve different enzymes and biochemical pathways, as well as different organelles.

D. Cells may utilize an anaerobic pathway (fermentation) that does not require O_2, or an aerobic pathway that does require O_2.

   1. Glycolysis is the first step of both pathways: This step does not require O_2.

2. Aerobic respiration has three additional steps, the second of which requires O_2 as the final electron receptor of the electron transport chain.

    i. The Krebs cycle takes place in the matrix of mitochondria.

    ii. The electron transport chain takes place in the inner membrane of mitochondria.

    iii. Chemiosmosis takes place across the inner membrane of mitochondria.

Figure 5.1 Location of Fermentation and the Steps of Cellular Respiration

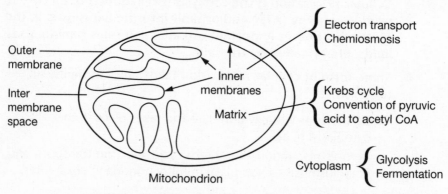

3. Anaerobic fermentation has one additional step following glycolysis that regenerates the oxidizing agent, NAD^+, to allow glycolysis to operate in the absence of O_2.

II. *Aerobic respiration* oxidizes glucose completely to CO_2 and H_2O.

A. *Glycolysis* is a series of biochemical reactions, catalyzed by a series of enzymes, which break one glucose molecule down to two molecules of *pyruvic acid (pyruvate)*.

1. The following are the most important *features* to remember about the glycolysis reaction series:

    i. Two ATP are used to add two phosphate groups to either end of glucose to energize it for subsequent reactions.

ii. Glucose is split in half to yield two 3-carbon compounds.

iii. As these compounds undergo oxidation, NAD⁺ is reduced to NADH, one of two electron carriers in cell respiration.

iv. The resulting 3-carbon compounds produce ATP when they are converted to pyruvic acid.

2. The *products* of glycolysis are as follows:

i. Two ATP: Four are produced, but two are used for a net yield of two ATP.

ii. Two NADH, which will travel to the mitochondria to donate electrons to the electron transport chain.

iii. Two pyruvic acid molecules, which are modified before entering the Krebs cycle.

Figure 5.2 Glycolysis

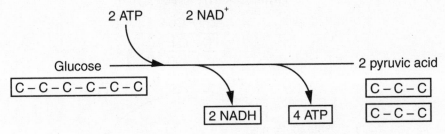

B. The *conversion of pyruvic acid to acetyl-CoA* occurs in the matrix of the mitochondria and involves three important features:

1. Coenzyme A (CoA) is added.

2. Pyruvate is oxidized, producing NADH.

3. The 3-carbon pyruvate is converted to the 2-carbon *acetyl CoA*, releasing a molecule of CO_2.

Figure 5.3 The Conversion of Pyruvic Acid to Acetyl CoA

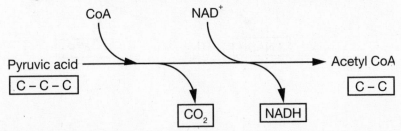

C. The *Krebs cycle* is a series of reactions that continually regenerates one of its first reactants, oxaloacetic acid.

1. The following are the most important *features* to remember about the Krebs cycle:

    i. Acetyl-CoA combines with oxaloacetic acid to produce citric acid at the start of the cycle.

    ii. Two CO_2, one ATP, three NADH, and one $FADH_2$ are produced during each turn of the cycle. (Like NADH, $FADH_2$ is an electron carrier that will donate electrons to the electron transport chain.)

    iii. Oxaloacetic acid is regenerated to begin the cycle again.

Figure 5.4 The Krebs Cycle

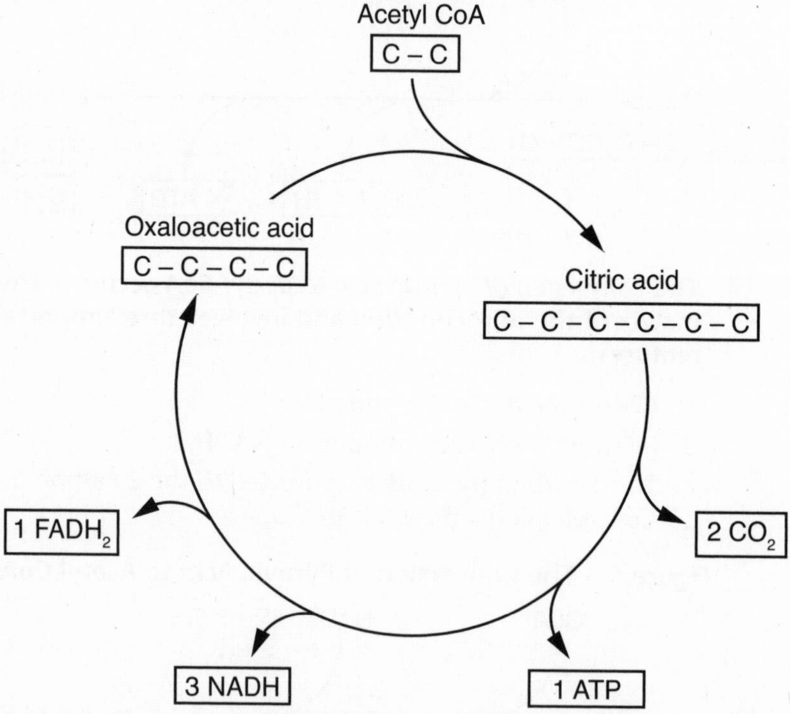

Acetyl CoA

C – C

Oxaloacetic acid

C – C – C – C

Citric acid

C – C – C – C – C – C

1 $FADH_2$

2 CO_2

3 NADH

1 ATP

2. For every glucose molecule that enters glycolysis, the Krebs cycle turns two times yielding the following *products.*

 i. Six CO_2 molecules are produced between glycolysis and the end of the Krebs cycle.

  a) Two CO_2 form during the conversion of two pyruvic acid molecules to two molecules of acetyl CoA.

  b) Four CO_2 form during two turns of the Krebs cycle.

  c) These six molecules of CO_2 account for all of the carbon atoms in the glucose molecule, $C_6H_{12}O_6$.

  d) The CO_2 diffuses out of the cells and is given off to the atmosphere.

 ii. Six NADH and two $FADH_2$ are produced per glucose molecule.

 iii. Two ATP are also produced directly in the Krebs cycle per glucose molecule.

D. *Electron transport* **is carried out by electron carriers that undergo a series of redox reactions as electrons are passed from one carrier to another.**

1. The following are the most important *features* to know about electron transport:

 i. The electron transport chains of photosynthesis and cell respiration are similar, but a different group of carriers is involved and the chains occur in different membranes within different organelles of the cell.

 ii. $FADH_2$ generates less ATP than NADH.

  a) 1 NADH is responsible for producing approximately three molecules of ATP. (Note: A very small amount of ATP is needed to move any NADH made in the cytoplasm into the matrix for processing by the electron transport chain.)

      b) One FADH$_2$ is responsible for producing two molecules of ATP.

   iii. Some of the energy of electron transport is used to transport H$^+$, released by the redox reactions, from the matrix to the inner membrane space.

      a) The H$^+$ comes from NADH and FADH$_2$.

      b) The resulting increase in H$^+$ in the inner membrane space represents potential energy that is used to make ATP by chemiosmosis.

   iv. The final electron acceptor of the electron transport chain is O$_2$, which combines with the spent electrons and protons of NADH and FADH$_2$ to produce H$_2$O:

$$O_2 + 4e^- + 4H^+ \rightarrow 2H_2O$$

E. *Chemiosmosis* relies on the H$^+$ difference across the inner membrane of mitochondria.

  1. H$^+$ ions move down their concentration gradient from the intermembrane space to the matrix.

  2. As they do this, they pass through the enzyme, ATP synthase, which causes the catalysis of ATP from ADP and P$_i$.

Figure 5.5 Electron Transport and Chemiosmosis of Cell Respiration

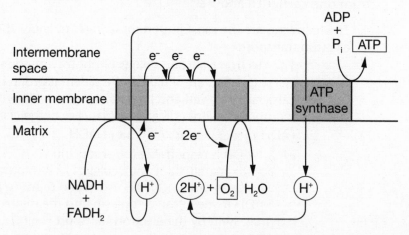

F. Flow summary: Aerobic respiration

1. Glucose is broken down by glycolysis into two pyruvic acid molecules, yielding a little ATP and NADH.
2. Pyruvic acid is converted to acetyl-CoA, yielding some NADH, and giving off CO_2.
3. Acetyl-CoA enters the Krebs cycle and its carbon atoms exit as CO_2.
4. The Krebs cycle also produces ATP, NADH, and $FADH_2$.
5. NADH and $FADH_2$ donate their electrons to the electron transport chain.
6. The donated electrons travel down the chain until they are finally accepted by O_2.
7. The movement of electrons causes H^+ to be pumped into the inner membrane space.
8. These H^+ travel back to the matrix through the ATP synthase in the inner membrane, producing ATP.

G. Energy summary: Electron transport is responsible for the great majority of ATP produced during aerobic respiration.

Table 5.1 Energy Summary of Aerobic Respiration

STEPS		Electron Transport	Subtotal
Glycolysis	2 ATP-----	------------------→	2 ATP
	2 NADH	2×3 →	6 ATP
Pyruvate to acetyl CoA	2 NADH	2×3 →	6 ATP
Krebs cycle	2 ATP ---	------------------→	2 ATP
	6 NADH	6×3 →	18 ATP
	2 $FADH_2$	2×2 →	4 ATP
Minus 2 ATP for ancillary NADH transport processes			−2 ATP
		Total	36 ATP

III. **Anaerobic fermentation provides a small amount of ATP in the absence O$_2$.**

A. **Glycolysis is the first step of both aerobic respiration and fermentation.**

   1. Two of the end products of glycolysis, pyruvic acid and NADH, can be processed anaerobically in the cytoplasm of certain cells.

   2. The second step of fermentation does not produce ATP directly.

   3. Rather, it regenerates NAD$^+$, which is required to keep glycolysis running and producing ATP.

B. *Lactic acid fermentation* **includes glycolysis plus an additional reaction that generates NAD$^+$ and lactic acid, as shown in Figure 5.6.**

   1. Certain fungi, bacteria, and muscle cells have special enzymes that carry out lactic acid fermentation.

   2. In the manufacture of dairy products, such as cheese and yogurt, lactic acid made by microorganisms adds tart flavors to the final product.

   3. In vigorously exercising muscle cells, lactic acid fermentation provides ATP when the circulatory system cannot keep up with the oxygen demands of muscle cell mitochondria.

C. *Alcoholic fermentation* **includes glycolysis plus additional reactions that produce NAD$^+$, ethanol, and CO$_2$ as shown in Figure 5.6.**

   1. Single-celled organisms, such as yeast and some plant cells, have special enzymes to carry out alcoholic fermentation.

   2. Yeast is used in bread making because CO$_2$ gas causes the bread to rise; the ethanol is removed by subsequent baking.

3. Yeast is used in beer making because it produces ethanol; CO_2 in an enclosed container produces carbonation.

Figure 5.6 Fermentation

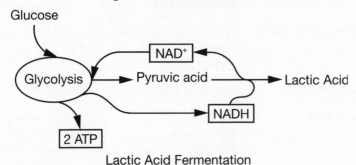

Lactic Acid Fermentation

Alcoholic Fermentation

Anaerobic fermentation produces much less energy than aerobic respiration: only 2 ATP per glucose processed, as compared to 36 ATP produced by aerobic respiration per glucose molecule.

Table 5.2 Comparison of Cellular Respiration and Photosynthesis

Item Compared	Cellular Respiration	Photosynthesis
Main purpose	Break down carbon compounds to make ATP	Use light energy to make carbon compounds
Organisms	Almost all organisms, including plants	Some bacteria, protists, and plants

(continued)

Table 5.2 (*continued*)

Item Compared	Cellular Respiration	Photosynthesis
Eukaryotic organelle	Mitochondria	Chloroplasts
Initial energy source	Organic compounds (chemical bond energy)	Light energy
Reducing power	NADH & FADH$_2$	NADPH
Order of steps	Glycolysis Krebs cycle Electron transport Chemiosmosis	Light absorption Electron transport Chemiosmosis Calvin cycle
Processes in common	Electron transport & chemiosmosis (ATP synthase)	
Cyclic processes	Krebs cycle	Calvin cycle
Gas used	O_2 (final electron acceptor)	CO_2 (Calvin cycle)
Gas released	CO_2 (mostly from Krebs)	O_2 (water splitting)

There is almost always at least one test question that requires comparing photosynthesis and cellular respiration. Also, keep in mind that plants carry out both photosynthesis and cellular respiration.

BIOLOGICAL CHEMISTRY, ENZYMES, AND BIOSYNTHESIS

I. Key Concepts

A. Because they are composed of matter, the basic rules of chemistry apply to all living organisms.

B. All organisms require an input of energy from the environment, as well as the means to control the orderly use of that energy.

   1. Organisms generally convert the energy they obtain to ATP, the cell's "energy currency," which they use to power all life processes, including biosynthesis.

   2. Biochemical reactions, catalyzed by a large array of enzymes that are specific for each reaction, control biosynthesis—the chemical reactions that produce the macromolecules of which an organism's cells are composed.

C. Biological molecules include carbohydrates, lipids, proteins, and nucleic acids that have a variety of important functions.

Table 6.1 Types, Functions, and Examples of Biological Molecules

Type of Biological Molecule	Examples	General Functions
Carbohydrates	Monosaccharides (sugars)	
	Glucose	Energy; building blocks of other carbohydrates
	Deoxyribose and ribose	DNA and RNA
	Polysaccharides	
	Starch and glycogen	Energy storage
	Cellulose	Plant cell wall structure
Lipids	Fats	Energy storage
	Phospholipids	Plasma membrane structure
	Waxes	Physical protection
	Steroids (cholesterol)	Hormones (part of cell membranes)
Proteins	Enzymes	Biochemical catalysts
	Other proteins	Structure, movement, signal reception, etc.
Nucleic Acids	DNA	Storage of genetic information
	RNA	Converts genetic information into proteins
	ATP	Energy currency of the cell

II. Biological Chemistry

A. These *biologically important elements* are found in all organisms.

1. *Carbon* (C), *hydrogen* (H), and *oxygen* (O) are found in all macromolecules.
2. Additionally, *nitrogen* (N) is found in significant amounts in proteins and nucleic acids.
3. *Sulfur* (S) is an element commonly found in proteins.

4. *Phosphorus* (P) is prominent in nucleic acids.

5. *Sodium* (Na), *potassium* (K), *magnesium* (Mg), and *iron* (Fe) are examples of important elements found in lesser quantities in most organisms.

B. An *atom* is the smallest unit of an element.

1. The *nucleus* of an atom contains positively charged *protons* and neutral *neutrons*.

   i. The *atomic number* of an element is its number of protons.

   ii. The *atomic mass* of an atom is its number of protons plus neutrons.

2. The *electrons* of an atom surround the nucleus, are negatively charged, and have virtually no mass.

   i. An electron can become excited and leave its atom. (See Light Absorption of Photosynthesis.)

   ii. Electrons can be passed from molecule to molecule. (See Electron Transport of Photosynthesis and Cell Respiration.)

   iii. Electrons in the outermost energy level of an atom are involved in chemical bonding.

C. Atoms join together by *chemical bonds* to form compounds and molecules.

1. *Ionic bonds* are formed when one atom transfers an electron to another atom.

   i. Ionic bonds are charge:charge interactions.

   a) The atom that loses the electron becomes a positively charged ion, and the atom that gains the electron becomes a negatively charged ion.

   b) Attraction of the opposite charges of the ions constitutes the ionic bond.

   ii. An example of an ionic bond is found in the compound NaCl.

Figure 6.1 Example of an Ionic Bond: Nacl

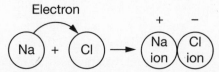

2. *Covalent bonds* are formed when two atoms share outer electrons.

    i. The majority of bonds within macromolecules are covalent.

    ii. In living organisms, covalent bonds do not normally form or break without the aid of enzymes.

    iii. Covalent bonds can be nonpolar or polar.

       a) In *nonpolar covalent bonds*, the shared electrons are fairly evenly distributed between the two atoms—carbon:carbon bonds and carbon:hydrogen bonds are examples.

       b) In *polar covalent bonds*, the shared electrons are not evenly distributed between the two atoms.

    iv. The bonds in a water molecule are examples of polar covalent bonds.

       a) Because of the unequal distribution of electrons, the hydrogen atoms carry a partial positive charge, and the oxygen atom carries a partial negative charge.

       b) This allows water molecules to form hydrogen bonds.

Figure 6.2 Polar Covalent Bonds of a Water Molecule

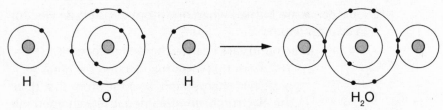

H   O   H H_2O

3. *Hydrogen bonds* are weak charge:charge attractions between a partial positive charge on a hydrogen atom of one molecule and a partial negative charge on an atom of another molecule.

Figure 6.3 Hydrogen Bonds Form Between Water Molecules

Dotted lines represent hydrogen
bonds between water molecules.

Test Tip

Generally, specific questions on atomic structure, bonding, atomic numbers, or atomic masses are not present on the test. Therefore you do not need to memorize the periodic table.

D. *Water* **has many characteristics of significance to living organisms.**

1. Water is the *aqueous solvent* in which biochemical reactions take place—within the cell and in its immediate environment (the space between cells in a multicellular organism).

2. The *pH* of the aqueous environment inside a cell and its organelles influence many biological activities such as the shapes of proteins, the creation of proton gradients across membranes, and the speed at which enzymes catalyze reactions.

    i. An acidic solution contains more hydrogen ions (H^+) than hydroxide ions (OH^-).

    ii. A basic solution contains more OH^- than H^+.

3. The cohesion and adhesion of water are important for water transport in plants.

    i. *Cohesion* is the attraction of two like substances; for example, the hydrogen bonding between two water molecules.

ii. *Adhesion* is the attraction of two unlike substances; for example, the attraction between water and the cell walls of vessel elements in plants.

4. Because water has a *high specific heat capacity*, it cools down and heats up slowly, allowing for temperature stability of organisms and the aqueous environments in which many organisms live.

III. Energy and Enzymes

A. *Free energy* is the energy available in a system to do work.

1. *Exergonic* reactions release free energy.

Reactant(s) → Product(s) + Energy

i. In *catabolic reactions*, reactant(s) are broken down to produce product(s) containing less energy.

ii. The energy released can be used for reactions that require energy.

2. *Endergonic* reactions require free energy.

Reactant(s) + Energy → Product(s)

i. In *anabolic reactions*, reactant(s) are joined together to produce product(s) containing more energy.

ii. The free energy required by anabolic reactions is often provided by ATP produced in catabolic reactions.

3. *Adenosine triphosphate (ATP)* carries energy in its high-energy phosphate bonds.

i. ATP is formed from adenosine diphosphate and inorganic phosphate.

$ADP + P_i + energy → ATP$

ii. Conversely, when ATP is broken down into ADP and P_i, energy is released that can be used in endergonic reactions.

iii. In addition, ATP can donate one of its phosphate groups to a molecule, such as a substrate or a protein, to energize it or cause it to change its shape.

Figure 6.4 ATP Stores Energy in its Phosphate Bonds

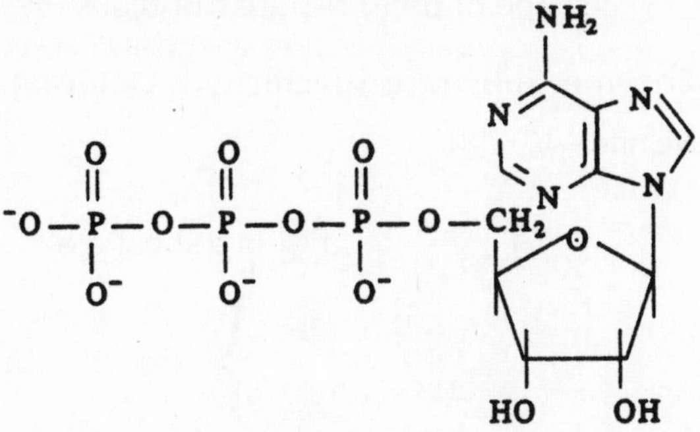

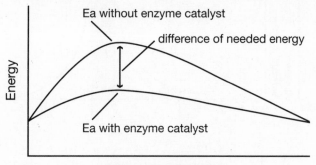

4. Almost all chemical reactions in organisms—exergonic and endergonic—are assisted by catalysts called enzymes.

B. *Enzymes* **are proteins that act as catalysts to speed up biochemical reactions.**

1. The function of enzymes is to *lower the activation energy of a reaction* = the energy required to initiate a chemical reaction.

Figure 6.5 Enzymes Lower the Activation Energy of Reactions

2. When a reactant (a *substrate*) binds to its enzyme, the enzyme and substrate are physically altered so that the substrate is more prone to react; this is called *induced fit*.

3. Enzyme specificity refers to the fact that an enzyme usually only catalyzes one specific reaction.

    i. *Specificity* is governed by the specific, physical, "lock and key" interaction between an enzyme and its substrate.

ii. The shape of the enzyme's reactive site matches the shape of the substrate molecule.

Figure 6.6 Enzyme–Substrate Specificity is Determined by Shape

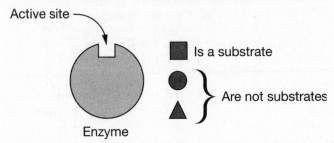

4. Enzymes are affected by pH, temperature, and substrate concentration.

    i. Enzymes have pH and temperature *optima* at which enzyme activity is greatest.

Figure 6.7 The Effect of pH and Temperature on Enzyme Activity

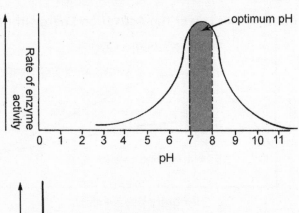

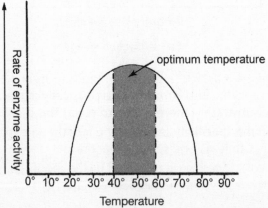

ii. As substrate concentration increases, the speed at which the reaction occurs increases up to a maximum level at which all enzyme molecules are processing substrate molecules as fast as possible.

Figure 6.8 The Effect of Substrate Concentration on Enzyme Activity

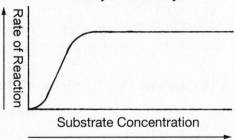

5. *Reduction–oxidation (redox) reactions* are a special type of enzyme catalyzed reaction in which electrons are transferred between molecules.

    i. When a molecule is oxidized it loses an electron, and when it is reduced it gains an electron.

    ii. Whenever a molecule is oxidized, another molecule is reduced.

    iii. An example of a redox reaction is the transfer of electrons from pyruvic acid to NAD^+ in the following reaction in which pyruvic acid is oxidized to acetyl CoA, and NAD^+ is reduced to NADH.

Figure 6.9 Redox Reactions Oxidize and Reduce Molecules by Transferring Electrons

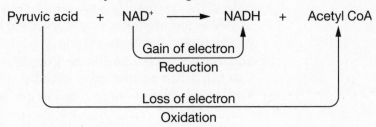

Biological Molecules

A. *Metabolism* **refers to all the reactions occurring in an organism.**

    1. *Condensation reactions* are responsible for the biosynthesis of polymers from monomers with the removal of water.

        i. *Monomers* are the building blocks of larger *macromolecules* called *polymers*.

        ii. A molecule of water is lost for each monomer that is added to a growing polymer.

Figure 6.10 Condensation Synthesis of a Polymer

New bond

H —◆—OH H—◇—◇—◇—OH ⟶ H_2O + H —◆—◇—◇—◇—OH

Monomer   Polymer

    2. Conversely, *hydrolysis* reactions break down polymers to their monomers with the addition of water, and is the reverse of the reaction shown in Figure 6.10.

B. **There are four classes of biological molecules.**

    1. *Carbohydrates* consist of monosaccharides, disaccharides, and polysaccharides.

        i. *Monosaccharides* are the monomers of carbohydrates, commonly called *sugars*.

        a) Sugars, particularly glucose, are key metabolites used in the synthesis of other organic molecules, as well as the substrates of glycolysis and the products of photosynthesis.

        b) Sugars have alcohol functional groups (−OH) that help them dissolve easily in water.

        c) They circularize to form ring shapes in solution.

Figure 6.11 Glucose—Example of a Monosaccharide

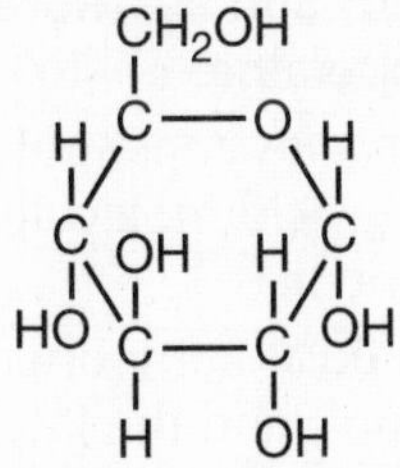

ii. *Disaccharides* are combinations of two monosaccharides.

Figure 6.12 Sucrose is a Disaccharide Formed from Glucose and Fructose

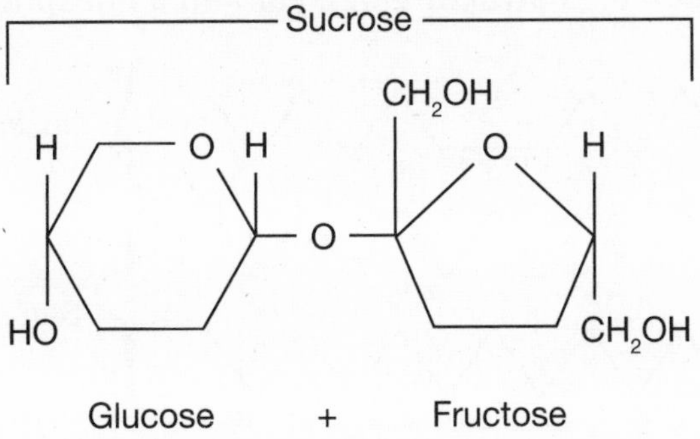

Glucose   +   Fructose

iii. *Polysaccharides* are long branched or straight chains of monosaccharides.

a) Starch and glycogen are polymers of glucose used in plants and animals, respectively, as energy reserves.

b) Cellulose is a polymer of glucose found in the cell walls of plants.

2. *Lipids* are water-insoluble molecules composed of glycerol and fatty acids.

i. *Fats (triglycerides)* are energy storage molecules consisting of one glycerol molecule with three fatty acid molecules attached.

a) *Saturated fatty acids* do not contain double bonds and are more likely to be solid at room temperature.

    b) *Unsaturated fatty acids* have one or more double bonds and are more likely to be fluid at room temperature.

  ii. *Phospholipids* consist of one glycerol molecule with two fatty acid molecules attached as well as a polar component.

    a) The polar component is *hydrophilic* (water loving), and the fatty acids are *hydrophobic* (water fearing).

    b) This amphoteric nature of phospholipids causes them to self-assemble into the classic bilayer arrangement that is the basis of all biological membranes.

Figure 6.13 Structure of a Fat and a Phospholipid

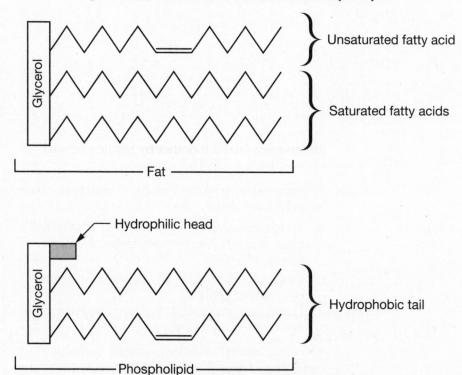

  iii. *Wax and steroids,* including cholesterol, are examples of lipids with more complex structures and have a variety of functions.

3. *Proteins* are polymers made up of different combinations of 20 commonly occurring amino acid monomers.
    i. *Amino acids* share the same basic structure.
        a) Each amino acid has a central carbon atom covalently bonded to four atoms or groups of atoms called *functional groups*.
            • One of the four is always a hydrogen atom.
            • A carboxyl (acidic) functional group ($-COOH$) and an amine (basic) functional group ($-NH_2$) are always present.
            • The fourth component bound to the central carbon is a variable R group, which is different for each amino acid.

Figure 6.14 Structure of an Amino Acid

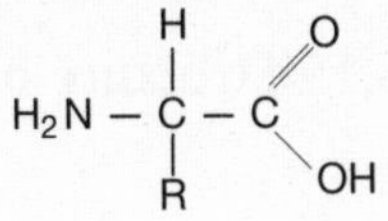

    ii. A *peptide bond* can form between two amino acids by dehydration synthesis to form a dipeptide.
    iii. *Polypeptides* are single chains of three or more amino acids linked together by peptide bonds.
    iv. Proteins have four levels of physical structure.
        a) *Primary structure* refers to the specific sequence of amino acids in a polypeptide.
        b) *Secondary structure* is the initial folding patterns of certain lengths of the polypeptide chain, such as alpha helices and beta-sheets.
        c) *Tertiary structure* refers to the overall shape into which a polypeptide eventually folds.
        d) *Quaternary structure* arises from the association of two or more folded polypeptides to form a multisubunit protein.
    v. Proteins have a wide variety of functions, including structural components of cells and tissues, transport proteins in the cell's membranes, and as catalysts called enzymes.

4. The *nucleic acids—DNA and RNA—*are made from monomers called *nucleotides.*

   i. A nucleotide has three parts.

      a) A *5-carbon sugar*, either deoxyribose (in DNA) or ribose (in RNA).

      b) Three *phosphate groups* are present on a nucleotide, only one of which remains in the DNA or RNA chain after a bond is formed between two nucleotides.

      c) One of four *nitrogenous bases* is present in each nucleotide.

         • Adenine, thymine, cytosine, and guanine are found in DNA.

         • Adenine, uracil, cytosine, and guanine are found in RNA.

Figure 6.15 Structure of a Nucleotide

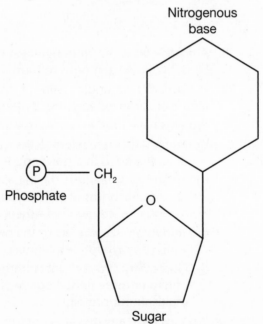

ii. *Phosphodiester bonds* form by dehydration synthesis, linking the sugar of one nucleotide to a phosphate of another nucleotide to produce the sugar–phosphate backbones of DNA and RNA.

iii. The function of DNA is to store genetic information, and the functions of RNA are to decode and express that genetic information as protein.

iv. *ATP* is a nucleotide that donates its energy to a wide variety of biochemical reactions and other processes that occur within cells.

Focus on the names, general structures, and functions of the various macromolecules.

PART III:
ECOLOGY

POPULATIONS

I. Key Concepts

A. **Ecology includes the study of organisms interacting with their environments at increasing levels of inclusiveness.**

1. *Individual organisms* may overcome changes in their environments by physical or behavioral adjustments.

2. A *population* is a group of individuals of the same species living in the same geographical location.

3. *Communities* are groups of interacting populations within an ecosystem.

4. An *ecosystem* includes a community (or communities) as well as the environment in which its members live.

5. The *biosphere* encompasses all organisms in all parts of the Earth including their interactions with their environments.

B. **Populations may experience exponential growth if there are no limiting factors in their environment, and logistic growth if there are limiting factors.**

C. **The smaller a population is, the more likely it is to become extinct.**

D. **Worldwide, the human population is currently experiencing exponential growth, but is expected to begin to level off in the near future.**

II. Individual organisms have mechanisms to withstand physical changes in their immediate environments.

A. The environment of an organism includes biotic and abiotic factors.

1. *Biotic* factors include all living organisms within the environment.

2. *Abiotic* factors are the physical factors of the environment and include temperature, precipitation, humidity, wind, salinity, and availability of oxygen, nutrients, and sunlight.

B. As abiotic factors change over time, or from place to place in an organism's environment, an organism may respond in a variety of ways.

1. A *tolerance curve* describes how able or active an organism is over the range of change it may experience for a particular factor in its environment; at the extreme limits of its range, an organism may not survive.

Figure 7.1 Temperature Tolerance Curve

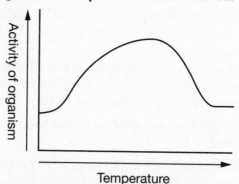

Temperature

2. An organism may *acclimate* (adjust its tolerance) to an environmental factor, such as when humans produce more red blood cells as their bodies adjust to higher elevation.

Don't confuse acclimation with adaptation. **Acclimation** *is a physical change in an individual organism in response to a changing environment, whereas* **adaptation** *is a genetic change in a population of organisms over time in response to a changing environment.*

3. *Regulators* are organisms that spend metabolic energy to internally regulate a physical factor, such as temperature or salinity, to keep it within a limited range even though their environment may exhibit a wider range for that factor.

4. In *conformers*, the factor is not internally regulated; instead, the conformer's internal factor changes to match the environmental factor as it increases or decreases.

Figure 7.2 Regulators and Conformers Respond Differently to Environmental Change

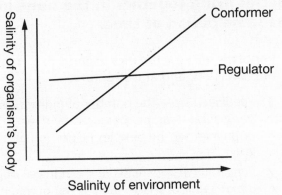

5. Individuals may respond to environmental change by temporary or permanent escape.

    i. An individual may move from location to location during the day, or *migrate* to another location.

    ii. An individual may become *dormant* through one of the following mechanisms.

       a) Some organisms may experience a period of inactivity called *torpor*: *hibernation* in cold weather or *estivation* in hot weather.

       b) Some organisms have resistant forms such as *spores* or *seeds*.

C. A *niche* refers to all of the roles of a species within its environment, including the biotic and abiotic features of its environment.

1. The *fundamental niche* of a species is the total range of environmental factors it can tolerate and the total range of resources it can potentially use.

2. The *realized niche* of a species is the actual extent to which it tolerates and uses its potential environment, due to the possibility that these resources are often reduced by biotic factors such as competition with other organisms.

3. *Generalists* are species with very broad niches, whereas the niches of *specialists* are more specific and limited.

 III. A population is a group of individuals of the same species living together in the same location during the same period of time.

A. Population characteristics include size, density, patterns of dispersion, and age structure.

1. *Population size*—the number of individuals in the population—can be measured by direct counting in small populations or by sampling a portion of the population if it is larger.

2. *Population density* refers to the number of individuals in a defined unit of space, such as the number of single-celled algae per milliliter of pond water, or ferns per square kilometer of forest floor.

3. *Dispersion* is the pattern of distribution of individuals within a population.

   i. A *uniform* (or *even*) dispersion pattern is one in which the members of the population are spaced at relatively equal distances from one another, and often occurs in species that defend a defined territory.

   ii. In a *random* dispersion pattern, each individual's position is independent of the locations of other individuals; for example, the dispersal of a plant's seeds by wind may result in the random location of the plant's offspring.

   iii. A *clumped* distribution pattern is the most common with most organisms in the population preferring to aggregate in the same area(s).

     a) Clumping can result from uneven distribution of the resources needed by the population's members.

     b) Clumping can also be the result of social behaviors that lead to swarming, flocking, or schooling among animals.

Figure 7.3 Dispersion Patterns

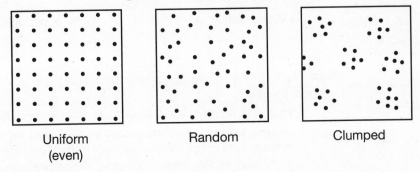

Uniform (even)   Random   Clumped

4. The *age structure* of a population is dynamic and changes over time due to varying birth rates, death rates, and life expectancies.

   i. A population with a greater number of younger, reproductively active members is expected to increase in size more rapidly than a population with fewer young individuals.

ii. If life expectancy increases, the number of older members in a population is expected to increase.

Figure 7.4 Age Structure in Two Different Populations

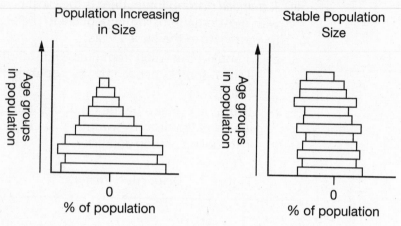

5. A *survivorship curve* shows the expected mortality (death) rates of members of a population over their potential life span.

  i. In a population with a *Type 1* curve—characteristic of species that have few young and invest a lot of energy caring for them—survivorship is high for early and midlife individuals, but drops precipitously in advanced age, indicating that most members of the population live out their potential, maximum life span.

  ii. *Type II* curves describe populations in which the members have more or less the same chance of dying regardless of age.

  iii. A *Type III* curve is characteristic of species that produce large numbers of offspring, most of which die before reaching maturity.

Figure 7.5 Survivorship Curves

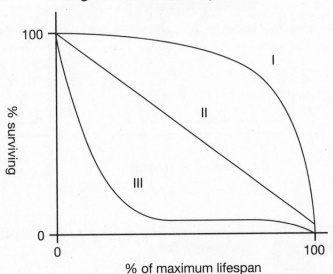

B. **A population's growth rate (birth rate minus death rate) is the change in a population's size per a defined unit of time; two models are used to describe population growth under different conditions.**

1. The *exponential growth model* predicts that a population will grow indefinitely without limit, and that its growth will increase exponentially.

2. The *logistic growth model* is more applicable to most populations in that it takes into account that few populations have the resources needed to increase growth indefinitely.

   i. Characteristics of the logistic growth model:

   a) At first, growth rate increases rapidly.

   b) Grow rate begins to slow down as resources decrease due to use by a larger number of members in the growing population.

   c) Finally, the growth rate levels off, neither rising nor falling, when the population has reached its maximum size, called its *carrying capacity*, which is determined by the resources available to the population.

Figure 7.6 Exponential and Logistic Growth Models

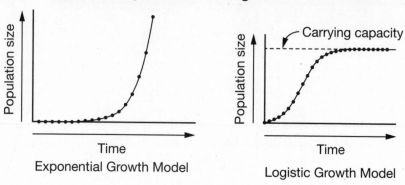

Exponential Growth Model

Logistic Growth Model

Test Tip

Be prepared to interpret population growth graphs and survivorship curves.

3. There are two types of factors that limit the growth of populations.

    i. *Density-independent factors*—such as fire, tornadoes, and hurricanes—limit population growth by affecting the same proportion of individuals in a population regardless of the density of the population.

    ii. *Density-dependent factors* limit population growth more severely at higher population densities than at lower densities.

        a) Limited resources reduce population size in a density-dependent manner, because competition for limited resources becomes more intense as the number of individuals using those resources increases.

        b) Poisoning due to accumulating waste materials becomes more likely, and affects more members of a population, as population density increases.

        c) Predation may be a density-dependent factor limiting a prey population if a predator increases its rate of predation when prey density is higher.

4. Small populations are more likely to become extinct than larger ones because inbreeding reduces the number, health, and genetic variability offspring, or a local natural disaster could eliminate the entire population.

5. After remaining steady for most of human history, the human population has been increasing exponentially since the 1600s due to increasing life expectancy and greater ability to exploit resources, but the growth rate has slowed since the 1960s due to reduction in birth rate in developed, as well as many developing, countries.

Even though the human growth rate has been decreasing since the 1960s, the human population continues to increase in size, because the base size of the population (the total number of humans) has become larger since that time.

COMMUNITIES

I. Key Concepts

A. A community is a group of interacting populations of different species that live in the same geographic area.

B. Species richness, species diversity, and community stability are major characteristics of communities.

C. Species interactions and competition for resources are the bases for community relationships.

D. A succession of different communities occurs over time on newly created areas or in habitats destroyed by natural disasters or human activities.

II. *Properties of communities* can be measured to understand how a community is structured.

A. *Species richness* is the number of different species in a community, while *species diversity* includes not only the number of each species but the size of each population, as well.

  1. Species richness increases as latitude decreases.

      i. Communities closest to the equator, such as those found in tropical rain forests, have the greatest number of species.

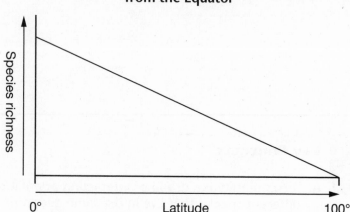

Figure 8.1 Species Richness and Distance from the Equator

ii. Three hypotheses may explain the greater number of species in lower latitudes.

    a) More available sunlight year-round promotes higher primary productivity—plant or phytoplankton growth—resulting in a greater base level at the lowest level of food chains.

    b) A more stable climate may lead to a greater number of niches available for exploitation.

    c) Tropical communities are older than those farther from the equator because they were not destroyed by recent ice ages.

2. The *species-area effect* shows that species richness increases as the number of habitats and the area they cover increases.

    i. Larger islands have more species than smaller islands.

    ii. Reduction in habitat area is a main cause of extinction of populations.

Figure 8.2 Species-area Effect

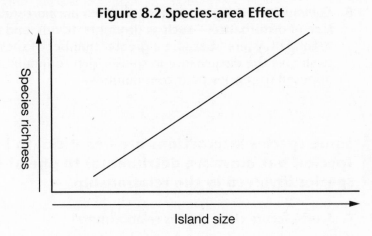

3. A *keystone predator* may increase species richness by preying on a successful competitor, thereby reducing competition between the prey species and its closest competitors and allowing those competitor populations to thrive.

Figure 8.3 Species Diversity with and without a Keystone Predator

Species Diversity with Keystone Predator

Species Diversity without Keystone Predator

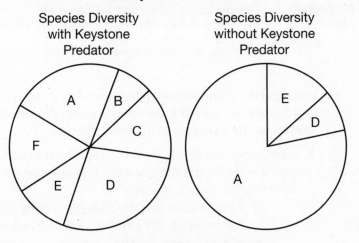

A–F represent different competing species in a community

B. *Communities with greater species richness are more stable* in the face of disturbances—such as droughts, floods, and other natural disasters—because a greater number of species tend to survive the disturbance in species-rich communities as opposed to species-poor communities.

III. Some species interactions are beneficial to both species, but most are detrimental to one of the species involved in the relationship.

A. *Symbioses* are close species relationships.

1. In *mutualism*, both species benefit from the relationship.
2. *Commensalism* is a relationship in which one species benefits while the other species is neither harmed nor helped.
3. *Parasitism* is beneficial to the parasite and detrimental—but not usually immediately fatal—to the host.

Symbioses may involve close coevolution where each species evolves in response to a change in the other species. (For more information, see Coevolution in Chapter 19.) Questions that require you to integrate material from different topics in biology are common on the test, so be aware of these relationships as you study; for example, ecology and evolution are closely related.

B. Interspecific competition, predator—prey interactions, and herbivore—plant interactions generally benefit one species at the expense of another species.

1. *Interspecific competition* is the competition between two species for the same limited resources when their fundamental niches overlap.
    i. If one species uses the shared resources more efficiently, it may gain a *reproductive advantage* as a result.
    ii. In *competitive exclusion*, one species competes so successfully for resources that the other species is

eliminated from the community by becoming extinct or by migrating.

Figure 8.4 Competitive Exclusion

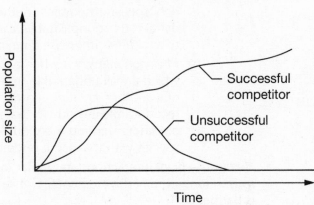

iii. *Character displacement* is the development of an advantageous, genetically determined trait—either physical or behavioral—resulting from the natural selective pressure of direct competition between two species that live in the same community (as opposed to similar species living in different communities who do not develop this type of difference because they are not in direct competition).

iv. Character displacement may result in *resource partitioning* where two or more species divide a common resource between them by feeding at different times on the same resource, or by feeding in different areas within a resource base, or on slightly different prey, etc.

2. *Predator—prey* interaction involves immediate benefits for the predator at the expense of the prey.

  i. *Natural selection* favors traits in the predator that increase the ability of the predator to find, capture, and utilize prey for nutritional needs, while favoring traits in prey that decrease its likelihood of being found, captured, and used for food.

  ii. *Camouflage (cryptic coloration)* is an adaptation common to both predators and prey.

iii. *Mimicry* is a common adaptation in prey species, which reduces their likelihood of being identified by a predator.

    a) In *Batesian mimicry*, a harmless or desirable prey species resembles another species that is dangerous or unpalatable, causing predators to avoid the otherwise desirable species.

    b) *Mullerian mimicry* is when two or more species, which are all undesirable to predators, resemble one another, creating a greater pool of easily recognizable individuals that may result in predators learning more quickly to avoid all species with that same resemblance.

3. *Herbivore—plant* interactions are similar to predator—prey interactions—the herbivore benefits while the plant species is harmed.

    i. Many plants have physical defenses such as thorns, spines, or thick outer coverings.

    ii. Many plants also produce chemical defenses, called *secondary compounds*, such as toxins or noxious substances.

Table 8.1 Types of Species Interactions

Species Interaction	Effect on: Species 1/Species 2	Examples
Mutualism	+/+	Human/intestinal bacteria Lichen (algae/fungi) Pollinators/flowing plants Acacia tree/ants
Commensalism	+/0	Barnacles/whales Birds/grazing animals
Parasitism	+/−	Tapeworm/human Fleas/cat
Competition	−/−	Any two species whose niches overlap

(continued)

Table 8.1 (*continued*)

Species Interaction	Effect on: Species 1/Species 2	Examples
Predator—prey	+/−	Snake/mice
		Spider/other insects
Herbivore—plant	+/−	Cattle/grass
		Caterpillar/plant leaves

Natural selection acting on a population is the mechanism by which species' characteristics change (evolve) over time. (Again, remember to think about how one topic in biology relates to another.)

IV. *Succession* **is a gradual progression of different communities over time that occurs on virgin territory or on habitat recovering from natural or manmade disturbances and involves species changing the environment as time goes on.**

A. *Primary succession* begins slowly and takes longer than secondary succession (hundreds to thousands of years), because it occurs in areas that have not supported life in the recent past.

1. Areas involved in primary succession may be newly exposed or newly formed rock, such as rock exposed by a glacier receding or islands produced by volcanic action.

2. Because there is little or no soil to begin with, rock must be gradually broken down by repeated freezing and thawing or other types of weathering.

3. Autotrophic bacteria, algae, and lichens that grow on rocks are common pioneer species—the first species to colonize the area.

4. Minerals leached from the rocks, as well as the remains of pioneer species, begin to produce some soil that can support small plants and insects.

5. Gradually, larger animals and plants add viable populations of species as they migrate to exploit newly available biotic resources, changing the community's composition of species as a result.

B. *Secondary succession* **occurs in areas where soil still remains and where communities used to exist but have been destroyed by disturbances such as fire, farming, mining, and so on.**

1. *Pioneer species* are usually *small, fast growing, and reproductively prolific.*

2. Windblown seeds or spores of plants, as well as insects, may be the first colonizers.

3. Eventually larger, more diverse plant and animal communities replace pioneer species—and the intermediate communities that have taken their place—in a somewhat predictable sequence.

4. A *climax community* is a stable community that may eventually arise and persist out of a disturbance event if additional disturbances do not occur.

In succession, existing species change the environment, making it more favorable for other species that outcompete them over time as a result.

ENERGY FLOW
AND NUTRIENT CYCLES

I. Key Concepts

A. An ecosystem includes groups of interacting communities and their environment; thus, it includes both *biotic* (living) and *abiotic* (nonliving) components.

B. A trophic level is an organism's nutritional position in a food chain.

C. Energy flows through an ecosystem in a one-way direction, from the sun to progressively higher trophic levels, passing along only about 10% of stored energy at each trophic level while traveling from lower to higher levels.

D. In contrast to a stream of energy running through an ecosystem, nutrients and water are recycled in an ecosystem.

II. *Energy flows through an ecosystem* from lower trophic levels to higher trophic levels.

A. *Producers* comprise the first trophic level and are almost exclusively dependent on solar energy.

  1. Producers are *autotrophs*, and the majority of autotrophs are photoautotrophs.

    i. *Chemoautotrophs* are rare and convert carbon dioxide to organic compounds using an energy source other than sunlight.

      ii. *Photoautotrophs* are the base of most food chains and use photosynthesis to convert carbon dioxide to organic compounds using sunlight as an energy source.

        a) *Plants* are the major producers in terrestrial ecosystems.

        b) *Photosynthetic bacteria and protists* are the major producers in aquatic ecosystems.

        c) Less than 5% of the *solar energy* available to photoautotrophs is used to make organic compounds.

2. *Gross primary productivity* is the rate at which producers capture energy.

      i. Producers use some of the energy they capture for their own cellular respiration.

      ii. This spent energy is not available to the next trophic level.

      iii. Therefore, *net primary* productivity is gross primary productivity minus the rate of cellular respiration of producers.

      iv. Net primary productivity results in the production of *biomass*—the organic material made by all organisms in one tropic level—therefore, net primary productivity determines how much energy is available to the next trophic level.

3. Different ecosystems have different levels of net primary productivity.

      i. Primary productivity is greatest in estuaries and tropical rainforests and lowest in deserts and the open ocean.

        a) The main factors affecting the net primary productivity of *terrestrial ecosystems* are sunlight, temperature, and precipitation.

        b) The main factors affecting the net primary productivity of *aquatic ecosystems* are sunlight and available nutrients.

B. *Consumers* **are the organisms which comprise subsequent trophic levels, and they are all ultimately dependent on producers for their energy needs.**

1. *Primary consumers* are heterotrophic herbivores that eat producers in order to obtain energy.
2. Consumers at higher trophic levels are either carnivores or omnivores.
    i. *Carnivores* eat other consumers.
    ii. *Omnivores* eat both consumers and producers.

Figure 9.1 Three Trophic Level Diagram

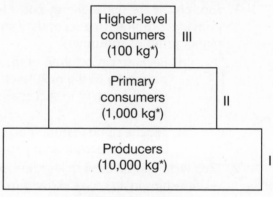

* approximate biomass

3. Only about 10% percent of the energy available at one trophic level is converted into biomass in the next trophic level, because some energy is always lost in the following ways:
    i. As heat every time a chemical reaction occurs within an organism.
    ii. By cellular respiration and other processes that do not produce biomass directly.
    iii. As organismal waste, such as urine and feces.
    iv. By the fact that not all of the organisms at a lower level are consumed by organisms at the next highest level.
    v. When part of the biomass of an organism, such as bones, teeth, or cellulose, cannot be eaten or digested for some consumers.

Because each question on the test has five possible answer choices, it is common for questions to be based on lists, such as the preceding one. Some of these questions ask you to pick out a "wrong" choice from a list and usually use the phrase, "all of the following are part of X EXCEPT. . . ." Other list-type questions ask you to pick out a "right" choice, because the other answer choices have been altered to make them incorrect answers.

C. **Food chains and food webs illustrate the energy interactions between members of a specific community.**

1. *Food chains* are single energy paths from a producer to a primary consumer to a secondary consumer, and potentially higher levels of consumers.

    i. Because almost 90% of the energy in a level is not passed up to the next level, fewer individuals are usually present in successively higher levels of a food chain.

    ii. For the same reason, food chains are usually fairly short, representing only three to four trophic levels.

2. *Food webs* can be used to illustrate interrelated energy relationships in an entire ecosystem.

    i. Some producers may be eaten by several consumers.

    ii. Some consumers may eat multiple producers and/or consumers.

    iii. Relationships with detritivores and decomposers can also be added to food webs.

    a) *Detritivores*, such as vultures and earthworms, are organisms that consume nonliving organic material, such as dead organisms, fallen leaves, and feces.

    b) A *decomposer*, such as a bacterium or fungus, is a type of detritivore that breaks down complex molecules, found in waste products and dead organisms, into simpler nutrients that can be recycled via nutrient cycles.

**Figure 9.2 An Example of a Food Chain (-----▶)
within a Food Web (——▶)**

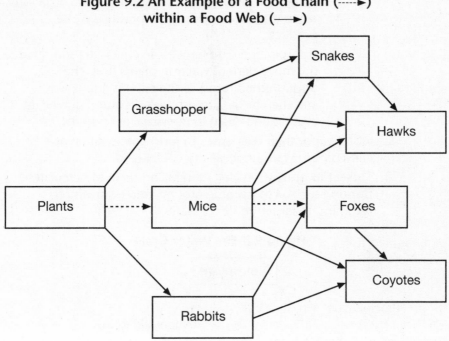

  **Test Tip**

The arrows in a food chain or web indicate the flow of energy. If all arrows originating from a species point away from it, it is most likely a primary producer. If all arrows point only toward a species, it is either a consumer or a decomposer.

III. *Nutrient cycles* **recycle water, carbon, nitrogen, and phosphorus, which move from the ecosystem's organisms to the abiotic portions of an ecosystem and back again.**

   A. The *water cycle* involves the processes of *evaporation, transpiration,* and *precipitation.*

      1. The sun's heat causes water to evaporate and enter the atmosphere as water vapor.

         i. The largest reservoirs of water on the Earth are oceans, lakes, rivers, and streams.

      ii. Water also evaporates from soil and from organisms when they sweat, exhale, or produce waste products.

      iii. Transpiration—the process in which the sun drives the movement of water in plants from the soil, through their roots, to their stems and leaves, and then to the atmosphere—is also a significant evaporation event in terrestrial ecosystems.

2. Water vapor then condenses to form precipitation as it is carried from warmer oceans to cooler land.

3. Subject to gravity, precipitation falling on land percolates through the soil to become ground water or runs off, returning to larger bodies of water.

Figure 9.3 The Water Cycle

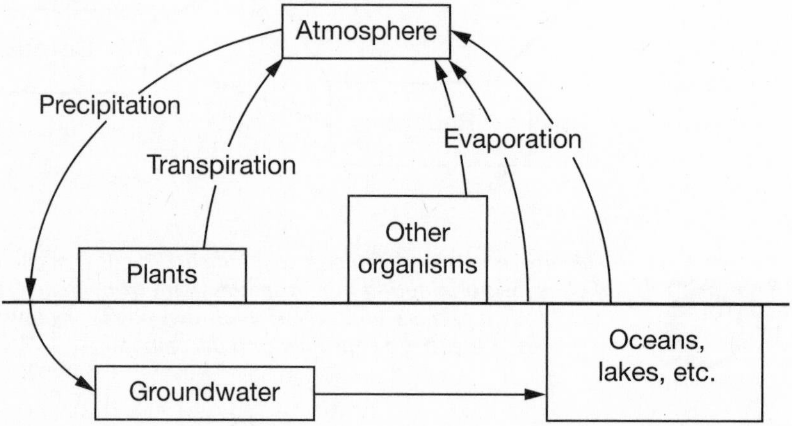

B. The *carbon cycle* involves the processes of *photosynthesis, cellular respiration,* and *combustion.*

1. Autotrophs take in carbon from the atmosphere as CO_2 and fix it into organic compounds by photosynthesis.

2. Organic compounds comprise the bodies of all organisms, as well as the starting compounds for cellular respiration.

3. All organisms break down some organic compounds in the process of cellular respiration, releasing CO_2 again to the atmosphere.

4. The combustion of carbon-based fuels—such as oil, coal, and natural gas—release carbon from geologic stores to the atmosphere as CO_2.

5. Some of this CO_2 enters the carbon cycle via photosynthesis, but the excess remains in the atmosphere.

Figure 9.4 The Carbon Cycle

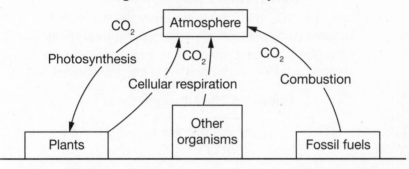

C. The *nitrogen cycle* involves a complex series of biochemical reactions in different organisms.

1. The key facts to remember about nitrogen and nitrogen metabolism are as follows.

   i. Nitrogen is needed by all organisms as an essential component of proteins and nucleic acids.

   ii. Most of the nitrogen on Earth is present in the atmosphere as N_2.

   iii. Another store of nitrogen is in the bodies and waste products of organisms themselves.

   iv. Plants cannot use N_2, but they can take in and use ammonia (NH_3) and nitrates (NO_3^-).

   v. Plants then pass nitrogen on to animals when they are eaten.

2. The *key processes* involved in the nitrogen cycle that make nitrogen available to plants are nitrogen fixation, ammonification, and nitrification.

   i. *Nitrogen fixation* is the process whereby *nitrogen-fixing bacteria* convert atmospheric N_2 to NH_3.

      a) Some nitrogen-fixing bacteria are free-living in the soil.

b) Others live symbiotically in root nodules of some
plants, such as peas, beans, clover, and alfalfa.

ii. *Ammonification* is the process whereby *decomposers*
break down nitrogenous compounds in dead
organisms, feces, and urine to produce NH_3.

iii. *Nitrification* is the process whereby *nitrifying bacteria*
convert NH_3 to NO_3^-.

3. NH_3 and NO_3^- made by these processes can then be
assimilated by plants and passed up the food chain to animals.

4. Nitrogen can be returned to the atmosphere by the process of
denitrification in which *denitrifying bacteria* convert NO_3^- to N_2.

Figure 9.5 The Nitrogen Cycle

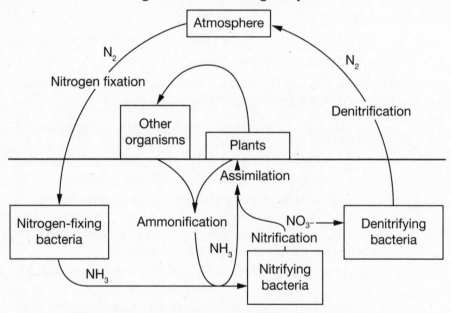

D. The *phosphorus cycle* provides an element needed by all
organisms as a component of nucleic acids and ATP.

1. Phosphorus is not present in the atmosphere, as are water,
carbon, and nitrogen.

2. Weathering of rocks releases phosphates to the soil and water,
making it available to producers.

3. Producers pass it on to consumers and then to decomposers,
who return it to the soil.

Figure 9.6 The Phosphorus Cycle

Weathering

Other organisms

Plants

Rock

Decomposition

Decomposers

P

Table 9.1 Comparison of the Different Nutrient Cycles

Nutrient Cycled	Use in Organisms	Major Reserves	Important Processes
Water	Most of the mass of an organism is water	Bodies of water (oceans, lakes rivers, streams)	Evaporation Transpiration Precipitation
Carbon	Organic molecules	Organisms Atmosphere	Photosynthesis Respiration Combustion
Nitrogen	Proteins Nucleic acids	Organisms Atmosphere	Nitrogen fixation Ammonification Nitrification Assimilation Denitrification
Phosphorus	Nucleic acids ATP	Rock, soil Organisms	Weathering Decomposition

Test Tip

Again, be on the lookout for material that can be converted into list-type questions as you study. Make flashcards with various important lists to test your knowledge.

ECOSYSTEMS AND BIOMES

I. Key Concepts

A. The earth has distinct ecological regions, covering large geographic areas, called *biomes*, which contain a number of smaller, interrelated ecosystems.

B. Terrestrial biomes are distinguished from one another by temperature, rainfall, flora, and fauna.

C. Aquatic ecosystems are distinguished primarily by salinity, and secondarily by availability of nutrients and sunlight.

II. There are seven major *terrestrial biomes*.

A. Although global distribution of biomes is generally related to latitude, biomes are not evenly distributed with respect to latitude due to global and local climatic variations.

1. Land masses are of different sizes and are separated by different amounts of open water.

2. The interior of land masses experience greater temperature extremes than coastal areas.

3. Seasonal temperature and sunlight variations occur because the Earth is tilted on its axis.

4. Wet and dry seasons also occur in some regions, while others experience regular precipitation throughout the year.

Figure 10.1 General Locations of Terrestrial Biomes

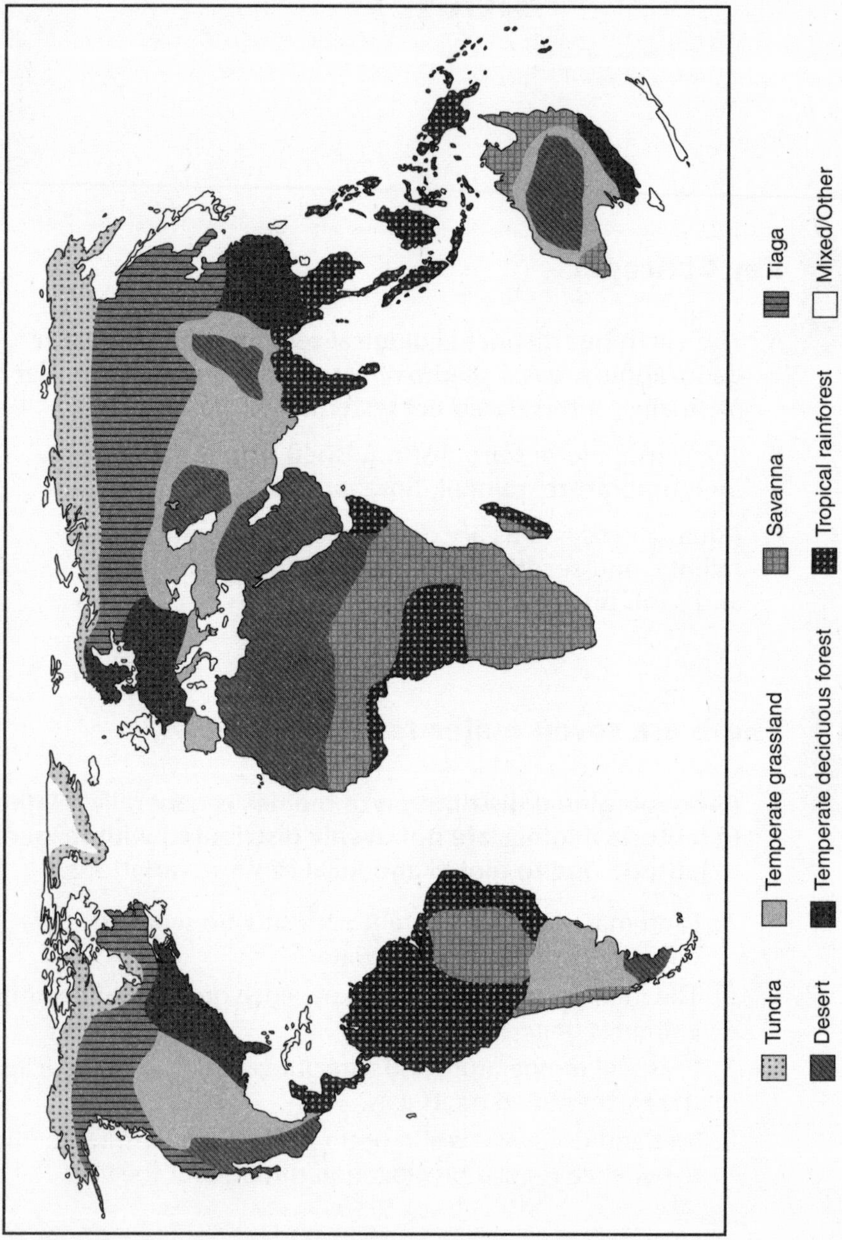

Tundra

Desert

Temperate grassland

Temperate deciduous forest

Savanna

Tropical rainforest

Tiaga

Mixed/Other

5. The rocks and soil in a particular area determine the availability of different inorganic nutrients.
6. Global wind patterns and ocean currents do not distribute moisture and heat evenly across the Earth's land masses.
7. Locations of mountain ranges affect local climate.

B. **Similar biomes are found on different continents.**

1. *Tundras* cover the most land of any biome, and are found above 60 degrees north latitude including northern portions of North America, Europe, and Asia.
2. *Tiagas* are south of tundras in the northern parts of North America, Europe, and Asia.
3. *Temperate deciduous forests* are found near 30 degrees north and south latitude in eastern North America, central Europe, eastern Asia, and eastern Australia.
4. *Temperate grasslands* are located in central North America, southern South America, eastern Europe, and central Asia.
5. *Deserts* are found in southern North America, southern South America, northern Africa, central Australia, and parts of Asia.
6. *Savannas* are found in central and southern Africa, central South America, and parts of Australia.
7. *Tropical rain forests* are found between the Tropics of Capricorn and Cancer in South America, Africa, and Asia.

C. **Rainfall and temperature are two major determinants of a biome's *flora* (plants) and *fauna* (animals).**

Test Tip

A tiaga is also called a **northern coniferous forest;** chaparral *is a less extensive biome found in some parts of California and in coastal areas surrounding the Mediterranean Sea.*

Table 10.1 Characteristics of Biomes

Biome	Temperature	Rainfall	Flora	Fauna	Terminology
Tundra	Low	Low	Small plants (grass, moss) almost no trees	Caribou, arctic fox, snowy owl	*Permafrost*: subsoil always frozen
Tiaga	Low	Low-moderate	Coniferous forest	Moose, bear, wolf	*Coniferous*: have cones, most evergreen
Temperate deciduous forest	Moderate	Moderate	Deciduous forest (beech, elm, oak, etc.) moss, ferns, herbs	Deer, fox, raccoon, snake, squirrels, birds	*Deciduous*: lose leaves in winter
Temperate grassland	Moderate	Low-moderate	Grasses, almost no trees	Bison, other grazers	*Grassland*: prairie, pampas, steppes, veldt
Desert	High	Low	Cactus, shrubs, succulents, CAM plants	Lizards, rodents, snakes	*CAM plants*: open stomata only at night
Savanna	High	Moderate	Grasses, some trees and shrubs	Zebra, lion, gazelle, giraffe	
Tropical rain forest	High	High	Very tall trees, epiphytes, highest biodiversity	Monkeys, snakes, insects, birds, sloth	*Biodiversity*: the number and variety of species present

III. *Aquatic ecosystems* **cover more of the Earth's surface than terrestrial ecosystems.**

A. *Marine biomes,* such as *oceans,* have about 3% salt concentration, and are divided vertically and horizontally into zones.

1. The *intertidal zone* occurs at the shorelines of oceans.

   i. Organisms in the intertidal zone are subject to strong waves and daily exposure to the air.

   ii. Species living in this zone include plankton, clams, oysters, mussels, crabs, sea anemones, whelks, and sea stars.

2. The *neritic zone* runs horizontally from the intertidal zone to the end of the continental shelf.

   i. Due to abundant sunlight and nutrients, the neritic zone has very high biodiversity.

   ii. Coral reefs form in warmer parts of the neritic zone.

   iii. Species include plankton, algae, coral, sponges, bryozoans, mollusks, sea turtles, squid, and numerous species of fish.

3. The *oceanic zone* is beyond the neritic zone and is divided into a number of additional zones according to depth.

   i. The *photic zone* is the upper level of the ocean that receives sunlight.

      a) For lack of nutrients, this zone is not as productive per unit area compared to the neritic zone, but because open ocean covers a much larger area, it has a greater total primary productivity.

      b) Species present include plankton, whales, dolphins, sea turtles, and many invertebrates and fishes.

   ii. The *aphotic zone* is below the photic zone and does not receive sunlight; it is divided into two areas.

      a) The *pelagic zone* supports communities that live mainly off of dead organisms that fall from the photic zone, and its members can stand low temperatures and high pressures.

b) The *benthic zone* (or *benthos*) is the ocean bottom and supports communities such as those living near volcanic, deep sea vents that rely on chemoautotrophic producers that use H_2S as an energy source to produce organic compounds.

Figure 10.2 Zones of Marine and Freshwater Biomes

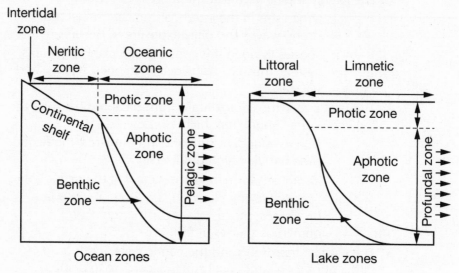

B. *Freshwater biomes* **usually have salt concentrations below 1%.**

1. *Lakes* and *ponds* contain standing freshwater.

   i. *Oligotrophic lakes* are deep and nutrient poor with clear water and are not as productive as shallower *eutrophic lakes*, which are nutrient rich.

   ii. The zones of lakes are similar to those of the ocean.

   a) The *photic zone* is divided into the *littoral zone* (closest to the shore) and the *limnetic zone* (farther from shore).

   b) The *aphotic zone* far from shore is called the *profundal zone*.

   c) The lake bottom is called the *benthic zone*.

       iii. Common species include plankton, crustaceans, fish, snakes, turtles, mammals, such as otter, muskrat, and birds.

2. *Streams* and *rivers* have a steady flow of moving water.

       i. At their sources, streams have few nutrients and the water flow is very rapid; species include insects, crustaceans, beaver, trout, and other fish.

       ii. As streams join to form larger rivers, water flow slows and runoff from the land produces a more nutrient-rich environment with less dissolved oxygen; species include underwater plants, algae, crustaceans, fish, and birds.

3. *Wetlands* include bogs, marshes, and estuaries.

       i. *Bogs* and *marshes* support water plants, such as cattails, water lilies, and sedges, and animals, such as birds and small fish.

       ii. *Estuaries* occur where rivers meet the ocean, and are thus a mixture of salt and freshwater patches.

          a) Tides cause water levels to rise and fall daily.

          b) Biodiversity is very high, and many species of fish and invertebrates, including shrimp and oysters, breed in estuaries.

          c) Autotrophs include grasses, algae, and some water-tolerant trees.

Test Tip

Be prepared to recognize biomes by their descriptions, major features, or types of organisms they support.

CONSERVATION BIOLOGY, BIODIVERSITY, AND EFFECTS OF HUMAN INTERVENTION

I. Key Concepts

A. Exponential growth of the human population has had effects on every aspect of the biosphere, from the global level to individual species.

B. Humans have cooperated to address problems of a global nature, such as the thinning of the ozone layer and the reduction of acid rain.

C. Global biodiversity, the number and variety of species on earth, is currently being reduced due to an increased rate of extinction mainly caused by pervasive habitat destruction.

D. A combination of conservation strategies are being applied to address biodiversity and other global issues that affect human welfare, including sustainable development, which focuses on the continued success of human populations and the ecosystems that sustain them.

II. The great growth of the *human population* in recent times has profoundly altered the biosphere from the global to the local level.

A. Human population has only risen to great numbers very recently.

  1. For most of the estimated 100,000 years humans have been on the Earth, the population has been well under half a billion individuals.

2. The size of the *human population has grown exponentially* since approximately 1650 CE.

3. Since 1650, it has taken only about 360 years (less than 0.4% of the total time humans have existed) for the population to rise from 0.5 billion to 7 billion.

4. At current growth rates, about 80,000,000 individuals are added to the human population each year.

Figure 11.1 Human Population Growth

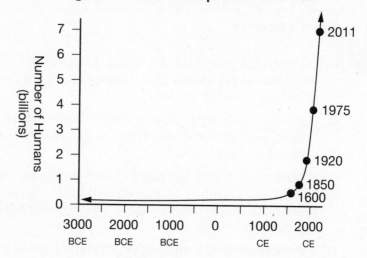

B. *Humans* have similar *needs* as other large mammals, but their numbers, worldwide distribution, and unique ability to extract and utilize resources have a greater impact on the Earth than most other organisms.

1. The *need for food* has resulted in the destruction of entire biomes, such as the grasslands of the Midwestern United States, which have been almost completely converted, over just the last 250 years, to agricultural and other uses.

2. The use of fossil fuels to supply *energy needed* for industry, and to heat and cool homes, has resulted in a global increase in atmospheric carbon dioxide, which is correlated with a rise in global temperature and severe weather.

3. The *need for space* to live has destroyed large areas of the habitats of other organisms in almost every part of the Earth where humans currently live, leading to the greatest rate of

extinction of species since the last major extinction event on the Earth 65,000,000 years ago, when about 50% of all species, including most dinosaur groups, became extinct.

4. The *disposal of* biological, industrial, and household *wastes* have significantly altered nutrient cycling and introduced either totally new, or otherwise rare, toxic molecules into the environment that have significant adverse affects on humans and other species.

III. Some success has been achieved in reversing several of the effects of human impacts at the global level through *international cooperation*.

A. Thinning of the protective *ozone layer* of the atmosphere has been addressed.

1. The Earth is surrounded by a layer of ozone (O_3), which protects all living organisms from ultraviolet (UV) radiation.

2. *UV radiation* causes *DNA mutations* that lead to *cancer* and other diseases in humans and other species.

3. *Chlorofluorocarbons (CFCs)*, used in refrigeration and other products and processes, contribute significantly to ozone depletion.

4. International agreements to discontinue CFC use starting in the 1990s, are expected to cause a reversal of thinning of the ozone layer within the next 50–100 years.

B. An *acid precipitation* reduction plan has been implemented in some countries, including the United States.

1. The pH of uncontaminated precipitation is about 5.6.

2. *pH levels* from 5.6 to 1.5 have been recorded in the United States; these low levels damage ecosystems by causing *leaching* of calcium and magnesium ions from soil, increasing *aluminum toxicity* in plants, and by direct effects on vulnerable aquatic and soil organisms at lower levels of food chains.

3. The main cause of acid precipitation is increased levels of sulfur oxides and nitrogen oxides released from the burning of fossil fuels—especially coal.

4. *Cap and trade,* and other reduction strategies put into place by the U.S. Environmental Protection Agency (EPA), have cut sulfur and nitrogen oxide emissions from electric generators by more than half in the past 30 years.

C. *Bans or reductions in toxins*—such as DDT, PCBs, and mercury—have been achieved in some countries.

1. Industrial waste chemicals released to the environment can be widely distributed in the environment via air and water.

2. Chemical wastes have a variety of serious toxic or developmental effects in organisms, including humans, and can affect entire ecosystems.

3. These effects are greatly increased by the process of *biological magnification* whereby toxins become more concentrated in the bodies of organisms at higher trophic levels, including humans; for example, DDT concentrations reach 10 million times the concentration in the tissues of a top predator compared to the minute concentrations found in its ecosystem's water source.

4. Not all toxins have been identified, studied in detail, or are easily removed from the environment, but bans on DDT in the United States and other countries, and reductions in other toxins, have been effective in reversing negative effects on some species and ecosystems.

D. *Climate change* due to the *rising temperature* of the Earth in recent decades has spurred development of models to predict the likely consequences and provide information for making appropriate plans where possible.

1. *Carbon dioxide* in the atmosphere from the burning of *fossil fuels*—oil, coal, and natural gas—has increased by 35% since the industrial revolution (beginning in the mid 1800s).

2. Carbon dioxide and other *greenhouse gases* trap heat within the Earth's atmosphere.

3. Even slight increases in the Earth's temperature have significant consequences.

   i. *Polar ice melts* cause a rise in sea level, which submerges low-lying land.

   ii. *More severe storms* due to the increased energy of the ocean and air masses can devastate larger areas more often.

   iii. Large changes in the *location of precipitation* can affect current agricultural areas.

   iv. *Acceleration of species extinction* may occur as species—plants in particular—are not able to move rapidly from changing habitats to more suitable ones.

4. International cooperation to reduce the emission of greenhouse gases including *energy conservation* and utilization of *alternative energy sources* such as wind, solar, and water power is being attempted.

5. Some countries, such as the low-lying Netherlands, are implementing plans to counter effects directly impacting their countries, such as the construction of additional protective structures and enhanced emergency preparedness.

Table 11.1 Major Effects of Human Intervention on a Global Level

Problem	Cause	Global Consequence	Solution Attempted
Depletion of ozone layer surrounding the Earth	Use of CFCs	–More UV radiation –Greater cancer risk in humans –Greater likelihood of DNA damage in organisms	Phase out use of CFCs
Acid precipitation (pH below 5.6)	Sulfur and nitrogen oxides released from burning fossil fuels, especially coal	–Increase in aluminum toxicity in plants –Death of vulnerable organisms –Damage to entire ecosystems	Reduce sulfur and nitrogen oxides through "cap and trade" programs

(continued)

Table 11.1 (*continued*)

Problem	Cause	Global Consequence	Solution Attempted
Toxins, such as DDT, PCBs, and mercury	Industrial and household waste	–Poisoning and death of species in multiple ecosystems –Toxicity to humans	–Ban the use of the toxin –Clear industrial waste of toxin before release
Global climate change	Increased greenhouse gases, mainly from the burning of fossil fuels	–Polar ice melts, sea level rises –More and larger storms –Extinction of organisms sensitive to altered temperatures –Negative effects on agriculture	–Reduce greenhouse gases –Alternative energy sources –Plan for flooding, intense weather, and effects on agriculture

 Habitat destruction, overexploitation, and introduction of exotic species and diseases are the greatest threats to biodiversity and are currently contributing to an increase in the rate of species extinction.

    A. *Biodiversity* is the degree of variation of species in a given area: the area can encompass a community or the entire biosphere.

        1. The basis of biodiversity is *genetic variation* within populations.

            i. Genetic variation is the raw material for *evolution* of populations.

            ii. Genetic variation within a population generally buffers a population against extinction.

2. *Species richness*—the number of different species in an area—and *species diversity*—the relative abundance of different species in an area—are general *measures of biodiversity*.

    i. Species richness in the biosphere varies among groups of organisms.

       a) Insects, plants, and crustaceans have the greatest number of different species.

       b) Fungi, fish, and mammals have lower numbers of different species.

    ii. Species richness in the biosphere varies among ecosystems.

       a) The rain forest, estuaries, and coral reefs generally have the greatest numbers of species.

       b) Deserts, open ocean, taiga, and agricultural land are examples of ecosystems with fewer numbers of species.

    iii. Species richness increases as latitude decreases.

    iv. Globally, *biodiversity hotspots* are relatively small areas with exceptionally high numbers of different species.

    v. Species that are *rare*—have small numbers of individuals—are found in all parts of the biosphere.

B. **Increasing *extinction rates* are currently decreasing biodiversity.**

1. Estimates of the biosphere's biodiversity are between 10 and 30 million species.
2. Extinction rates vary for different groups of organisms, but the overall extinction rate across all species is currently estimated at about 20%.

C. **The major causes of decreasing biodiversity are over-exploitation, introduction of exotic species and diseases, and habitat destruction.**

1. *Overexploitation*—overhunting and overharvesting, mostly of plants and animals—contribute to the extinction, or near extinction of species; examples include dodo birds, American bison, whales, cod, sassafras, elephants, and wolves.

2. The intentional or unintentional introduction of an *exotic species*—one that is not *endemic* (not native) to a particular ecosystem—contributes to extinction through competition with native species or predation on native species; examples include the reduction in biodiversity of cichlid fish species following the introduction of Nile perch to Lake Victoria, the release of exotic pets in the Florida Everglades, and the replacement of native North American bird species by the introduction of starlings and pigeons.

3. The introduction of a *disease-causing organism* to an area where it was not previously present also reduces biodiversity.

4. *Habitat destruction* or reduction through immediate or gradual processes is the major cause of decreasing biodiversity.

   i. *Wars and natural, or human-caused, disasters* may result in immediate or gradual habitat destruction; examples include the use of the defoliant, agent orange during the Vietnam War, which destroyed large patches of rain forest habitat, hurricane effects on islands, and the radioactivity released by the Chernobyl nuclear meltdown.

   ii. *Global changes,* such as the thinning of the ozone layer, global warming, and acid precipitation can affect producers in an ecosystem, resulting in large-scale changes in habitat characteristics.

   iii. The gradual increase in land converted to *agriculture* and living space directly eliminates or fragments extremely large habitat areas.

   iv. The release of *organic* (nitrogen-rich sewage and fertilizer runoff) and *toxic waste* into the environment alters or destroys aquatic habitat.

D. **Reasons for preservation of biodiversity include utilitarian and nonutilitarian consideration.**

1. *Utilitarian* reasons for maintaining biodiversity are those that benefit humans physically or economically.

   i. Biodiversity maintains the health of ecosystems, thus preserving the services they provide, such as the protection of coastal regions from excessive flooding provided by wetlands, or removing harmful substances from the water and atmosphere.

      ii. Maintaining biodiversity provides ready supplies of food and materials currently used, e.g., wide varieties of seafood, game, plants, and lumber.

      iii. Maintaining biodiversity provides a future store of genetic diversity used by businesses from pharmacology to food, textile, and energy manufacturing.

  2. *Nonutilitarian* considerations are reasons dealing with religious, moral, or aesthetic values, such as the beauty and belief in the intrinsic value of all beings, responsibility to ancestors, children, and future generations, and the protection and stewardship of the Earth.

E. ***Conservation biology* focuses on maintaining biodiversity and includes strategies targeting all ecological levels.**

  1. *At the individual and population levels*, rare species are targeted for protection.

      i. The U.S. *Endangered Species Act* provides various protections for a species that is in danger of extinction throughout all or a significant portion of its range.

      a) Pesticide use is restricted within the species' area.

      b) The species is prohibited from being killed, harmed, or harvested.

      c) Federal agencies are prohibited from authorizing, funding, or carrying out any action that likely jeopardizes the species' continued existence or destroys or modifies its critical habitat.

      ii. Isolated populations of a species may be united by creating *habitat corridors* to join fragmented habitat patches.

      iii. Other strategies to protect individual species may include the following:

      a) *Reintroduction* of a species to an existing habitat that may involve raising individuals of a species in captivity and releasing them

      b) Creating a *protected area* for the species to live and procreate

      c) *Restoring habitat* that has been used for human activities, and then reintroducing species

      d) *Monitoring* the movement of individuals in a population

2. *Community and ecosystem-level* strategies primarily seek to protect biodiversity by protecting, reclaiming, or expanding critical habitat.

    i. Biodiversity hotspots are especially targeted for protection as *nature reserves* due to the large variety of species often found only within the small area.

    ii. Restoring entire ecosystems may involve reclaiming polluted, radioactive, or otherwise damaged areas; contouring land; re-establishing waterways; and reintroducing biotic components to the environment.

    iii. Restoration may involve *bioremediation*—the use of special plants or bacteria that break down toxic substances.

    iv. Protection of a critical habitat may involve purchasing and restoring surrounding areas.

V. Limiting further damage to biodiversity and the environment involves sustainable development.

A. The goal of *sustainable development* is to manage the ecosystems of the biosphere in a way that supports the prosperity of human populations in the long term.

B. A continuing goal in this process is to study how ecological systems work in order to provide the best information for making decisions as to how to best manage and utilize the Earth's resources in a way that continues to replenish vital resources for future generations, such as clean air and drinking water.

Pay attention to italicized terminology, potential lists that could be turned into questions, and connections with material in other chapters.

PART IV:
GENETICS

MEIOSIS

I. Key Concepts

A. Sexual reproduction creates greater genetic variation in offspring compared to asexual reproduction.

B. The sexual life cycle involves two key processes: meiosis—the production of haploid gametes—and fertilization—the union of two gametes to form a single-celled zygote.

C. Meiosis involves two cell divisions, the first of which, meiosis I, differs in very significant ways from mitosis.

D. Sexual reproduction produces genetic variation by three mechanisms: independent assortment of chromosomes, crossing over, and random fertilization.

II. Greater genetic variation is found in the offspring produced by sexual reproduction as opposed to asexual reproduction.

A. In *asexual reproduction*, a single parent gives rise to two genetically identical offspring, by the processes of mitosis or binary fission.

　1. Most prokaryotes reproduce by *binary fission* in which the parent's single chromosome is copied and each new cell receives an almost identical copy of that chromosome.

2. Asexual reproduction also occurs in some multicellular eukaryotes when a certain cell, or group of cells, produced by mitosis, gives rise to an almost identical offspring called a *clone.*

    i. This process is called *budding* in some organisms, such as yeast (a fungus) and hydra (an animal).

    ii. This process is called *vegetative reproduction* in plants, most of which also reproduce by sexual reproduction.

3. A small amount of genetic variation between parents and offspring in asexual reproduction occurs by *mutation* during DNA replication when the chromosome(s) is copied.

4. Additional genetic variation occurs during asexual reproduction in prokaryotes by *transformation, transduction,* and *conjugation.* (For additional information, see Prokaryotes in Chapter 21.)

Figure 12.1 Asexual Reproduction in Yeast and Plants

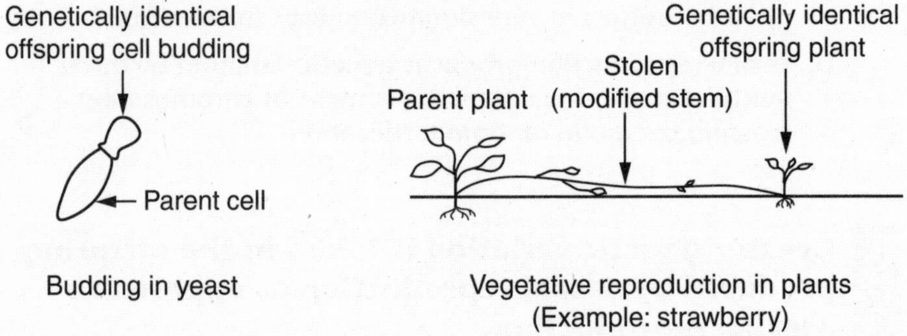

Genetically identical offspring cell budding

Parent cell

Budding in yeast

Parent plant

Stolen (modified stem)

Genetically identical offspring plant

Vegetative reproduction in plants (Example: strawberry)

B. *Sexual reproduction* **occurs in most eukaryotes, and produces offspring with much greater genetic variation due to meiosis and fertilization, which are the key processes of the sexual life cycle.**

III. **The *sexual life cycle* involves the production of haploid gametes and the union of gametes during fertilization to produce a single cell, called a *zygote*, which is diploid.**

A. The sexual life cycle in *animals* includes a *multicellular diploid* form of the organism.

1. *Somatic cells*—the cells of the body—of a sexually reproducing animal are diploid.

    i. Each *diploid cell* contains a set of chromosomes derived from the female parent (n), and a set of chromosomes derived from the male parent (n).

    ii. The total number of chromosomes in a diploid cell is thus $2n$.

2. Two alternating processes in the sexual lifecycle maintain a constant number of chromosomes from generation to generation.

    i. *Meiosis* occurs in testes and ovaries to produce *haploid cells*—called *gametes*—that contain half the number of chromosomes as diploid cells.

      a) Female gametes are called *eggs*, or *ova* (sing. *ovum*).

      b) Male gametes are called *sperm* or *spermatozoa*.

    ii. *Fertilization* is the union of a sperm and an egg cell to produce a *zygote*, which is diploid.

      a) Because each gamete has a haploid number of chromosomes (n), when a sperm and an egg combine, the zygote produced is diploid ($n + n = 2n$).

      b) The zygote then divides by mitosis many times to produce a multicellular organism composed of diploid cells, including its own testes or ovaries in which meiosis can occur to produce the next generation.

B. All sexual life cycles include the alternating processes of meiosis and fertilization, but those occurring in organisms other than animals differ in regard to whether or not the multicellular form(s) of the organism are diploid or haploid.

  1. The only *multicellular* form of most *fungi* and some *algae* is *haploid*.

      i. The haploid, multicellular organism produces haploid gametes by mitosis.

      ii. Union of the gametes during fertilization produces a diploid zygote.

      iii. The single-celled zygote undergoes meiosis almost immediately to produce haploid spores.

      iv. The haploid spores undergo repeated mitoses to produce the haploid, multicellular organism.

  2. *Plants* and some *algae* have a sexual life cycle called *alternation of generations* that involves *two multicellular forms*: one of which is haploid and the other diploid.

      i. The haploid, multicellular form of the organism produces gametes by mitosis.

      ii. These gametes then fuse during fertilization to produce a diploid zygote.

      iii. The diploid zygote undergoes repeated mitoses to produce the diploid, multicellular form of the organism.

      iv. This diploid, multicellular form then produces haploid spores by meiosis.

      v. The spores undergo repeated mitoses to form the haploid, multicellular form.

Figure 12.2 Sexual Life Cycles

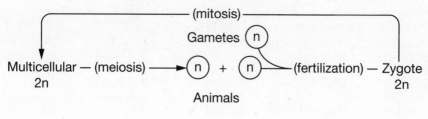

Animals

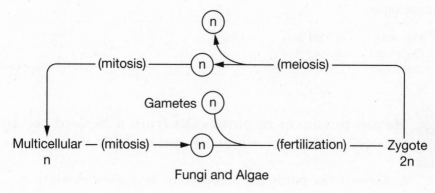

Fungi and Algae

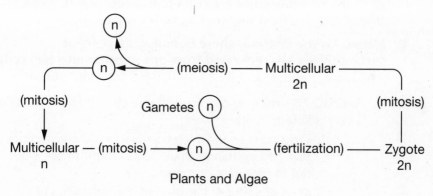

Plants and Algae

Table 12.1 Comparison of Sexual Life Cycles

Organism	Multicellular Form(s)	Meiosis Produces Haploid Cells	Gametes Produced by Meiosis	Gametes Produced by Mitosis
Animals	Diploid only	Always	Yes	No
Fungi and some algae	Haploid only	Always	No	Yes
Plants and some algae	Diploid and haploid forms	Always	No	Yes

 IV. *Meiosis* **produces haploid cells from a diploid cell by two cell divisions: meiosis I and meiosis II.**

A. Meiosis, like mitosis, is preceded by an *S phase* in which all of the chromosomes are copied; the two copies, called *chromatids*, are held together at their centromeres.

B. *Meiosis I* is the division where homologous pairs of chromosomes are separated from one another into two cells which are haploid, and it can be divided into four stages.

  1. *Prophase I* is similar to prophase of mitosis in a few ways, but is very different in other ways.

     i. *Crossing over*, in which homologous chromosomes pair and exchange DNA, occurs in prophase I, but not in prophase of mitosis.

        a) A diploid cell has pairs of chromosomes of maternal and paternal origin called *homologous chromosomes* (or homologues).

        b) *Homologues* such as maternal chromosome 1 and paternal chromosome 1 pair with each other.

    c) Chromosome 2 pairs with its homologue; chromosome 3 pairs with its homologue, and so on.

    d) This pairing of homologues is called *synapsis*.

    e) Because each chromosome was copied before prophase I, each homologue consists of two chromatids; therefore, each pair of homologues has four units and is called a *tetrad*.

    f) Because the homologues in a pair are so close together, they can exchange DNA with each other.

    g) This produces chromosomes in which the maternal and paternal DNA are mixed (see Figure 12.5).

  ii. Several aspects of prophase I are the same as prophase of mitosis.

    a) The chromosomes are condensed.

    b) The nuclear envelope disassembles.

    c) A spindle forms and is composed of both kinetochore and polar fibers.

2. During *metaphase I*, orientation of each tetrad with respect to the two poles of the cell is random.

  i. Each tetrad moves to the center of the cell.

  ii. Kinetochore fibers attach to the centromeres of each chromatid pair.

    a) For each tetrad, kinetochore fibers from one pole attach to one chromatid pair, and kinetochore fibers from the other pole attach to the chromatid pair of the other homologue.

    b) The orientation of each maternal and paternal homologue in different tetrads is random with respect to which pole it is attached.

3. In *anaphase I*, the homologues are separated from each other.

  i. Each tetrad splits, causing its homologues (consisting of two chromatids) to move to opposite sides of the cell.

  ii. The random separation of one pair of homologues is independent of the random separation of any other pair of homologues.

  iii. Centromeres do not split as in mitosis, so both chromatids (copies) of one homologue move to the same side of the cell.

4. During *telophase I*, the movement of chromosomes is completed.

      i. In some species, *cytokinesis*—separation of cytoplasm and formation of new cells—follows telophase I.

     ii. In other species, cytokinesis does not occur between meiosis I and meiosis II.

C. *Meiosis II* **occurs after meiosis I.**

1. No DNA replication occurs between meiosis I and meiosis II.
2. Meiosis II occurs in each of the two new cells.
3. Meiosis II has four stages.

      i. In *prophase II*, the chromosomes are already condensed and new spindle fibers form.

     ii. In *metaphase II*, each pair of chromatids lines up in the middle of the cell, and kinetochore fibers attach to the centromeres of each pair.

    iii. In *anaphase II*, the centromeres holding the chromatids together split, and one chromatid moves to each side of the cell.

     iv. In *telophase II*, nuclear envelopes reform around the chromosomes.

D. *Cytokinesis* **follows telophase II, resulting in gametes.**

1. If sperm are produced, meiosis usually produces four sperm cells.
2. If ova are produced, meiosis often produces a single egg cell, while the other three cells die or have other functions in reproduction.

Figure 12.3 Meiosis I and Meiosis II

Early
prophase I

Late
Prophase I
(synapsis
begins)

Later
prophase I
(synapsis
has occurred)

Later
prophase
(cross-over
occurring)

Anaphase I

Telophase I

Prophase II

Metaphase II

Anaphase II
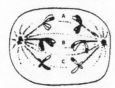

After
telophase II

V. Sexual reproduction produces *genetic variation* in three ways during sexual reproduction.

A. The first two *genetic recombination* events happen during meiosis I.

1. *Independent assortment* of homologous chromosomes happens during *metaphase I and anaphase I*, creating a variety

of outcomes (gametes) that contain *different combinations of* an organism's maternal and paternal *chromosomes.*

Figure 12.4 Independent Assortment of Homologous Chromosomes in Meiosis I

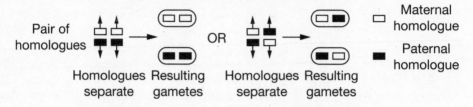

Depending on how homologues align during meiosis I, gametes with different combinations result.

2. *Crossing over* occurs between homologous chromosomes during *prophase I,* creating entirely new chromosomes on which the organism's maternal DNA is mixed with his or her paternal DNA so that *newly created chromosomes* may be passed on to offspring.

Figure 12.5 Crossing Over in Meiosis I

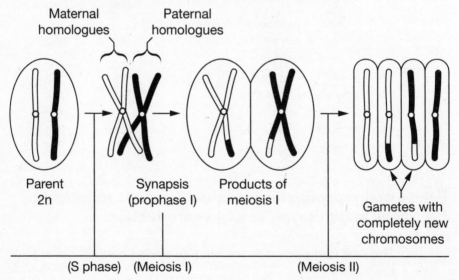

B. *Random fertilization* **creates further genetic variation.**

1. One sperm, out of the large variety of sperm a male can produce, joins with any of a large number of different eggs a female can produce.
2. This creates a large variety of different possible offspring.

 VI. *Comparison of mitosis and meiosis* **highlights key differences between them.**

A. *Similarities* **include the following:**

1. All chromosomes are replicated during the S phase of the interphase preceding both mitosis and meiosis.
    i. Copies of the chromosomes are called *chromatids* in both processes.
    ii. The chromatids are attached to each other at their centromeres in both processes.
    iii. The replication of chromosomes results in a doubling of the total amount of DNA within the cell that begins mitosis or meiosis.
        a) The amount of DNA present at the start of each process is twice the amount present in a diploid cell of the organism.
        b) In humans, for example, $2n = 46$, so 46 chromosomes are present in diploid cells, and 92 chromatids are present at the beginning of both mitosis and meiosis.
2. Cytoskeletal components called *kinetochore fibers* are responsible for moving chromosomes during metaphase and anaphase.
3. Nuclear envelopes disassemble and reform.
4. The chromosomes are condensed during prophase.

B. *Differences* between the two processes result in different outcomes.

   1. Mitosis has one division, while meiosis has two.

      i. The two cells produced by mitosis are diploid (2*n*), while the four cells resulting from meiosis are haploid (*n*).

      ii. For example, in humans where 2*n* = 46, the 92 chromatids present after the S phase prior to mitosis are divided into two diploid cells containing 46 chromosomes each, while the same 92 chromatids present at the start of meiosis are divided into four haploid cells containing 23 chromosomes each.

   2. Mitosis produces cells that are almost genetically identical, while meiosis produces cells that are very different genetically from either parent or from each other.

      i. Homologous chromosomes do not pair during prophase of mitosis, but they do pair to form tetrads during prophase I of meiosis I, allowing the genetic recombination called crossing over.

      ii. During metaphase of mitosis, homologous chromosomes do not pair when they line up at the metaphase plate, but in metaphase I of meiosis I they do.

      iii. Mitosis does not separate homologues during anaphase, but meiosis I does separate them during anaphase I so that each cell gets a different mixture of paternal and maternal homologues resulting in the genetic recombination of chromosomes called *independent assortment*.

   3. Meiosis II is very similar, but not identical, to mitosis.

      i. Sister chromatids are separated from one another in each.

      ii. The difference is that half the number of chromatid pairs is present in the cells at the start of meiosis II, as opposed to mitosis.

Table 12.2 Comparison of Mitosis and Meiosis in Animal Cells

Item to Compare	Mitosis	Meiosis
Purpose in animals	Creates somatic cells	Creates gametes
Number of cells produced	2	4
Number of cell divisions	1	2
DNA in starting cell during G_1 (before S phase)	$2n$	$2n$
DNA in starting cell during G_2 (after S phase)	$4n$	$4n$
DNA in resulting cells	$2n$	n
Synapsis of homologous chromosomes resulting in crossing over	No	Yes (prophase I)
Separation of homologous chromosomes resulting in independent assortment	No	Yes (anaphase I)

MENDELIAN GENETICS

I. Key Concepts

A. In the mid-1800s, without knowledge of chromosomes or genes, but with careful experimentation and statistical analysis, Gregor Mendel worked out the basic rules of heredity—the inheritance of characteristics from generation to generation—that occur during sexual reproduction.

B. The law of segregation is the principle that the two determinants of a characteristic, called *alleles* of a gene, are separated during meiosis and are distributed to separate gametes.

C. The law of independent assortment is the principle that the segregation of one set of alleles into gametes, which determine one characteristic, is independent of the segregation of a second set of alleles governing a second characteristic.

D. Genes are located on chromosomes, and in sexually reproducing organisms, alleles—different versions of the same gene—are located at the same position on homologous chromosomes.

E. Understanding the use of probabilities and punnett squares is important for determining the likelihood of different outcomes in genetic crosses.

Gregor Mendel carefully planned and carried out experiments involving the *inheritance* of characteristics during sexual reproduction in garden peas.

A. Garden peas propagate by *sexual reproduction* and can be either self-pollinated or cross-pollinated.

1. Peas have flowers with both male and female reproductive structures.

   i. The male gamete, *sperm*, is contained in *pollen*, which is produced by *anthers*.

   ii. Female gametes, *ova*, are located in the ovaries of female reproductive structures called *pistils*.

   iii. *Pollination* occurs when pollen is transferred from anthers to the tips of pistils.

   iv. *Fertilization*, the union of gametes, follows pollination.

2. *Self-pollination* results in the fertilization of a plant's ova by its own sperm.

3. *Cross-pollination* results in the fertilization of a plant's ova by the sperm of another plant.

B. Mendel preformed crosses in peas involving seve*n* *characteristics* that have two distinct, *contrasting traits*.

Table 13.1 The Contrasting Traits for Seven Characteristics of Pea Plants Mendel Used in His Experiments

Characteristic	First Trait	Second Trait
Plant height	Tall	Dwarf (short)
Flower position	Axial (along stem)	Terminal (at top of stem)
Flower color	Purple	White
Pod shape	Inflated (rounded)	Constricted (contoured)
Pod color	Green	Yellow

(continued)

Table 13.1 (*continued*)

Characteristic	First Trait	Second Trait
Seed shape	Smooth	Wrinkled
Seed color	Yellow	Green

1. A *trait* is also called a *phenotype*: both refer to some variation of a characteristic that is determined by heredity.
2. The clear difference between the traits of the characteristics Mendel chose made it easy to determine the phenotype of the *progeny* (offspring) of a cross.
3. Using seven traits allowed for *experimental repetition*, which strengthened Mendel's final conclusions.

C. **Mendel started each of his experiments using plants that were pure-breeding (also called true-breeding) for a particular trait.**

1. A *pure-breeding* plant for a particular trait always produces progeny that have the same trait for that characteristic if it is self-fertilized.
2. For the characteristic of plant height, *for example*, a pure-breeding tall plant that is self-pollinated (or crossed to another pure-breeding tall plant) produces all tall progeny; the same occurs with pure-breeding dwarf plants.

tall × tall = all tall progeny

dwarf × dwarf = all dwarf progeny

 III. The law (or principle) of segregation was determined by performing monohybrid crosses for each of the seven characteristics.

A. A *monohybrid cross* involves looking at only one characteristic at a time.

1. In the *P* (parental) *generation*, a pure-breeding plant for one trait is crossed with a pure-breeding plant for the contrasting trait.

2. *For example*, for the characteristic of plant height, one parent in the P generation is a true-breeder for the tall phenotype, and is cross-pollinated with a true-breeder for the dwarf phenotype.

P generation	tall × dwarf

B. **For each of the seven crosses between parents with contrasting traits, all of the progeny showed only one of the two traits.**

1. The progeny of the P cross are called the F_1 (1st filial) *generation*.
2. *For example*, when true-breeding tall and dwarf plants were crossed, all of the progeny in the resulting F_1 generation were tall; none were dwarfs.

P generation	tall × dwarf
F_1 generation	**all tall**

3. Because one trait appeared to mask the other, Mendel referred to one trait as dominant (the *dominant phenotype* in modern terminology), and the trait not exhibited by the F_1 he called the recessive trait (*recessive phenotype*).
4. *For example*, the tall phenotype is dominant to the dwarf phenotype.

C. **Mendel then self-pollinated the F_1 plants to produce the next generation and found the same general result regardless of the characteristic he was examining.**

1. The progeny of a self-pollination of an F_1 plant are called the F_2 (2nd filial) *generation*.
2. For each of the seven self-pollinations of F_1 individuals, the F_2 progeny showed a *3:1 ratio* of the dominant phenotype to the recessive phenotype.

3. *For example,* when an F$_1$ tall plant was self-pollinated, 3/4 of the progeny were tall and the remaining 1/4 of the progeny were dwarfs, yielding a *3:1 ratio* of phenotypes.

Table 13.2 Summary of Mendel's Results for a Monohybrid Cross

P generation	tall × dwarf
F$_1$ generation	all tall
F$_2$ generation	**3 tall: 1 dwarf**

Table 13.3 P, F$_1$, and F$_2$ Generations for Each of Mendel's Seven Monohybrid Crosses

Characteristic	P Generation	F$_1$ Generation (dominant trait only)	F$_2$ Generation (3:1)
Plant height	Tall × dwarf	All tall	3 tall : 1 dwarf
Flower position	Axial × terminal	All axial	3 axial : 1 terminal
Flower color	Purple × white	All purple	3 purple : 1 white
Pod shape	Inflated × constricted	All inflated	3 inflated : 1 constricted
Pod color	Green × yellow	All green	3 green : 1 yellow
Seed shape	Smooth × wrinkled	All smooth	3 smooth : 1 wrinkled
Seed color	Yellow × green	All yellow	3 yellow : 1 green

D. Because the results were consistent for each characteristic, Mendel concluded that the same process applied to all these inherited characteristics; this principle is known as the "*law of segregation*."

   1. From his data, Mendel inferred that each trait must be the result of two distinct factors and that these *factors separate from each other during reproduction and are incorporated into separate gametes.*

   2. The modern synthesis of this principle has the following features.

      i. Each diploid has two forms of a gene, called *alleles*, which determine the expression of its trait for a particular characteristic.

        a) A *dominant allele* may mask a *recessive allele* when the two are both present in an organism's cells, causing the individual to manifest the dominant phenotype.

        b) A dominant allele is often represented by a capital letter, such as "*T*" for the tall allele for plant height, and a recessive allele is then represented by a lower case letter, such as "*t*" for the dwarf allele.

        c) An organism with two different alleles is called a *heterozygote*; *for example*, the tall F_1 plants are *heterozygous* for the plant height characteristic and their *genotype* (allele composition) can be designated by the letters *Tt*.

        d) An organism having two dominant alleles (genotype *TT* in our example) exhibits the dominant phenotype and is called a *homozygote*, specifically a *homozygous dominant* individual.

        e) An organism having two recessive alleles (genotype *tt*) exhibits the recessive phenotype and is called a *homozygous recessive*.

      ii. During meiosis, alleles are separated from each other and are incorporated into different gametes, with only one of the parent's alleles going to any one gamete.

        a) If the organism is a homozygote, only one type of gamete is possible.

b) If the organism is a heterozygote, two types of gametes are possible with a 50% chance of the gamete receiving the dominant allele and a 50% chance of it receiving the recessive allele.

— For a *TT* parent, all gametes will receive a *T* allele.

— For a *tt* parent, all gametes will receive a *t* allele.

— For a *Tt* parent, 1/2 of the gametes will get a *T* allele and the other 1/2 will get a *t* allele.

iii. Each progeny inherits only one allele from each parent.

3. *Punnett squares* can be used to determine the genotypes and phenotypes of progeny from a genetic cross.

i. The alleles of one parent's gametes are placed on the side of a Punnett square, and the alleles of the other parent's gametes are written across the top.

ii. The grid inside the square is filled in to determine the possible progeny.

iii. The progeny can then be categorized and counted to determine both *genotypic* and *phenotypic ratios*.

iv. For a monohybrid cross, only one set of alleles needs to be considered for each parent.

Figure 13.1 Punnett Square for a Typical P Generation Cross

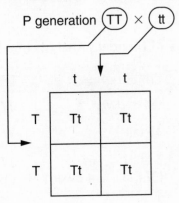

v. The probabilities of each possible gamete and each possible progeny can be included in Punnett square analyses.

a) For F_1 parents, 1/2 of the gametes of each parent are dominant and the other 1/2 are recessive.

b) When calculating the probability of each F_2 progeny, the respective gamete probabilities are multiplied, in this case $1/2 \times 1/2 = 1/4$ for each possible progeny.

Figure 13.2 Punnett Square for a Typical F_1 Generation Cross

F_1 generation: $Tt \times Tt$

	T (1/2)	t (1/2)
T (1/2)	TT (1/4)	Tt (1/4)
t (1/2)	Tt (1/4)	tt (1/4)

4. Based on Punnett square analysis, the typical results of one of Mendel's monohybrid crosses can be summarized in Table 13.4.

Table 13.4 Summary of Mendel's Analysis of a Monohybrid Cross

Generation	Phenotypes	Genotypes
P generation	tall × dwarf	$TT \times tt$
F_1 generation	All tall	Tt
F_2 generation ratio (probability)	3 tall:1 dwarf (3/4 tall, 1/4 dwarf)	$1TT : 2Tt : 1tt$ (1/4 TT, 1/2 Tt, 1/4 tt)

IV. **Mendel also preformed dihybrid crosses, and, based on the results, drew the conclusion known as the law (or principle) of independent assortment.**

A. A *dihybrid cross* follows the same order of crosses as Mendel's monohybrid crosses, but involves examining the inheritance of *two characteristics* at the same time instead of just one.

1. It starts with a P generation cross of pure-breeding parents for contrasting traits for both characteristics.

2. *For example*, for the characteristics of seed color and seed shape, one parent in the P generation is a true-breeder for the yellow seed phenotype and the round seed phenotype, and is cross-pollinated with a true-breeder for the green and wrinkled seed phenotypes.

3. The F_1 progeny exhibit only the dominant phenotypes for both characteristics: yellow, round seeds.

4. The F_2 progeny exhibit a new phenotypic ratio of 9 progeny with both dominant phenotypes: 3 with one dominant and one recessive phenotype: 3 with the other dominant and recessive phenotypes: and 1 with both recessive phenotypes (*a 9:3:3:1 ratio*).

Table 13.5 Summary of Mendel's Results for a Dihybrid Cross

Generation	Phenotypes
P generation	Yellow, round $\times$ green, wrinkled
F_1 generation	All yellow, round
F_2 generation	9 yellow, round
	3 yellow, wrinkled
	3 green, round
	1 green, wrinkled

B. The results of these crosses demonstrate what Mendel called the "law of independent assortment."

1. The law of independent assortment is the principle that *a set of alleles for one characteristic gets incorporated into gametes without regard to how another set of alleles for a different characteristic segregates.*

2. This is consistent with the idea of independent assortment of chromosomes during meiosis.

    i. Because homologous chromosomes assort independently during meiosis, if the alleles of two genes are on separate chromosomes, it makes sense that their alleles would also assort independently.

Figure 13.3 Independent Assortment of Alleles of Genes Located on Different Chromosomes

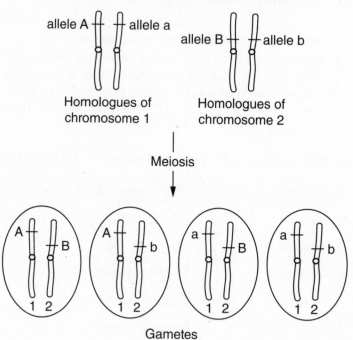

    ii. A Punnett square shows the expected genotype of the F_2 generation and illustrates the principle of independent assortment.

3. *For example,* if an F₁ parent (always a *double heterozygote*) has the genotype *YySs*, the law of independent assortment predicts that four types of gametes will be created with equal likelihood: 1/4 *YS*, 1/4 *Ys*, 1/4 *yS*, and 1/4 *ys*.

Test Tip

Each gamete gets one *allele for each characteristic, i.e., combinations like SS and Yy would not occur for this gene pair.*

Figure 13.4 Results in the F₂ Generation of a Dihybrid Cross for Alleles that Demonstrate Independent Assortment
(Y-yellow allele, y-green allele, S-smooth allele, s-wrinkled allele)

$YySs \times YySs$ (F₁)
yellow, smooth × yellow, smooth

F₂ progeny

	YS (1/4)	**Ys** (1/4)	**yS** (1/4)	**ys** (1/4)
YS (1/4)	**YYSS** yellow smooth	**YYSs** yellow smooth	**YySS** yellow smooth	**YySs** yellow smooth
Ys (1/4)	**YYSs** yellow smooth	**YYss** yellow wrinkled	**YySs** yellow smooth	**Yyss** yellow wrinkled
yS (1/4)	**YySS** yellow smooth	**YySs** yellow smooth	**yySS** green smooth	**yySs** green smooth
ys (1/4)	**YySs** yellow smooth	**Yyss** yellow wrinkled	**yySs** green smooth	**yyss** green wrinkled

Test Tip

Mendel's rule of independent assortment occurs for genes on different chromosomes. Genes near enough to each other on the same chromosome are linked to one another and do not assort independently. (See Linkage in Chapter 14.)

V. Understanding probability and the use of Punnett squares is important for quickly determining the likelihood of the results of a genetic cross.

A. *Probability* (*p*) is the number of times an event is expected to occur divided by the number of opportunities for the event to occur.

  1. A probability can be expressed as a fraction, a percent, or a decimal; *for example*:
    i. 1/4 = 0.25 = 25%
    ii. 1/2 = 0.5 = 50%
    iii. 1/1 = 1 = 100%.
  2. The *product rule* of probability is applicable to a situation in which two or more independent events occur at the same time; the probability of two independent events occurring simultaneously is the product of their individual probabilities.
    i. Example:
      a) The probability that a *Yy* × *Yy* cross will produce a recessive individual is 1/4. (*Yy* × *Yy* = 1/4 *yy*)
      b) The probability that an *Ss* × *Ss* cross will produce a recessive individual is 1/4. (*Ss* × *Ss* = 1/4 *ss*)
      c) Therefore, the probability of both independent events occurring simultaneously is 1/4 × 1/4 = 1/16. (*YySs* × *YySs* = 1/16 *yyss*)
    ii. The advantage of using the product rule is that it is more rapid to calculate probabilities during dihybrid crosses.

B. **Small Punnett squares can be rapidly drawn during a test to examine crosses involving a single pair of alleles.**

   1. All of the characteristics examined by Mendel are examples of *complete dominance* (also known as *simple dominance*).

        i. If there are two alleles of a gene, and one (*A*) shows complete dominance over the other allele (*a*), then there are three possible genotypes and two possible phenotypes.

        ii. The *AA* and *Aa* genotypes have the dominant phenotype.

        iii. The *aa* genotype has the recessive phenotype.

Test Tip

It is essential that you be familiar with the Punnett squares in Figure 13.5.

Figure 13.5 Punnett Squares for Important Types of Crosses

a)
$Aa \times Aa$
(dominant × dominant)

	A	a
A	AA	Aa
a	Aa	aa

Genotypes: 1/4 AA, 2/4 Aa, 1/4 aa
Phenotypes: 3/4 dominant, 1/4 recessive
Genotypic ratio: 1:2:1
Phenotypic ratio: 3:1

b)
$AA \times aa$
(dominant × recessive)

	A	A
a	Aa	Aa
a	Aa	Aa

Genotype: all Aa
Phenotype: all dominant

(*continued*)

Figure 13.5 (*continued*)

c)   *Aa* × *aa*
(dominant × recessive)

	A	a
a	Aa	aa
a	Aa	aa

Genotypes: 1/2 *Aa*, 1/2 *aa*
Phenotypes: 1/2 dominant, 1/2 recessive
Genotypic ratio: 1:1
Phenotypic ratio: 1:1

2. A *test cross* is often performed to determine the genotype of an individual with a dominant phenotype. (The question being asked is, "Is the individual *AA* or *Aa*?")
    i. The individual with the dominant phenotype is crossed with a homozygous recessive (genotype *aa*).
    ii. If the individual is *AA*, all the progeny will have the dominant phenotype.
    iii. If the individual is *Aa*, 1/2 of the progeny will have the dominant phenotype and 1/2 will have the recessive phenotype.
    iv. Compare the preceding Punnett squares (b) and (c).
3. In *incomplete dominance*, the heterozygote has a phenotype intermediate between the contrasting phenotypes of the two homozygotes.
    i. An example is flower color in some plants where the flowers of the *AA* genotype are red, the *aa* genotype has white flowers, and the flowers with the *Aa* genotype are pink.
    ii. In the case of incomplete dominance, the phenotypic ratios always directly match the genotypic ratios.

iii. Compare the following Punnett square results with those for complete dominance in an *Aa* × *Aa* cross.

Figure 13.6 Punnett Square for Incomplete Dominance

Aa × *Aa*
(red × red)

	A	a
A	AA	Aa
a	Aa	aa

Genotypes: 1/4 AA, 2/4 Aa, 1/4 aa
Phenotypes: 1/4 red, 2/4 pink, 1/4 white
Genotypic ratio: 1:2:1
Phenotypic ratio: 1:2:1

4. In *codominance*, the heterozygote also has a unique phenotype, but this phenotype results from the expression of the traits of both alleles.

   i. An example is found with the I^A and I^B alleles of the ABO blood group, where individuals with the $I^A I^A$ genotype produce the A antigen and have type A blood, those with the $I^B I^B$ genotype produce the B antigen and have type B blood, and the heterozygote, $I^A I^B$, produces both antigens resulting in type AB blood.

   ii. As with incomplete dominance, the phenotypic ratios in codominance always directly match the genotypic ratios: $I^A I^B$ × $I^A I^B$ results in 1/4 $I^A I^A$ (type A), 1/2 $I^A I^B$ (type AB), and 1/4 $I^B I^B$ (type B).

Practicing a variety of genetics problems is an essential test preparation activity. Some genetics problems give you information about parents and ask about phenotypic ratios of their progeny; others give information about progeny and ask about the parents' genotypes or phenotypes. On the test, work out genetics problems in three steps: 1) Read the question, making sure you know what is being asked (genotype? phenotype? progeny's phenotype? parent's genotype? question about gametes? etc.); 2) Apply the correct strategy for the problem (use the right Punnett square, ratio, probability, etc.); and 3) Take a little time to recheck your strategy and your math work right away, because the wrong answer choices usually correspond to common strategy or math errors.

OTHER INHERITANCE PATTERNS

Key Concepts

A. The sex chromosomes, X and Y, determine the sex of mammals and many insects.

B. Genes on the X and Y chromosomes have special patterns of inheritance called *X-linkage* and *Y-linkage*.

C. Genes on the same chromosome do not assort independently if they are linked.

D. Linkage can be used to map the relative locations of genes on a chromosome.

E. Pedigree analysis is used to study the inheritance of human genes.

Sex is determined by the *sex chromosomes*, *X* and *Y*, in fruit flies and humans.

A. A *female* has two X chromosomes and has the genotype *XX*.

B. A *male* has an X and a Y chromosome and has the genotype *XY*.

C. As shown in the Punnett square in Figure 14.1, these genotype combinations are the basis for the 1:1 ratio of sexes.

Figure 14.1 Inheritance of Sex Chromosomes

XY × XX
male × female

	X	Y
X	XX	XY
X	XX	XY

1/2 female: 1/2 male

D. The rest of an organism's chromosomes are homologous autosomes.

III. Genes located on the sex chromosomes show a pattern of inheritance, called *sex linkage*, which is different from genes located on autosomes.

A. *X-linkage* occurs for genes located on the X chromosome.

1. Because males only receive one X chromosome, their phenotype is determined by a single allele inherited from their mother.

2. This is because most, if not all, of the alleles on the X chromosome do not have matching alleles on the Y chromosome.

3. The X chromosome (and all its alleles) that a male receive always comes from his mother, and his Y chromosome always comes from his father.

4. Females receive one X chromosome from their mother and one from their father.

5. The special types of results for crosses involving genes on the X-chromosome are shown in the following Punnett squares, using an eye color gene in the fruit fly, *Drosophila*.

     i. A set of alleles in *Drosophila*, located on the X-chromosome, determines red and white eye color.

    ii. The red color allele (*R*) is dominant to the white color allele (*r*).

   iii. When a male has the genotype X^RY, he has red eyes, and, if his genotype is X^rY, his eyes are white.

   iv. A female can have three genotypes.

      a) The homozygous dominant genotype, X^RX^R, and the heterozygous genotype, X^RX^r, both result in red eyes.

      b) The homozygous recessive genotype, X^rX^r, results in white eyes.

6. When a male with the dominant phenotype (red eyes) is crossed with a female with the recessive phenotype (white eyes), instead of all the offspring having red eyes as would be the case if the gene were located on an autosome, all the females have the dominant phenotype and all the males have the recessive phenotype as shown in Figure 14.2.

Figure 14.2 P Generation Cross—Red-eyed Male × White-eyed Female

P generation

$X^RY \times X^rX^r$

male × female

	X^R	Y
X^r	X^RX^r	X^rY
X^r	X^RX^r	X^rY

F_1 generation

genotypes: 1/2 X^RX^r, 1/2 X^rY

phenotypes: 1/2 red-eyed females, 1/2 white-eyed males

7. When a male and a female from the F_1 generation are crossed, the F_2 females have red eyes and white eyes in equal proportion, and so do the males.

Figure 14.3 F₁ Generation Cross—White-eyed Male × Heterozygous Female

F$_1$ generation
$X^rY \times X^RX^r$
male × female

	X^r	Y
X^R	X^RX^r	X^RY
X^r	X^rX^r	X^rY

F$_2$ generation

genotypes: 1/4 X^RX^r, 1/4 X^rX^r, 1/4 X^RY, 1/4 X^rY
phenotypes: 1/4 red females, 1/4 white females, 1/4 red males, 1/4 white males

8. When a male with the recessive phenotype is crossed with a female who is homozygous for the red allele, all the offspring have the dominant phenotype.

Figure 14.4 P Generation Cross—White-eyed Male × Red-eyed Female

P generation
$X^rY \times X^RX^R$
male × female

	X^r	Y
X^R	X^RX^r	X^RY
X^R	X^RX^r	X^RY

F$_1$ generation

genotypes: 1/2 X^RX^r, 1/2 X^RY
phenotypes: all offspring, regardless of sex, have red eyes

9. When a male and a female from the F_1 generation are crossed, all of the females have red eyes, but the males show a 1:1 ratio of red eyes to white eyes.

Figure 14.5 F_1 Generation Cross—Red-eyed Male × Heterozygous Female

F_1 generation

$X^R Y \times X^R X^r$

male × female

	X^R	Y
X^R	$X^R X^R$	$X^R Y$
X^r	$X^R X^r$	$X^r Y$

F_2 generation

genotypes: 1/4 $X^R X^R$, 1/4 $X^R X^r$, 1/4 $X^R Y$, 1/4 $X^r Y$

phenotypes: 1/2 red females, 1/4 red males, 1/4 white males

B. Y-linkage occurs for genes located on the Y chromosome.

1. Not very many genes have been found on the Y chromosome.

2. Those genes that are present on the Y chromosome are inherited only from father to son, because only fathers have a Y chromosome and only sons receive it.

Test Tip

As for Mendelian inheritance in Chapter 13, it is essential that you practice doing genetics problems that utilize sex-linked traits, because there is almost certain to be at least one problem on the test involving a sex-linked allele.

IV. The alleles of two genes located on the same chromosome often do not show independent assortment; instead, they exhibit a special type of inheritance called *linkage*.

A. If two genes are located close together on the same chromosome, they do not assort independently, because they are physically linked to each other.

    1. A back cross for *two genes that **are not** on the same chromosome produces four types of offspring in equal proportions*, because four types of gametes are produced by the double heterozygote parent.

        i. A back cross is one type of test cross in which one parent is heterozygous for both characteristics and the other parent is a recessive for both characteristics.

        ii. If the genes for these characteristics are on different chromosomes, they are incorporated independently into gametes, producing four types of offspring.

            a) Consider the Mendelian dihybrid cross for the two characteristics of seed color and seed shape discussed in Chapter 13.

            b) For seed color, the yellow allele (Y) is dominant to the green allele (y).

            c) For seed shape, the smooth allele (S) is dominant to the wrinkled allele (s).

            d) Because these genes are on different chromosomes, they do show independent assortment, and a cross between a heterozygote for both characteristics ($YySs$) and a double homozygous recessive plant ($yyss$) would produce four types of progeny in equal numbers.

Figure 14.6 Backcross for Two Genes on Separate Chromosomes

YySs × yyss

(yellow, round × green, wrinkled)

gametes for YySs: meiosis produces equal numbers of *YS, ys, Ys,* and *yS*
gametes for yyss: meiosis produces all *ys*

	YS	ys	Ys	yS
ys	YySs	yyss	Yyss	yySs

genotypes: 1/4 *YySs*, 1/4 *yyss*, 1/4 *Yyss*, 1/4 *yySs*
phenotypes: 25% yellow, round
25% green, wrinkled
25% yellow, wrinkled
25% green, round

2. However, a back cross for *two genes that **are** located close together on the same chromosome produces only two types of offspring,* because only two types of gametes are produced by the double heterozygote parent.

   i. Because the genes are physically linked on the same chromosome, the two alleles present on a chromosome travel along with that single chromosome and are incorporated into the same gamete.

Figure 14.7 Assortment for Alleles of Genes Located on Different Chromosomes Compared to Alleles of Genes Located on the same Chromosome

When genes are on different chromosomes . . .

. . . four different types of gametes are produced

Two chromosomes are involved

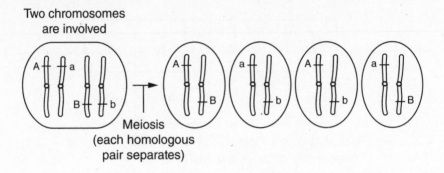

Meiosis (each homologous pair separates)

When genes are on the same chromosome . . .

. . . only two different types of gametes are produced

One chromosome is involved

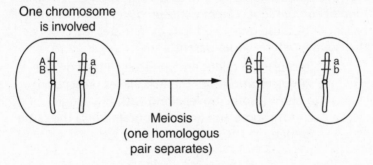

Meiosis (one homologous pair separates)

ii. Only two types of gametes are produced, resulting in two types of progeny in equal numbers.

   a) Consider a back cross, in which two genes are located on the same chromosome.

   b) For the first characteristic, the *A* allele is dominant to the *a* allele.

   c) For the second characteristic, the *B* allele is dominant to the *b* allele.

   d) Because these alleles are on the same chromosome, and thus do not show independent assortment, a cross between a heterozygote for both characteristics (*AaBb*) and a double homozygous recessive individual (*aabb*) would produce only two types of progeny.

Figure 14.8 Backcross for Two Genes on the Same Chromosome (with no crossover)

AaBb × *aabb*
(both dominant × both recessive)

gametes for AaBb: meiosis produces equal numbers of *AB* and *ab*
gametes for aabb: meiosis produces all *ab*

	AB	ab
ab	AaBb	aabb

genotypes: 1/2 *AaBb*, 1/2 *aabb*
phenotypes: 50% both dominant, 50% both recessive

B. In summary, if two genes are linked on the same chromosome, they do not exhibit independent assortment.

 V. **Linkage can be used to map the locations of genes on a chromosome.**

A. If two genes on the same chromosome are right next to each other they always are inherited together, but if they are further apart they are not always inherited together due to crossing over during meiosis. (Additional information about crossing over can be found in Chapter 12.)

1. When two genes are very close together on the same chromosome, there is no possibility of them getting separated during crossing over during meiosis.

2. However, when two genes are farther apart on a chromosome, crossing over may occur during meiosis.

Figure 14.9 Crossing over Creates Some Gametes with Different Combinations of Alleles

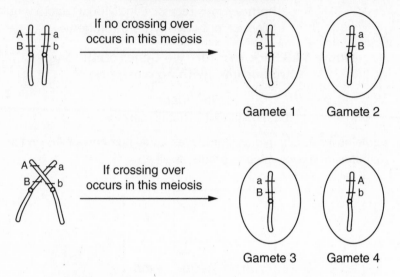

Gamete 1   Gamete 2

Gamete 3   Gamete 4

3. Crossing over results in deviation from the 1:1 ratio of offspring in a back cross that would occur if the genes were always inherited together.

Figure 14.10 Backcross for Two Genes on the Same Chromosome (with crossing over)

AaBb× aabb
(both dominant × both recessive)

gametes for AaBb: meiosis produces mostly *AB* and *ab* gametes, but also can produce some *Ab* and *aB* gametes
gametes for aabb: meiosis produces all *ab*

	without crossing over		with crossing over (recombinants)	
	AB	*ab*	*Ab*	*aB*
ab	*AaBb*	*aabb*	*Aabb*	*aaBb*

genotypes: most progeny are *AaBb* and *aabb*, but some are *Aabb* and *aaBb*
phenotypes: most progeny have the double dominant phenotype or the double recessive phenotype, but some are recombinants

i. Crossing over in this type of cross is called *recombination*, and progeny with mixed phenotypes are called *recombinants*.

ii. The farther apart the genes are, the more likely it is for recombination to occur.

B. Recombination due to crossing over can be used to construct a genetic *linkage map* showing the locations of genes on a chromosome.

i. Through back crosses, the *percent recombination* for two genes can be calculated and used to construct a chromosome linkage map that shows the locations of their genes.

ii. Recombination is the percent of recombinants present in the back cross progeny.

iii. Each percent recombination is equal to one *map unit*.

iv. The location of a gene on a chromosome is called its *locus* (pl. *loci*).

Figure 14.11 A Linkage MAP for Three Genes Located on the Same Chromosome

% recombination
Gene A + Gene B = 5%
Gene B + Gene C = 20%
Gene A + Gene C = 25%

5 mu   20 mu

A   B   C

Test Tip

For the test, is important to understand how the concept of linkage is related to crossing over, and how the concept of recombination is related to creating a linkage map.

VI. **Other deviations from Mendelian inheritance patterns include multiple alleles, polygenic inheritance, sex-influenced genes, and environmental influence.**

A. Some characteristics are determined by genes that have more than two alleles.

    1. An example of a gene having *multiple alleles* is the ABO blood group, which has three alleles: I^A, I^B, and i.

        i. The I^A and I^B alleles are codominant: when they are both present in an individual, they are both expressed.

        ii. Both the I^A and I^B alleles show complete dominance over the i allele.

    2. Even though the population as a whole has three possible alleles that could be at an individual's ABO blood group locus, a single individual can only have two alleles at any one locus.

        i. The genotypes, $I^A I^A$ and $I^A i$, have the phenotype of A type blood.

        ii. The $I^B I^B$ and $I^B i$ genotypes have the B blood type.

        iii. The $I^A I^B$ genotype expresses both A and B phenotypes, and has the AB blood type.

        iv. An individual with the ii genotype has O type blood.

B. Some characteristics are determined by the additive effect of many genes and are called *polygenic* characteristics; skin color and height in humans are examples.

C. Many characteristics have genetic components, but are also heavily influenced by *environmental* or other *factors*.

    1. Height, size, and weight are examples of characteristics that have a genetic basis, but are also highly influenced by such factors as nutrition, sunlight, disease, and other environmental factors.

    2. Flower color in some species, such as hydrangea, is influenced by the pH of the soil in which the plants grow.

3. Some characteristics are *sex influenced,* where the same genotype in males and females leads to a different characteristic due to the influence of sex hormones.

VII. *Pedigree analysis* is used to study inheritance in humans.

A. **A pedigree is a family tree with genetic information showing individuals who have a trait, or do not have a trait, for a particular characteristic.**

1. Individuals who have the trait are often represented by shaded symbols, while individuals without the trait are represented by open symbols.
2. The symbols that represent males are squares, and females are represented by circles.
3. A marriage is represented by a horizontal line between a male and a female, and children are shown in a grouping below their parents.
4. If an allele cannot be determined for an individual, the allele is represented by an underscore (_) mark.

B. **Most pedigrees are for *recessive traits,* and exhibit a specific pattern of inheritance.**

1. Only homozygous recessive individuals (*aa*) have the trait, and thus their symbol will be shaded.
2. Individuals with the trait can be either male or female.
3. Individuals with heterozygous genotypes (*Aa*) do not have the trait, but they carry one allele for the trait, and are thus called *carriers.*
4. The defining feature of a pedigree for a recessive trait is that two individuals **without** the trait can have a child **with** the trait.
5. Because they are both carriers (*Aa*), the parents can each contribute a recessive allele (*a*) to produce a child with an *aa* genotype.

Figure 14.12 Autosomal Recessive Pedigree

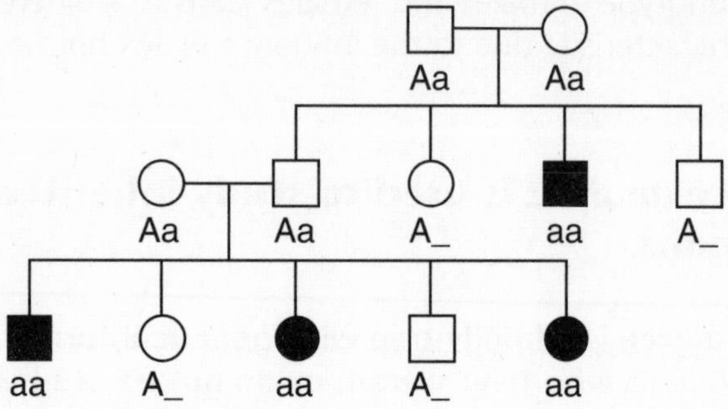

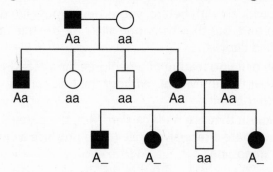

C. **Pedigrees for *dominant traits* also show their own specific inheritance pattern.**

1. Individuals that are homozygous recessive (*aa*) are the only individuals who do not have the trait.

2. Both homozygous dominant (*AA*) and heterozygous (*Aa*) individuals have the trait, and this is shown by their shaded symbols.

3. Just as for recessive pedigrees, individuals with the trait can either be male or female.

4. The defining feature of a pedigree for a dominant trait is that two individuals **with** the trait can have a child **without** the trait.

5. As in a recessive pedigree, the parents of that child are both heterozygous (*Aa*), but their child who is homozygous recessive (*aa*) does **not** have the trait.

Figure 14.13 Autosomal Dominant Pedigree

D. Pedigrees for *X-linked recessive* traits show a different pattern of inheritance than either autosomal dominant or autosomal recessive pedigrees.

    1. An X-linked pedigree may exhibit several defining features.

        i. While females can have the trait, it is much more likely for males to be the ones with the trait.

        ii. Males never get the trait from their father, because their father does not give them an X chromosome on which the allele is located.

        iii. If a father does not have the trait (X^AY) but the mother does (X^aX^a), all their sons will have the trait (X^aY), but none of their daughters will (X^AX^a).

    2. Color-blindness and hemophilia are examples of X-linked traits in humans.

Figure 14.14 X-Linked Recessive Pedigree

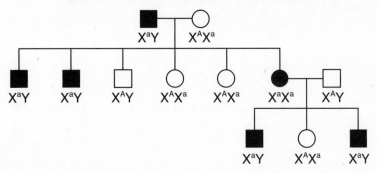

E. A *Y-linked pedigree* also has several defining features.

    1. Only males have the trait, because only males have a Y chromosome.

    2. If a male has the trait, all of his sons will have it.

    3. If a male does not have the trait, all of his sons will not have it.

Figure 14.15 Y-Linked Pedigree

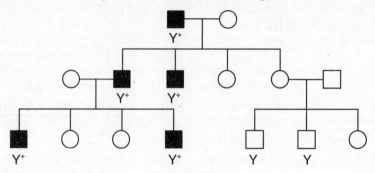

You will be expected to know how to read and analyze a pedigree on the test.

MOLECULAR GENETICS

I. Key Concepts

A. The structure of a DNA molecule is the key to understanding how each strand of DNA can act as a template for the replication of the other strand during DNA replication, and for the production of RNA during transcription.

B. DNA replication produces two new DNA molecules, each of which consists of one old strand and one newly synthesized complementary strand, and which are checked for errors by proofreading and repair processes.

C. RNA transcription produces rRNA, tRNA, and mRNA, all of which have different roles during the process of translation.

D. In its sequence of nucleotides, mRNA carries the genetic information present in an organism's DNA (also in the form of sequences of nucleotides) from the nucleus to the ribosome.

E. Translation (protein synthesis) converts the information in the nucleotide sequences of mRNA into information in the form of the amino acid sequences of proteins that are critical to the structure and functioning of cells.

F. Many different types of mutations of nucleotides and chromosomes can occur during DNA synthesis and meiosis, resulting in different effects.

G. Mutations in somatic cells and germ cells can lead to the formation of cancer.

H. Control over gene expression is important for determining when, and in which cells, a protein will be made.

I. Gene regulation in bacteria involves control over the transcription of operons, and in eukaryotes involves multiple levels before, during, and after transcription and translation.

J. DNA technology has created many powerful tools for basic research, as well as for commercial use in agriculture and medicine.

Figure 15.1 Nucleotides are the Building Blocks of DNA

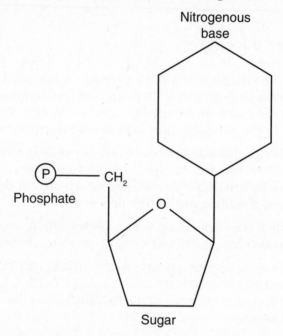

II. **The structure of a *deoxyribonucleic acid (DNA)* molecule is based on the pairing of *nucleotides* along the lengths of two complementary DNA strands, each of which has a sugar–phosphate backbone and twists to form a double helix.**

A. The *sugar–phosphate backbone* of each DNA strand is a repeating chain of the 5-carbon sugar, *deoxyribose*, and a *phosphate group* composed of a phosphorus atom surrounded by 4 oxygen atoms.

1. The sugar–phosphate chains are held together by *covalent bonds* that are generally only broken or formed by *enzymes*.
2. The sugar–phosphate backbone of each strand is an identical feature of all DNA molecules.

B. **Attached to each sugar is one of four *nitrogenous bases* composed of carbon and nitrogen rings.**

1. The *purines*, adenine (A) and guanine (G), consist of two rings.
2. The *pyrimidines*, thymine (T) and cytosine (C), have a single ring.

Figure 15.2 The Four Nitrogenous Bases Found in DNA

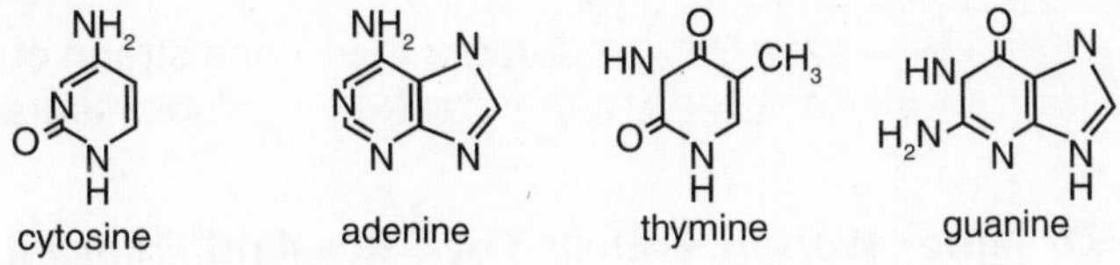

cytosine   adenine   thymine   guanine

C. **The *complementary pairing* of nitrogenous bases is the basis of the double-stranded structure of a DNA molecule.**

1. *Base pairing* involves the formation of *hydrogen bonds* between the bases that are located toward the center of each DNA molecule, and they serve to hold the two strands together.
    i. Hydrogen atoms in a base on one strand form hydrogen bonds with an electronegative atom (either nitrogen or oxygen) located on a base of the other strand facing it.
    ii. Hydrogen bonds are weaker than covalent bonds, allowing the two strands of the DNA molecule to be separated for DNA replication and transcription.
    iii. A pyrimidine can only pair with a purine due to their sizes and the types of hydrogen bonds possible between the bases.
        a) *Base pairing rules* are simple: adenine pairs with thymine (*A:T*), and guanine pairs with cytosine (*G:C*).

b) Guanine forms three hydrogen bonds with cytosine, while adenine only forms two hydrogen bonds with thymine.

c) Because purines are larger than pyrimidines, the base pairing rules serve to maintain a constant width along the length of the double helix.

2. Base pairing occurs along the entire length of the two DNA strands and results in one strand being an exact complement of the other.

3. Knowing the sequence of one strand of DNA, the sequence of its complement can be deduced by the use of the base pairing rules.

Figure 15.3 Complementary Base Pairing in DNA

-----G A T T C G T A A G G C------ one strand of DNA
-----C T A A G C A T T C C G------ complementary strand of DNA

D. James *Watson*, Francis *Crick*, Rosalind *Franklin*, and Maurice *Wilkins* contributed to constructing the double helical model of DNA structure.

1. *X-ray crystallography*—a technique used to measure the shapes of molecules—was contributed by Franklin and Wilkins.

2. Watson and Crick used this and other data to construct a *three-dimensional model*.

   i. Two strands of complementary DNA twist to form a *helix* often described as a spiral ladder with each base pair representing a single step.

   ii. Each turn of the double helix contains 10 base pairs and is 34 angstroms long.

   iii. The width of the helix is uniform and is 10 angstroms across.

Figure 15.4 The DNA Double Helix

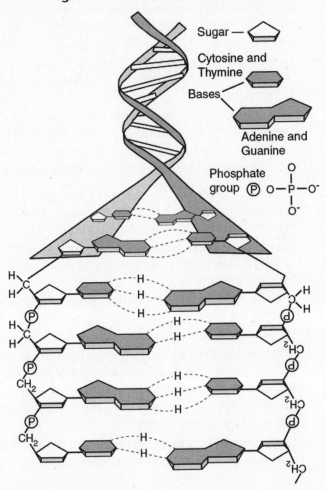

 III. **During *DNA replication*, each strand of a DNA molecule acts as a template for the synthesis of the other strand, and when errors do occur, proofreading and repair mechanisms keep mutation rates low.**

A. All of the chromosomes of an organism's *genome* (all of an organism's DNA), are copied prior to each cell division.

1. Each strand acts as a *template* for the synthesis of its complementary strand through the addition of nucleotides to the growing end of the complement.
2. DNA replication begins at *origins of replication* distributed at many sites along the length of each eukaryotic chromosome, and usually at a single site on the chromosome of prokaryotes.
3. *DNA polymerase* is the enzyme that catalyzes the addition of nucleotides to the ends of a growing strand of DNA.

B. The process of DNA replication occurs as follows.

1. Enzymes, called *helicases,* unwind the helix at origins of replication and help break the hydrogen bonds holding the strands together, creating a *replication fork.*
2. An enzyme called *primase* then synthesizes a short segment of *RNA* called a *primer* that is complementary to nucleotides on the DNA strand.
3. *DNA polymerases* bind to each separated strand and begin adding the proper complementary nucleotides to the primer to produce a new copy of each strand.
4. The bond formed between two nucleotides is a covalent bond between the deoxyribose sugar of one and the phosphate of the other.
5. Another enzyme, called *DNA ligase,* helps seal gaps between the many growing strands.
6. DNA polymerases keep moving along the strands until synthesis of both strands are completed.

C. Each new molecule of DNA consists of one of the original DNA strands hydrogen bonded to its newly synthesized complement.

Test Tip

Know the names and functions of enzymes involved in DNA replication and RNA transcription, and those used in DNA technology. Most all enzyme names end in –ase.

D. *Proofreading* during DNA replication, *and repair* of damaged DNA, result in low mutation rates at the nucleotide level.

1. DNA polymerase makes mistakes at a rate of about 1/10,000 base pairs, but proofreading and repair mechanisms reduce that rate to 1/1,000,000,000.

2. Errors are usually corrected by enzymes that move along the new DNA molecule and replace any base that has been mismatched.

3. DNA molecules are also susceptible to damage by chemicals or radiation, and are repaired in a similar manner. (See also Mutations in this chapter: Section VI.)

IV. The three types of *RNA* have different structures and functions, but are all made during the process of *transcription*, and all are important in the subsequent production of proteins during translation.

A. *Ribonucleic acid (RNA)* structure is similar to DNA in some ways, but has very important differences.

1. RNA and DNA are both composed of nucleotides and both have strands consisting of a *sugar–phosphate backbone* with nitrogenous bases attached to their sugars.

2. RNA and DNA differ in the following significant ways.

   i. The 5-carbon sugar in RNA's backbone is *ribose*, instead of deoxyribose.

   ii. Instead of thymine, RNA uses the pyrimidine base, *uracil*.

Figure 15.5 Structure of Uracil

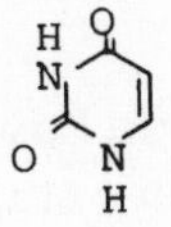

iii. RNA does not form a stable double helix along its entire length with a complementary strand of RNA as DNA does.

    a) RNA often is present in a *single-stranded* state, *but it also can base pair* with DNA, with itself, and with other RNA molecules.

    b) When it does form base pairs through hydrogen bonding, guanine pairs with cytosine, and *adenine pairs with uracil.*

Figure 15.6 Complementarity of DNA and RNA

```
-----G A T T C G T A A G G C------ D N A
-----C U A A G C A U U C C G------ R N A
```

B. The functions of RNA and DNA are different.

1. *DNA stores genetic information* on how to make RNA and proteins, and it passes this information from cell to cell and from parents to offspring.
2. Different types of RNA function in different ways.

    i. *Messenger RNA (mRNA)* transfers genetic information from DNA in the nucleus to ribosomes in the cytoplasm, where its information is translated into proteins.

    ii. *Ribosomal RNA* (rRNA) is incorporated into large protein complexes, called *ribosomes*, which are the sites of protein synthesis in the cytoplasm.

    iii. *Transfer RNA (tRNA)* carries amino acids to a ribosome so they can be assembled into proteins.

C. *Transcription* is the process whereby information contained in the nucleotide sequences of genes is transferred to RNA molecules.

1. Transcription has three basic steps and occurs in the nucleus of eukaryotes and the cytoplasm of prokaryotes.

    i. The *initiation* of transcription is controlled by interactions between various proteins and various regions of a gene. (See also Gene Expression in this chapter: Section VII.)

a) During initiation, the enzyme *RNA polymerase,* binds to the promoter and opens a portion of the gene, to create a *transcription bubble.*

b) RNA polymerase begins to synthesize an *RNA transcript* complementary to only one strand of DNA called the *template.*

ii. During *elongation,* RNA polymerase moves along the template DNA, adding nucleotides to the elongating strand of RNA.

a) RNA polymerase catalyzes the formation of a covalent bond between each new nucleotide by joining the ribose of one nucleotide to the phosphate of another.

b) Each incoming nucleotide base pairs with its complementary pyrimidine or purine in the DNA template sequence on the gene.

iii. When a *termination* sequence, or *terminator,* at the end of the gene is reached, RNA polymerase leaves the promoter, and the RNA transcript is released.

Figure 15.7 RNA Transcription

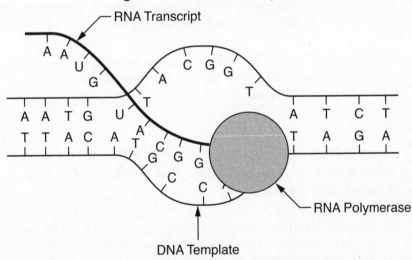

2. In eukaryotes, before RNA leaves the nucleus, it is modified.

i. The initial mRNA transcript that is synthesized contains regions that will be translated into protein, called *exons,* interspersed with regions that are not translated, called *introns.*

ii. Before leaving the nucleus, mRNA undergoes *splicing* to remove its introns.

Figure 15.8 Splicing of mRNA to Remove Introns

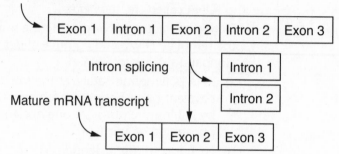

a) A special enzyme complex, called a *spliceosome*, cuts the ends of introns and joins two exons together.

b) In some cases, the mRNA molecule itself acts as a catalyst (called a *ribozyme*) and splices out its own introns.

iii. Splicing of specific regions of rRNA transcripts and tRNA transcripts also occurs.

3. rRNA—as a part of ribosomal subunits—plus mRNA and tRNA all travel through the nuclear pores of the nuclear envelope to the cytoplasm where they all participate in protein synthesis.

V. *Translation*, also called *protein synthesis*, occurs on ribosomes in the cytoplasm of prokaryotic and eukaryotic cells.

A. *Proteins* act as critical structural components of cells, as well as controlling such processes as catalysis, movement, and communication between cells.

1. Proteins are made of subunits called *amino acids*.

i. There are about *20 different amino acids* that are linked together by *covalent bonds*, called *peptide bonds*, in a manner specified by the sequence of nucleotides present in mRNA.

ii. The information determining the sequence of amino acids in a protein is carried in units of *three nucleotides*, called *codons*, present in a distinct sequence along the mRNA transcript.

2. Each codon specifies only one amino acid (or a stop or start signal).

    i. The *genetic code* specifies which codon codes for each amino acid (or signal).

       a) The genetic code used by all organisms is almost identical.

       b) This near *universality of the genetic code* suggests an ancient origin of the genetic code during evolution.

    ii. One codon, *AUG*—called a *start codon*—specifies the amino acid, *methionine*, and functions as a start signal, telling the ribosome where to start translating an mRNA.

    iii. The three possible *stop codons*—*UGA, UAA*, and *UAG*—signal the ribosome to stop because the end of the protein has been reached.

    iv. Although each codon always specifies one amino acid, most amino acids have more than one codon.

       a) For example, UUU on an mRNA transcript always means that the amino acid phenylalanine should be placed at that specific location.

       b) But, at another location in the transcript, a UUC codon may be used to specify that phenylalanine should be placed at the other location as well.

       c) This feature of the genetic code is called *redundancy*.

Test Tip

It is not necessary to memorize the codons and which amino acids they code for. If a question asks you to translate an mRNA sequence into amino acids, a codon table will be provided for you.

Table 15.1 The Genetic Code

		Second Position of Codon					
		U	C	A	G		
F I R S T P O S I T I O N	**U**	UUU Phe	UCU Ser	UAU Tyr	UGU Cys	**U**	**T H I R D P O S I T I O N**
		UUC Phe	UCC Ser	UAC Tyr	UGC Cys	**C**	
		UUA Leu	UCA Ser	UAA Ter [stop]	UGA Ter [stop]	**A**	
		UUG Leu	UCG Ser	UAG Ter [stop]	UGG Trp	**G**	
	C	CUU Leu	CCU Pro	CAU His	CGU Arg	**U**	
		CUC Leu	CCC Pro	CAC His	CGC Arg	**C**	
		CUA Leu	CCA Pro	CAA Gln	CGA Arg	**A**	
		CUG Leu	CCG Pro	CAG Gln	CGG Arg	**G**	
	A	AUU Ile	ACU Uhr	AAU Asn	AGU Ser	**U**	
		AUC Ile	ACC Thr	AAC Asn	AGC Ser	**C**	
		AUA Ile	ACA Thr	AAA Lys	AGA Arg	**A**	
		AUG Met	ACG Thr	AAG Lys	AGG Arg	**G**	
	G	GUU Val	GCU Ala	GAU Asp	GGU Gly	**U**	
		GUC Val	GCC Ala	GAC Asp	GGC Gly	**C**	
		GUA Val	GCA Ala	GAA Glu	GGA Gly	**A**	
		GUG Val	GCG Ala	GAG Glu	GGG Gly	**G**	

3. The order of nucleotides in the template of a gene corresponds to the order of nucleotides in an mRNA transcript, which in turn corresponds to the order of amino acids in a protein.

Figure 15.9 Co-linearity of DNA, mRNA, and Protein Sequences

—A A A　T C G　A A G　G G C— template DNA
—U U U　A G C　U U C　C C G— mRNA
—P h e—S e r —P h e—P r o— protein

B. Co-linearity of mRNA and protein is the result of the structure and function of *tRNA molecules*.

Test Tip *An understanding of the concepts of templates and co-linearity are core concepts usually included on the test.*

1. The *function of a tRNA* molecule is to carry the correct amino acid to the ribosome.
2. Two features of *tRNA structure* are responsible for this function.
    i. One part of a tRNA molecule is a *site for the attachment of a specific amino acid.*
    ii. Another part of a tRNA is a three-nucleotide sequence called an *anticodon*.
        a) The anticodon has a complementary sequence to the codon for the specific amino acid it carries.
        b) Thus, it brings the corresponding amino acid to the correct location in the mRNA.
3. There are enough types of tRNA molecules to carry every amino acid to the ribosome in response to its specific codon(s).

Figure 15.10 Example of a tRNA Molecule

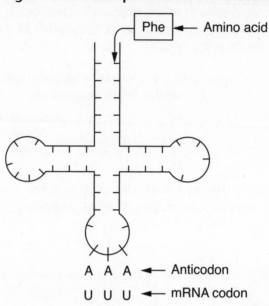

Phe ◄── Amino acid

A A A ◄── Anticodon

U U U ◄── mRNA codon

C. *Ribosomes* are the sites of translation.

1. *Free ribosomes*—those in the cytoplasm that are not attached to the ER—are the sites of synthesis for proteins that will be used inside a cell.

2. *Bound ribosomes* are attached to the ER, and are the sites of synthesis for proteins that will become part of the plasma membrane or will be exported from the cell.

3. Ribosomes are large complexes of rRNA molecules and proteins, and they provide *binding sites* for the actors involved in translation.

    i. One site holds the mRNA that is being translated.

    ii. Two other sites each hold one tRNA molecule at a time.

4. More than one ribosome can move along a single mRNA molecule, allowing multiple copies of the protein to be made at one time.

Test Tip

Know the different types of RNA and their functions for the test.

D. The process of *translation* has three major steps.

Figure 15.11 Translation (Protein Synthesis)

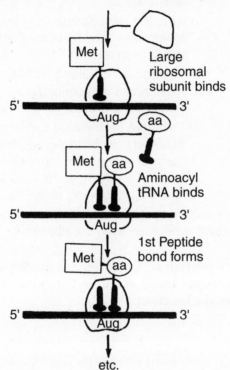

1. Translation is *initiated* when the start codon on an mRNA transcript is recognized by the ribosome.
   - i. A tRNA—which carries the amino acid methionine and has the anticodon UAC—attaches to the ribosome at one of the sites set aside for tRNA on the ribosome, and its anticodon hydrogen bonds to the start codon, AUG.
   - ii. Methionine is the first amino acid specified by all mRNA transcripts, but is often removed, sometimes along with other amino acids, after translation.
2. *Elongation* is a series of repeating steps which add amino acids to the elongating protein.
   - i. A tRNA, with the anticodon matching the next codon on the mRNA, hydrogen bonds to that codon as it sits at the second tRNA binding site of the ribosome.

ii. This brings the first amino acid in close contact with the second amino acid in the protein, allowing for the formation of a peptide bond between the two amino acids.

iii. After the peptide bond is formed between the two amino acids, the tRNA for the first amino acid leaves the ribosome.

iv. The ribosome—along with the remaining tRNA—then moves one codon forward on the mRNA transcript: a process called *translocation*.

v. The tRNA for the next codon now takes its own place on the ribosome, and the steps repeat themselves with the formation of the next peptide bond, the release of the used tRNA, translocation, and the positioning of the next tRNA.

3. *Termination* occurs when the stop codon is reached and the protein is released from the ribosome.

E. After a protein is translated it is modified, folded, and sent to its proper location within the cell where it will carry out its specific function.

Test Tip

An understanding of the similarities and differences between DNA replication, transcription, and translation is a popular topic for test questions.

VI. *Mutations* **are genetic changes in the DNA of an organism and have effects on either specific proteins or other aspects of an organism's phenotype.**

A. Mutations of one or a few nucleotides in DNA are called *point mutations* **and usually occur during** *DNA replication.*

1. *Substitution mutations* occur when a nucleotide has been altered, or incorrectly paired during DNA synthesis, thereby changing it to another nucleotide.

i. If a substitution occurs within the *coding region* of a gene (within its exons), it may or may not cause a change in the amino acid in that position of the protein, depending on the specific change and its specific location in a codon.

Figure 15.12 Substitution Mutations

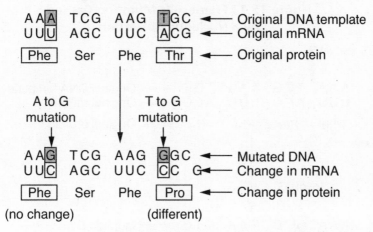

ii. Some substitutions that change a single amino acid result in significant detrimental effects, such as single amino acid changes in the blood protein hemoglobin that result in the sickle cell anemia disease.

iii. Other substitutions have no detrimental effects.

2. *Insertion* or *deletion point mutations* occur when one or a few nucleotides are inserted or deleted.

    i. Insertion or deletion of groups of *three nucleotides* within the coding region of a gene may simply cause insertion or deletion of amino acids in a protein.

    ii. Insertion or deletion of *one* nucleotide, or groups of nucleotides that are *not divisible by three*, result in *frameshift mutations*.

        a) The term, *reading frame*, refers to the fact that the coding region of a gene is divided into codons of three nucleotides.

        b) If one nucleotide is deleted or inserted, the reading frame changes such that all codons after the mutation are changed, causing all of the amino acids after the site of the mutation to also be altered.

c) A frameshift mutation, especially near the start of a gene, almost always results in a completely defective protein.

Figure 15.13 Frameshift Mutation Caused by a Nucleotide Insertion

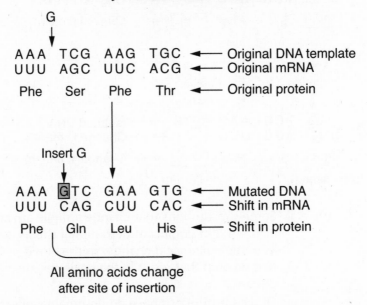

All amino acids change after site of insertion

B. Mutations occurring during *meiosis* (as opposed to those that occur during DNA replication) can involve parts of chromosomes or whole chromosomes.

1. Mutations in *chromosome structure*—where regions of DNA much larger than those involved in point mutations are involved—are due to chromosome breakage.

   i. If a region of a chromosome (that does not contain a centromere) is broken and does not rejoin the chromosome, a chromosome *deletion* results.

   ii. If a broken portion of a chromosome becomes incorporated into its homologous chromosome, a chromosome *duplication* results on the homologue.

iii. The broken portion of the chromosome may also be inverted and then reattached to the same chromosome, resulting in a chromosome *inversion*.

iv. If a portion of a chromosome is moved from one chromosome to a chromosome that is not its homologue, a chromosome *translocation* results.

Figure 15.14 Chromosomal Mutations: Alterations of Parts of Chromosomes

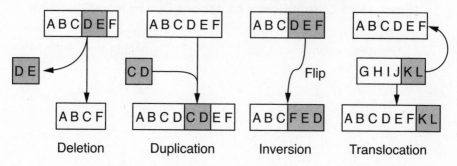

Deletion   Duplication   Inversion   Translocation

2. Mutations in *chromosome number* involve the loss or gain of whole chromosomes, or duplication of whole genomes (all of an organism's chromosomes).

   i. *Nondisjunction*—the failure of chromosomes to separate properly during meiosis—can result in the production of cells with abnormal numbers of chromosomes.

      a) Nondisjunction can occur during meiosis I or meiosis II.

         ▸ *When nondisjunction occurs during meiosis I, a complete tetrad of one pair of homologous chromosomes moves to one side of the cell.*

         ▸ *When nondisjunction occurs during meiosis II, a pair of sister chromatids fails to separate, pulling both chromatids to one side of the cell.*

      b) Regardless of whether nondisjunction occurs during meiosis I or meiosis II, the result is that some gametes are missing one chromosome and others have two copies of that chromosome.

▶ *A normal gamete and a gamete missing one chromosome (n − 1) join to create a zygote with a missing chromosome that is called a monosomic.*

▶ *A normal gamete and a gamete with an extra chromosome (n + 1) may join to create a zygote with an extra chromosome that is called a trisomic.*

Figure 15.15 Chromosomal Mutations Due to Nondisjunction

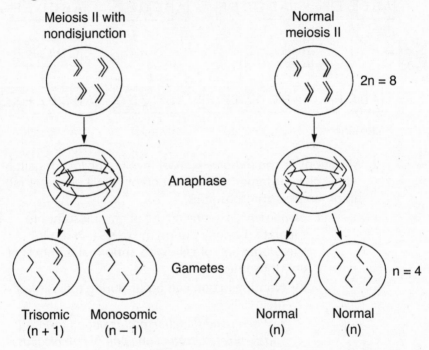

c) Monosomic chromosomal abnormalities involving the sex chromosomes occur in humans.

▶ Monosomics *receiving only one X chromosome (genotype XO) have the condition known as* Turner's syndrome.

▶ *Monosomics receiving only one Y chromosome are not viable because they lack all of the necessary genes present on the X chromosome.*

d) Trisomic chromosomal abnormalities involving autosomes and sex chromosomes also occur in humans.

▸ *Individuals with trisomy-21 have three copies of chromosome 21 and have* Down syndrome.

▸ *Trisomics who receive two X chromosomes and a Y chromosome (genotype XXY) have the condition known as* Klinefelter's syndrome.

2. *Polyploidy*—multiple sets of all chromosomes—occurs in plants and some other organisms, and can result in the formation of new species.

   i. When meiosis fails to occur during gamete formation, diploid gametes can result.

   a) *Autopolyploidy* occurs when two abnormal diploid gametes (2*n*) fuse to form a viable zygote (4*n*) that can reproduce with like individuals (4*n*), but not with members of its parent species (2*n*).

   b) *Allopolyploidy* occurs when two species contribute to the formation of a third species and also involves the formation of diploid gametes.

   ii. Plants tolerate polyploidy more than most other organisms, and polyploid species are not uncommon in plants.

C. *The effects of mutations* **run the gamut from neutral to lethal, but mutations also provide the raw material for evolution by natural selection.**

1. Mutations can occur in *somatic cells* or *germ cells*.

   i. If a mutation occurs in a germ cell, it can be inherited because the products of germ cells are gametes.

   ii. If a mutation occurs in somatic cells, it is not inherited through sexual reproduction, but it may have other effects in the organism in which it occurs, such as the development of cancer.

2. Germ cell mutations that do not impact the fitness of an organism are known as *neutral mutations*.

   i. Neutral mutations result in *neutral variation*—variations between organisms that do not seem to impact evolutionary fitness.

    ii. Many, if not most, of the DNA differences between members of the same species, such as those revealed by DNA fingerprinting, may not impact an organism's fitness.

    iii. Neutral variation may be important during evolution, because environmental conditions vary over time, and a variation that is neutral under one set of conditions may be beneficial under a different set of conditions.

3. *Polyploidy*, as occurs in plants, can create *new species* in one or a few generations.

4. Germ cell mutations create the *allelic variation* that underlies *phenotypic variation*.

    i. A mutation in the regulatory parts of genes, such as a promoter, can affect when, where, and how much of a protein is produced in different cells in a body.

    ii. A mutation in a gene important as a regulatory component in processes such as metabolism, cell to cell communication, growth, development, and so on can create significant differences between individuals and between species.

    iii. Mutations that alter the expression of proteins or their amino acid sequences can result in *lack of a protein* or in a *nonfunctional protein* that may cause *inherited diseases*.

5. Some germ cell mutations—called *lethal mutations*—can include point mutations or the loss of parts of chromosomes or whole chromosomes, and result in the death of an organism before birth.

6. A combination of germ cell and somatic cell mutations are involved in the development of cancer.

    i. *Tumor cells* undergo cell division much more often than normal cells because they lack control over the cell cycle and other cell growth processes.

        a) Cells normally undergo cell division during activities such as development, growth, maintenance, and repair of an organism's body.

        b) Some cells divide repeatedly to produce masses of cells called *tumors*.

        c) Tumors become dangerous if they interfere with normal body functions, and if they

        spread—*metastasize*—to multiple locations
        within the body, causing *cancer.*

ii. Mutations that cause tumors can occur in germ cells or somatic cells.

    a) A mutation in a germ cell can be inherited, and people with inherited mutations are more susceptible to developing some types of cancer.

    b) Mutations in somatic cells add to the effects of inherited mutations, making the development of cancer more likely.

iii. There are several *types of genes* that, when mutated, can result in cancer.

    a) Genes that normally regulate the cell cycle or a cell's response to growth hormones—called *proto-oncogenes* in this context—mutate to form *oncogenes.*

    b) Other normal genes, called *tumor-suppressor genes*, exert negative control over cell division processes, and when they are mutated, they may fail to keep cell growth under control.

    c) The *accumulation* of mutated genes over an organism's lifetime can turn otherwise normal cells into cancerous cells.

iv. Exposure to carcinogens and mutagens are the most likely causes of the somatic mutations that contribute to cancer development, but mutagens may also cause germ cell mutations that are carried by gametes.

    a) *Carcinogens* are substances in the environment that increase the risk of cancer.

    b) Most carcinogens are mutagens.

    c) *Mutagens* are substances that cause mutations.

    d) Examples include tobacco, asbestos, x-rays, ultraviolet light, and a host of other chemical substances in the environment.

v. Some *viruses* can contribute to cancer development by transferring oncogenes to host cells, or causing mutations in proto-oncogenes or tumor-suppressor genes of host cells.

Know the names, descriptions, and effects of the different types of mutations.

VII. **Gene expression—the transcription and translation of a gene into protein—is controlled by DNA sequences surrounding the coding region of a gene and by regulatory proteins that bind to these sequences.**

A. In *prokaryotes*, such as *bacteria*, the single chromosome contains many genes that are organized into operons.

1. An *operon* contains a promoter, an operator, and a group of structural genes.

i. Several *structural genes*, often coding for proteins involved in the same metabolic process, are under the control of a promoter and operator.

ii. A *promoter* is the part of the operon to which RNA polymerase binds in order to begin transcribing the structural genes.

iii. An *operator* is the part of the operon to which a repressor protein can bind in order to stop expression of the structural genes.

2. *Repression* occurs when a regulatory protein, called a *repressor*, binds to the operator, thereby blocking RNA polymerase from transcribing the genes.

3. *Induction* occurs when a substance, called an *inducer*, binds to the repressor protein, inactivates it, and keeps it from binding to the operator, thereby activating transcription of the genes.

Figure 15.16 Regulation of a Bacterial Operon: The Lac Operon

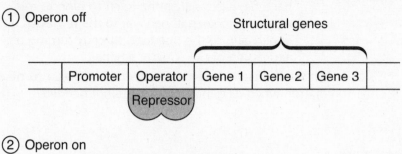

① Operon off

Structural genes

Promoter	Operator	Gene 1	Gene 2	Gene 3
	Repressor			

② Operon on

Genes expressed

Promoter	Operator	Gene 1	Gene 2	Gene 3

RNA Polymerase

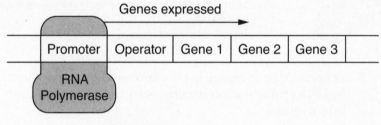

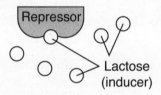

Repressor

Lactose (inducer)

4. The *lac operon* is induced by the sugar, lactose.

    i. The structural genes of the *lac* operon control the utilization of lactose by the bacteria, *Escherichia coli* (*E. coli*).

    ii. When lactose is not present in its environment, *E. coli* has no need to turn on the *lac* operon because there is no lactose to metabolize; so the repressor is bound to the operator, and the genes are turned off.

    iii. If lactose becomes available, it acts as an inducer by binding to the repressor and inactivating it so that RNA polymerase can bind to the promoter and transcribe the structural genes.

    iv. When the structural genes are translated into proteins, the proteins help the bacteria use lactose as an energy source.

v. As the lactose is broken down and used by the bacteria, eventually none is left to bind to the repressor to keep it inactive; so the repressor binds once again to the operator, thereby turning off expression of the structural genes.

5. In this way, bacteria save resources and energy by turning off an operon when its gene products are not needed.

Test Tip

Know the basic parts of an operon and how operons are turned on and off.

B. *Eukaryotic gene expression* **is controlled at many levels as DNA's information is converted to mRNA and then into protein.**

Figure 15.17 Opportunities for Control Over Eukaryotic Gene Expression

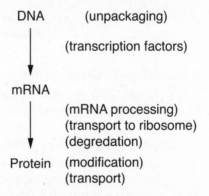

DNA   (unpackaging)

(transcription factors)

mRNA

(mRNA processing)
(transport to ribosome)
(degredation)

Protein   (modification)
(transport)

1. Only a small fraction of the genes in the genomes of multicellular organisms need to be expressed in any given cell type at any given time.

2. Eukaryotic genes are not organized into operons as in bacteria.

i. Each gene has its own *promoter* and other *control elements* present in the DNA sequences surrounding the gene.

    ii. Many types of *regulatory proteins* bind to these elements to determine the timing and level of expression of any particular gene.

3. Controls over gene expression can occur before, during, or after transcription and translation.

    i. *Before transcription* can occur, the region of the genome in which the gene is located needs to be *unpackaged* to allow access to regulatory proteins.

        a) During interphase, some DNA remains as tightly packed as it was during mitosis and is called *heterochromatin*; genes in these regions of the genome are not able to be expressed.

        b) The uncoiling of DNA in a region—which is partly controlled by *histone proteins* associated with DNA—produces less tightly packed *euchromatin*, allowing regulatory proteins to access genes in that region.

    ii. To allow for *transcription* after a region of DNA has been unpackaged, regulatory proteins, such as *transcription factors*, bind to the regulatory elements of the gene, thereby allowing access to the promoter by RNA polymerase.

        a) Some transcription factors bind directly to the promoter to assist the binding of RNA polymerase.

        b) Other transcription factors bind to DNA regions surrounding the gene, called *enhancers*, to further assist RNA polymerase binding.

        c) Once *RNA polymerase* binds to the promoter, transcription can occur.

        d) By controlling the synthesis and activity of transcription factors, a cell determines which gene will be expressed and when.

    iii. *After transcription*, opportunities for control of gene expression can occur during *RNA processing*, which may involve the speed or types of splicing that occur to remove introns and join exons together to produce the mature mRNA.

    iv. *Before translation*, the amount of mRNA sent to the ribosome can be controlled by how efficiently it is *transported from* the *nucleus* to the ribosome, or by how many *mRNA transcripts* are *degraded* along the way.

  v. After translation, opportunities for further regulation of gene expression may involve *protein modifications* and *transport*, such as clipping off small parts of the protein, adding sugars to the protein, or reading signals located in the protein's amino acid sequence that determine where the protein is to be transported.

 VIII. **DNA *technology* is a collection of procedures for manipulating and analyzing DNA that aid in all aspects of biological research and in developing technical applications for a wide range of purposes.**

  A. Manipulating DNA, cloning genes, transferring genes to other organisms, and examining genomes are the *key techniques* of molecular biology.

  1. *Restriction endonucleases* (RENs) are used to cut DNA molecules at specific locations.

     i. RENs are generally isolated from bacteria that use them as a defense mechanism to cut, and thus destroy, foreign DNA that enter their cell.

     ii. An REN cuts DNA at a specific nucleotide sequence called the REN's *recognition sequence*.

        a) Dozens of RENs are available, and each REN has a different recognition sequence.

        b) Recognition sites are generally *palindromic*, meaning that the order of their nucleotides on one DNA strand is the same when read backwards on the complementary strand; for example, the REN called *Eco*RI has the following recognition sequence.

-----GAATTC-----

-----CTTAAG-----

    c) Some RENs cut DNA to produce jagged ends, called *sticky ends*; for example, *Eco*RI cuts at its recognition sequence in the following way:

        -----G   AATTC-----

        -----CTTAA   G-----

    d) When DNA from two sources has been cut with the same REN, sticky ends help the DNA from one source to *anneal* to the DNA from the other source by hydrogen bonding.

    e) Two pieces can be permanently joined using the enzyme *DNA ligase*, which creates covalent bonds between their sugar–phosphate backbones.

2. *Gene cloning* involves isolating a gene from one source, placing it in a cloning vector, and then placing the cloning vector into an organism that rapidly reproduces, such as a bacterium, virus, or yeast cell.

    i. Bacterial *plasmids* are small circular pieces of DNA— much smaller than a bacterial chromosome—that can be used as *cloning vectors*.

    ii. The process of cloning a gene in a plasmid involves the following steps.

        a) A gene of interest (the gene to be cloned) and the plasmid DNA are cut with the same REN.

        b) The two DNAs are then mixed together in the presence of DNA ligase to form bonds between the plasmid DNA and the gene of interest, producing a *recombinant DNA molecule*, called a *recombinant plasmid*.

        c) The recombinant plasmid is placed in a bacterium.

        d) When the bacterium reproduces, the recombinant plasmid is copied so that each new bacterial cell receives a copy of the recombinant plasmid.

        e) Billions of bacteria can be grown in a matter of hours, and each will contain the plasmid with the new gene.

f) Each of the recombinant bacteria is a *transgenic organism* because it carries a gene that came from another organism.

Figure 15.18 Gene Cloning in a Bacterial Plasmid

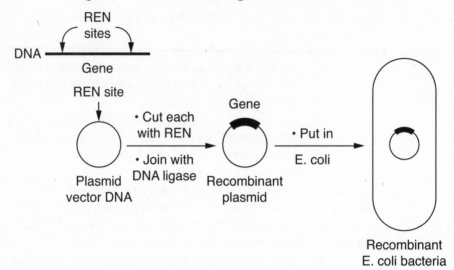

iii. If a copy of the gene of interest is not available, a *plasmid library* containing all of the organism's DNA can be cloned by a similar method, and the clone carrying the gene of interest can be identified by a variety of special techniques.

Test Tip

Remember that antibiotics are often used to identify recombinant bacteria by the presence of antibiotic genes that are carried on the plasmids used for cloning.

3. As well as the transfer of genes to bacteria, similar techniques are routinely used to make *transgenic plants* and *animals* that contain genes from other organisms.
4. *Expression vectors* are special cloning vectors used to create large amounts of *transgenic protein*.

    i. An expression vector usually carries a *strong promoter* next to which the gene of interest can be placed during cloning.

    ii. The vector's host (the bacteria, virus, or yeast) provides all the enzymes and other substances required to transcribe and translate the *transgene*'s protein.

    iii. Genes containing introns cannot usually be expressed in bacteria, because prokaryotic cells do not have the molecular machinery required to carry out intron splicing.

    iv. Special vectors that work in eukaryotic cells, such as yeast, may be able to better express eukaryotic genes.

5. *Restriction fragment length polymorphism (RFLP) analysis* is a technique used to compare the DNA of different members of the same species, or members of different species.

    i. *DNA fingerprinting* in humans is a type of RFLP analysis used in the criminal justice system to identify suspects and to exonerate people unjustly incarcerated.

    ii. RFLP analysis involves the following steps.

Figure 15.19 RFLP Analysis

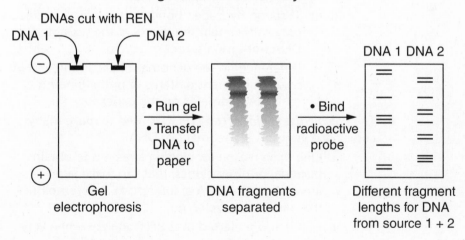

a) DNA from two sources is cut with specific RENs, creating thousands of fragments of DNA of different lengths.

b) Each sample is then subjected to *gel electrophoresis*, which separates the fragments by size.

  ▸ *Each sample is placed in a separate depression in the gel, called a* well.

  ▸ *An* electric current *is run through the gel for a certain amount of time.*

  ▸ *Because DNA is negatively charged, it moves toward the positive* electrode, *but larger fragments move slower than smaller fragments.*

  ▸ *The* porosity *of the gel, the* strength *of the* electric current, *and the* size of the fragments *determine the final locations of the fragments when electrophoresis is completed.*

  ▸ *(Note: This same technique can be used to separate proteins of different sizes and charges.)*

c) The DNA from the gel is next transferred to a special type of *paper*.

d) The paper is then soaked in a solution containing a *probe*—a piece of DNA of known sequence that has been made *radioactive*.

e) Through hydrogen bonding, the probe interacts only with certain sequences of the separated DNA from each source.

f) Differences in the genomes of each source DNA result in different patterns of probe-binding to the DNA fragments on the paper.

6. The *polymerase chain reaction (PCR)* is used to make many copies of a very specific segment of DNA.

  i. One main reason for cloning a gene is to obtain bacteria, or other clones, that can make large amounts of the DNA of interest; PCR accomplishes that task without cloning.

  ii. PCR is also preferred over RFLP analysis when very minute quantities of a sample are available for analysis and has a multitude of applications.

Figure 15.20 The Polymerase Chain Reaction (PCR)

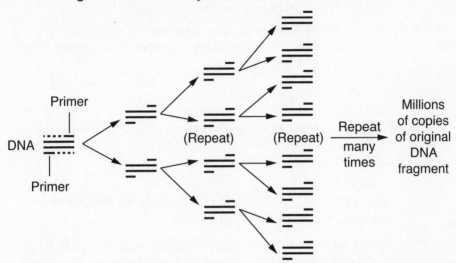

iii. *PCR makes many copies of a specific DNA segment between two specially chosen fragments of DNA called primers* and involves the following steps.

a) Two single-stranded fragments of DNA, called *primers*, are synthesized corresponding to 15–20 nucleotides present at either end of the specific DNA segment that is to be copied.

b) These *primers* are added to the *source DNA* along with the components needed to synthesize DNA: *nucleotides* and *a special, heat-stable DNA polymerase.*

c) The primers bind to either end of the segment to be copied from the source DNA, and DNA polymerase synthesizes two copies of the segment.

d) The reaction is repeated over and over again, doubling the number of copies in each round of DNA synthesis.

e) Repeated rounds of heating and cooling are employed in PCR: heat to separate DNA strands, and cooler temperatures to allow the primers to anneal to the new DNA for another round of DNA synthesis.

f) In less than an hour, millions of copies of the DNA segment are produced.

iv. Compared to other methods for copying DNA, which may take days or weeks, PCR is much faster and less expensive.

Test Tip

A general understanding of the previous DNA technologies is required for the test.

B. *Applications of DNA technology* **include basic biological research, medicine, and agriculture.**

1. The techniques for manipulating and analyzing DNA have created an explosion in *basic* biological *research* affecting all subdisciplines from ecology to evolution to medicine.

   i. RFLP analysis can be used to compare the DNA of individual organisms in a population to determine the amount of genetic diversity that is critical to preservation efforts of specific species.

   ii. PCR analysis can be used to examine the DNA of fossils, as well as living species, to determine evolutionary relationships, and aids in more correct classification of species.

   iii. Cloning, RFLP analysis, PCR, and related chromosome mapping techniques have been used to map the entire human genome (as well as the genomes of many other organisms critical to basic research), creating computer databases that are widely available to researchers in all fields including medicine, mathematics, engineering, computer technology, and other biology disciplines.

2. *Practical uses* of DNA technology in *medicine* include production of *vaccines* and other *pharmaceutical products.*

   i. Genetic analysis and transgenic organisms are used to create more effective vaccines that have less of a chance of causing disease than traditionally manufactured vaccines.

     ii. *Cloning human genes* into bacteria using expression vectors has resulted in larger supplies of important *medicines* such as *insulin* to treat diabetes, and *interferons* and *interleukins* to treat acquired immunodeficiency syndrome (AIDS).

3. *Transgenic plants* are used in *agriculture* to raise crop yields, reduce pesticide and fertilizer use, improve nutritional quality of grains, and create plants tolerant to extreme weather conditions such as drought.

It is helpful to be familiar with examples of how DNA technologies are used to solve practical problems, so that you will understand why a certain technique is being used on application-type questions on the test.

PART V:

ORGANISMAL BIOLOGY

ANIMAL STRUCTURE, FUNCTION, DEVELOPMENT, AND BEHAVIOR

I. **Key Concepts**—See also the summary of core concepts following each individual system.

A. Each cell of a multicellular organism has the same genome, but cells differ from each other because they express different genes of the genome.

B. The body of a multicellular animal is organized into groups of cells called *tissues*, groups of tissues called *organs*, and groups of organs called *organ systems*.

C. Body systems coordinate their activities (e.g., heart rate and respiration rate increase if the muscles need more oxygen).

D. Homeostasis—the maintenance of stable internal conditions in the body—is generally controlled by a group of body sensors, the nervous system, and the endocrine system, which coordinately control several body systems (e.g., thermoregulation involves the hypothalamus sensing body temperature, causing shivering of muscles and constriction of blood vessels to the skin if the body is cold; or dilation of blood vessels to the skin, which produces sweat if the body is hot).

E. A large surface area for a critical activity is created by multiple identical units and/or folding or coiling of structures to be able to fit a tissue into a minimum amount of space (e.g., multiple units of alveoli for gas exchange; folding of the lining of small intestine for adsorption; and coiled seminiferous tubules in testes for sperm production).

F. The structure of a component of a body system underlies its function.

Use the tables and core concepts provided with each organ system for a quick review a day or two before the test. If there is material you still feel you do not know well enough, go back to the text material provided for each separate system and study the appropriate explanations.

II. The bodies of most animals are organized on four basic levels of coordinated cooperation: cells, tissues, organs, and organ systems.

A. *Cells* are the most basic units of organization of all animals.

1. All *animals* are *multicellular*, being composed of many different types of *eukaryotic* cells.

2. The cells of an organism all have the *same genome*, but are different from one another because they *express different genes*.

3. Because different genes code for *different proteins*, the structure and function of each cell type is different.

B. *Tissues* are composed of many cells of the same type and fall into four major categories.

1. *Epithelial tissue* consists of one or more layers of tightly packed cells—forming protective sheets—that line the outer surface of an organism, as well as the surfaces of internal organs and body cavities.

   i. The shapes and arrangement of the cells vary from surface to surface.

Figure 16.1 Examples of Epithelial Tissue

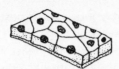
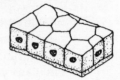

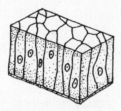

    ii. Examples of epithelial cell functions include *protection* (e.g., skin), *absorption* and *secretion*, (e.g., lining of small intestine) and *rapid diffusion* (walls of capillaries and alveoli).

2. *Connective tissues* are a *diverse* group and consist of cells dispersed throughout an extracellular *matrix* that may be a solid, gel, or liquid.

    i. *Bone* cells are embedded in a solid matrix.

    ii. *Cartilage, tendons, ligaments,* and *adipose* tissues consist of cells embedded in a gel matrix that includes fibrous proteins.

        a) Cartilage, ligaments, and tendons provide support, connection, and protection to surrounding structures.

        b) Adipose tissue stores fat in adipose cells.

    iii. *Blood* and *lymph* cells are dispersed in liquids.

3. *Muscle tissue* contains cells capable of *contraction*, and it functions in *movement* of substances within the body or movement of the body itself.

    i. *Skeletal* muscles (also called *striated* muscles) are attached to the skeleton and are responsible for limb, trunk, head, and similar motions.

        a) The functional unit of skeletal muscle cells is the *sarcomere*, which is composed of *actin* and *myosin filaments*.

b) Skeletal muscles exhibit voluntary movement—i.e., contraction is under conscious control.

ii. *Smooth* muscles throughout the digestive system contract and relax without conscious control (involuntary) to move food and waste; in the circulatory system, they control the distribution of blood to different regions of the body as required.

iii. Specially enervated to contract simultaneously without conscious control, *cardiac* muscle of the heart moves blood within the circulatory system.

4. *Nervous tissue* consists of nerve cells, called *neurons,* which receive and transmit *electrical* and *chemical signals* to provide coordinated *communication* between different parts of the body.

i. *External sensory neurons* in the skin, eyes, nose, mouth, and ear sense stimuli and transmit it to the brain via nerves.

ii. *Internal sensory neurons* monitor body conditions and send information to the brain and endocrine glands.

iii. The *brain* stores information, integrates sensory input, and coordinates responses in conjunction with *spinal nerves.*

C. *Organs* **consist of an integrated group of different types of tissues that coordinate to perform specific functions in an organ system.**

D. *Organ systems* **consist of a group of organs, and other related structures, that work together to carry out an overall process such as digestion or excretion.**

E. **Organ system processes, in turn, work together in a coordinated fashion to allow integration of the body's activities.**

F. *Summary* of *core concepts* of animal *body organization.*

1. Organization of the multicellular animal body involves a hierarchy of lower to higher levels of structure starting with eukaryotic cells, which are grouped into tissues, organs, and organ systems.

2. Four types of tissues—epithelia, connective, muscle, and nervous—are present in the bodies of most animals and have different structures and functions.

    i. Epithelial tissue generally takes the form of sheets that serve as protective, secretory, and/or diffusion surfaces.

    ii. Connective tissues consist of living cells dispersed throughout a matrix and have diverse functions.

    iii. Muscle tissue is capable of contraction and moves substance through the body or moves body parts.

    iv. Nervous tissue senses stimuli, transmits electrical and chemical signals, and integrates responses.

 III. **The *digestive system* is a collection of structures, organs, and glands that work in concert to ingest food, break it into molecules that can be absorbed by the circulatory system, and eliminate solid waste from the body.**

A. *Nutritional needs* vary among animals, but common needs include carbohydrates, proteins, lipids, vitamins, minerals, and water.

1. *Carbohydrates* provide energy and carbon skeletons for *metabolism*—the chemical reactions carried out by cells within the body.

    i. Sugars can be readily broken down to produce ATP during cellular respiration.

    ii. Polysaccharides, such as starch, are broken down into sugars.

    iii. The polysaccharide, cellulose—abundant in plants—cannot be readily broken down to sugars in humans, but provides roughage needed to move wastes through the lower digestive tract.

2. *Lipids* store energy, insulate the body from cold, and provide fatty acids for membrane synthesis.

3. *Proteins* are broken down into the amino acids necessary to build an organism's own specific proteins.

      i. *Nonessential amino acids* are ones that an organism
      can synthesize within its own body.

      ii. *Essential amino acids* must be obtained from the diet.

4. *Vitamins* are complex organic molecules needed by the body
in lesser amounts and most must be obtained from food;
they are used in a variety of processes, including by enzymes
to catalyze specific reactions.

      i. *Fat-soluble* vitamins—such as vitamins A, D, E,
      and K—can be stored in the body.

      ii. *Water-soluble* vitamins—such as B and C—are
      not stored and must be replenished.

5. *Minerals* are inorganic substances—such as *iron*, *sodium*,
calcium, iodine, phosphorus, potassium, and *magnesium*—
that are essential for a variety of processes including nerve
function, enzyme catalysis, and as components of important
molecules such as *hemoglobin* and some *hormones*.

6. *Water* is essential as the medium in which chemical reactions
occur, for maintaining body temperature, and for its role in
chemical reactions, such as *hydrolysis*.

**B. The locations and functions of important organs and
structures in the human digestive system are summarized
in Figure 16.2 and Table 16.1.**

Figure 16.2 The Human Digestive System

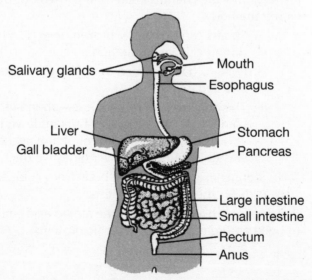

For each organ system, be prepared to identify organs and related structures displayed on figures similar to the ones provided, and be able to associate these components with their functions.

Table 16.1 Functions of the Components of the Human Digestive System

Component	Structure	Function
Mouth (Oral Cavity)	Teeth for tearing and grinding, tongue for tasting and manipulation	Ingestion; mechanical and chemical (starch) digestion (see Salivary Glands)
Salivary Glands	Three pairs; mucus contains amylase	Starch digestion; moisten food
Esophagus Pharynx/ Epiglottis	Longitudinal and circular muscles for peristalsis; movable cartilage flap	Transports food from mouth to stomach; directs food to esophagus
Stomach	Three muscle layers; low PH, pepsin, protective mucus; cardiac and pyloric sphincter	Mechanical digestion; chemical digestion of protein; *bolus*[1] and *chyme*[2] movement
Pancreas (functions in digestion as an *exocrine gland*[3])	Duct delivers enzymes and bicarbonate ions (low pH) to small intestine	Provides enzymes that digest proteins, lipids, carbohydrates and raises pH of chyme
Gallbladder (not a gland)	Saclike; duct delivers bile to small intestine	Stores bile salts made by the liver that emulsify fats
Small Intestine (sections: duodenum, jejunum, and ileum)	Walls of lining secrete mucus and enzymes; villi and microvilli increase absorptive surface area	Produces digestive enzymes for completion of digestion; absorption of nutrients and water

(continued)

Table 16.1 (*continued*)

Component	Structure	Function
Liver	Large organ; has functions in different organ systems	Produces bile; stores energy as *glycogen*[4]; removes toxins
Large Intestine (Colon)	Ascending, transverse, descending (*cecum*[5] and *appendix*[6]); contains bacteria	Removes additional water; absorption of vitamins produced by bacteria
Rectum	Involuntary and voluntary sphincters near anus	Stores and eliminates solid waste (feces)
Anus	Posterior opening	Feces pass to exterior

[1]*bolus*—ball of food that is swallowed; [2]*chyme*—name of partially digested material that leaves the stomach for the small intestine; [3]*exocrine gland*—gland that secretes substances via small tubes called *ducts*; [4]*glycogen*—storage polysaccharide of animals found in the liver; [5]*cecum*—a portion of the colon (generally smaller in carnivores and omnivores than in herbivores) that is involved in fermentation and processing plant material; [6]*appendix*—tiny fingerlike projection of the cecum in humans

   C. Digestion is a *stepwise* process as food moves from one specialized compartment to another.

    1. The *digestive tract* is a compartmented *tube* in which food and food waste move *linearly* from the mouth, through the esophagus, to the stomach, the small intestine, the large intestine (colon), rectum, and out through the anus.

        i. Alternate contractions of *longitudinally* and *circularly* arranged *smooth muscle* in the esophagus, small intestine and colon, result in *peristalsis*, which moves substances through the tract.

        ii. *Sphincter muscles*, all under involuntary control except one near the anus, open to allow the controlled movement of substances from one compartment to another.

    2. The *nutritive substances* in food, as well as *most of the water ingested*, pass through the lining of the *small intestine* into

the *bloodstream*, which, because of its length and internal structure, possesses an *extremely large surface area.*

    i. The wall of the small intestine itself is *highly folded.*

    ii. In addition, *villi*—small fingerlike projections of epithelial tissue—cover the inside wall.

        a) Each villus contains a *lacteal* to absorb *fats* into the *lymphatic system.*

        b) Each villus also contains a network of *capillaries* to absorb the rest of the fully digested food molecules.

    iii. At the *cellular level*, the *plasma membrane* also has fingerlike projections called *microvilli* that serve to multiply the surface area even further.

3. *Mechanical digestion* is the breakdown of food by the *physical* action of teeth and stomach muscles.

    i. *Incisors* (sharp teeth) tear food, and *molars* (flat teeth) grind food in the mouth.

    ii. The three *muscle layers* of the *stomach* mix and *fragment food.*

4. *Chemical digestion* is the breakdown of food by enzymes and other *chemical means.*

    i. The *low pH* of stomach acid serves to degrade larger food particles within the stomach.

    ii. *Bile salts* made by the liver, stored in the *gallbladder*, and secreted into the small intestine, *emulsify fats* into tiny droplets to aid exposure to digestive enzymes.

    iii. Key *enzymes* include the following:

        a) *Amylase*, which is produced by the salivary glands and secreted into the mouth where it starts to break down starch to sugars

        b) *Pepsin*, which is produced by the lining of the stomach, begins the digestion of proteins, and requires low pH to become activated and to function properly

        c) Other *enzymes produced by* the *pancreas* and lining of the *small intestine* digest protein, carbohydrates, and fats to monomers in the small intestine before absorption

5. Viscous *mucus* is secreted by glands and the linings of the digestive tract to aid the movement of substances and to protect the epithelial lining from excessive degradation.

6. pH changes drastically from the stomach (pH of 2) to the small intestine (pH near neutral); the stomach lining produces *hydrochloric acid,* and the pancreas secretes *bicarbonate ions* to neutralize the acidic chyme entering the small intestine.

7. *Bacteria* that live in the colon metabolize waste to produce various substances including *vitamin K*

D. *Summary* of *core concepts* of the human *digestive system.*

1. Larger fragments of food are broken down into the monomers of carbohydrates, proteins, and lipids—sugars, amino acids, and fatty acids—and used for energy and to build the body's own cellular components.

2. Food is ingested by the mouth, digested in the stomach and small intestine, absorbed into the bloodstream by the small intestine, further processed in the colon, and waste is eliminated through the anus.

3. Both physical and chemical means are used to digest food.

4. Exocrine organs and the linings of the stomach and small intestine contribute enzymes and mucus of different pH levels to accomplish digestion.

5. The large surface area of the small intestine greatly facilitates the absorption of nutrients and water.

6. Bacteria in the colon produce some required nutrients.

7. Solid waste is eliminated, not excreted. (Excretion involves waste crossing plasma membranes, such as urea in the kidneys or CO_2 in the lungs.)

The *respiratory system* consists of the lungs and related structures; it delivers oxygen to, and removes carbon dioxide from, the circulatory system in humans via the functional units known as the *alveoli*.

Figure 16.3 The Human Respiratory System

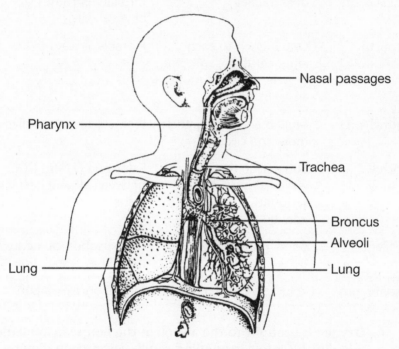

Nasal passages

Pharynx

Trachea

Broncus

Alveoli

Lung

Lung

**Table 16.2 Functions of the Components
of the Human Respiratory System**

Component	Structure	Function
Nose, Nasal Passages	Nose hairs; compartmented; moist surface; epithelial cells have cilia	Protects airway to pharynx; moisten, warm, and filter air
Pharynx Glottis/ Epiglottis	Air opening/ movable flap	Protects airway to trachea/ directs air to trachea

(continued)

Table 16.2 (*continued*)

Component	Structure	Function
Trachea	Cartilage rings; moist, ciliated epithelia	Directs air to bronchi; protects airway in neck/chest; traps and removes debris
Larynx/ Vocal cords	Two ligaments stretched over trachea	Vocalizations: air forced thru larynx causes vibration of vocal cords
Bronchi	One branch to each lung; cartilage; smooth muscle; epithelia moist and ciliated	Protects airways to lungs
Bronchioles	Multi-branching; epithelia moist and ciliated	Protects airways to alveoli
Alveoli	600 million tiny, thin-walled air sacs; each surrounded by a capillary network	Exchange O_2 and CO_2 between air and circulatory system
Ribcage	Bone; muscle between ribs	Protects thoracic cavity; inhalation /exhalation
Diaphragm	Voluntary skeletal muscle	Inhalation/exhalation

A. Oxygen is brought to the alveoli of the lungs via inhalation and diffuses into surrounding capillaries; carbon dioxide diffuses from the capillaries to the alveoli and is exhaled into the atmosphere.

   1. Air from the atmosphere is brought into the lungs through the air passageways by *inhalation* (*inspiration*) and removed by *exhalation* (expiration), a process called *ventilation*.

      i. When the *diaphragm* and *rib muscles contract*, the chest cavity expands, causing air pressure in the chest cavity to drop, which *pulls air into* the lungs.

      ii. When the diaphragm and rib muscles *relax*, the chest cavity compresses, causing an increase in pressure, which *pushes air out* of the lungs.

Figure 16.4 Structure of an Alveolus

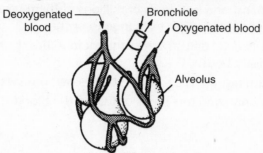

2. The *functional unit* of the respiratory system is the *alveolus* (pl. alveoli).

    i. *Hundreds of millions* of alveoli comprise a very large *surface area* for the exchange of gases between the atmosphere and the circulatory system.

        a) Alveoli are *thin-walled sacs* of epithelia tissue surrounded by incoming and outgoing *capillaries*.

        b) Blood low in O_2 and rich in CO_2 enters the pulmonary capillary beds from the heart.

        c) CO_2 from the capillaries *diffuses* into the alveoli, and O_2 from the alveoli diffuses into the capillaries.

        d) The CO_2 that was transferred to the alveoli *leaves* the body during exhalation.

    ii. The O_2 that *enters* the capillaries is transported back to the heart where it is pumped through the arterial system to the rest of the body.

        a) Most O_2 is carried by *hemoglobin molecules* within *red blood cells*.

        b) Some CO_2 is dissolved in blood plasma, but most of it reacts with water in blood vessels to form *carbonic acid*.

3. *Breathing rate* is controlled by the *brain*, which monitors CO_2 levels and increases breathing rate when the tissues, such as muscles, need more O_2.

B. **Summary of core concepts of the human respiratory system.**

1. Ventilation of the lungs is accomplished by contraction (inhalation) and relaxation (exhalation) of the diaphragm and rib muscles.

2. The alveoli are the functional units of gas exchange in humans, and hundreds of millions of them provide a large surface area for gas exchange to occur.
3. CO_2 and O_2 diffuse across the membranes of alveoli and their capillary beds.
4. Breathing rate is controlled by the nervous system, which primarily monitors levels of CO_2 in the blood.

V. **Nutrients absorbed by digestion, wastes to be removed by the excretory system, oxygen gained through respiration, immune system components, hormones secreted from endocrine glands, and lymph fluid are the prime substances moved through the *circulatory system* from one part of the body to another.**

A. The *cardiovascular system* includes the heart, blood vessels, and blood.

B. The *lymphatic system* includes lymph vessels, lymph nodes, and lymph fluid.

Table 16.3 Functions of the Components of the Human Circulatory System

Component	Structure	Function
Heart	SA node and AV nodes; right and left sides divided by septum	Self stimulating; separate systemic and pulmonary circuits
Ventricles	Two muscular chambers	Pump blood
Atria	Two thin-walled chambers	Collect blood from veins
Valves	Valves: flexible tissue flaps that open in only one direction	One-way flow of blood
Arteries	Thick-walled to withstand high pressure, muscular	Carry blood away from the heart under pressure

(continued)

Table 16.3 (*continued*)

Component	Structure	Function
Veins	Walls are thinner; valves properly oriented to prohibit backflow of blood; surrounded by the body's skeletal muscles	Carry blood toward the heart; keep blood from flowing backward; contraction of skeletal muscles provide force
Capillaries	Numerous, very thin-walled, small diameter	Exchange substance with nearby tissues, generally by diffusion
Blood		
Red blood cells (erythrocytes)	Iron in hemoglobin carries 4 O_2 molecules, made in bone marrow	Carry O_2
White blood cells (leukocytes)	Various (see Immune System)	Protect against infections
Platelets	Stimulate fibrin production at wound sites	Clot blood
Plasma	Liquid with dissolved substances	Carries nutrients, wastes, antibodies, and hormones;
	Proteins (albumin)	Regulates osmotic pressure
Lymph Vessels	Similar to veins; valves oriented to prohibit backflow of lymph; lacteals pick up fats in small intestine	Carry lymph from tissues to heart; transport digested fat to cardiovascular system
Lymph Nodes	Connective tissue; white blood cells in fibrous matrix	Filter lymph to remove microorganisms and debris
Lymph	Water and proteins lost from blood to tissues	Return lost fluid and protein to cardiovascular system

C. The circulatory system moves blood and lymph throughout the body.

Figure 16.5 The Human Heart

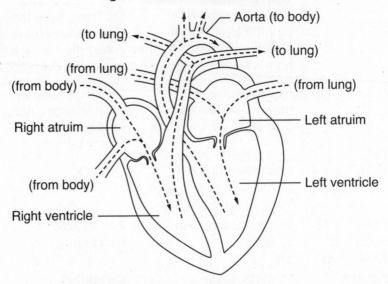

1. The *heart* moves blood in the cardiovascular system by contraction of both atria first, and then both ventricles; the contractions are controlled by electrical signals generated by specialized muscle tissue in the walls of the right atrium and ventricle called *nodes*.

    i. The right atrium is connected to the right ventricle by a special *valve* that only lets blood flow in one direction—from the atrium to its ventricle; the left atrium and left ventricle also have a similar connection through a separate valve.

    ii. The cardiac muscle of the right atrium of the heart contains specialized cells called the *SA node* (or *pacemaker*) of the heart.

    iii. When the SA node generates an electric signal, it spreads quickly to both *atria*, causing them to *contract simultaneously*.

    iv. As the atria contract, they push blood coming from the body or lungs into their respective ventricles.

    v. The *AV node* (located between the right atrium and the right ventricle) then generates a similar electrical signal that spreads quickly to both *ventricles*, causing them to also *contract simultaneously*.

   vi. As the ventricles contract, they push blood into the arteries, which pump blood away from the heart.

  vii. Ventricular contraction is called *systole*, and atrial contraction is called *diastole*: *blood pressure* readings are reported as systolic pressure/diastolic pressure.

Figure 16.6 Systemic and Pulmonary Blood Flow of the Circulatory System

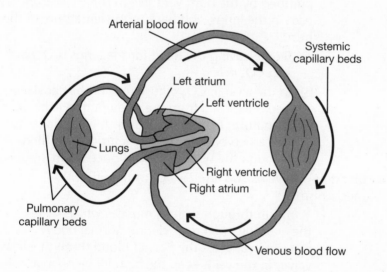

2. There are two separate *circuits* in the cardiovascular system.

    i. In the *systemic circuit*, oxygenated blood is carried from the left ventricle of the heart, through arteries to *capillary beds* located *throughout the body*, and back to the right atrium of the heart via veins.

      a) The *left ventricle* of the heart is larger and *more muscular* than the right ventricle, because it must supply the pressure to move blood farther, and to more capillary beds, than the right ventricle.

b) Blood leaving the heart (the main artery being the *aorta*) in the systemic system is O_2 *rich* and CO_2 *poor*.

c) The O_2 *diffuses* across the thin-walled *capillaries* into the body's tissues and CO_2 *diffuses* from the tissues into the capillaries to be carried back to the heart (the main vein being the *vena cava*) and then the lungs.

ii. In the *pulmonary circuit,* the *deoxygenated* blood from the body that enters the right atrium is pumped by the right ventricle to the *alveoli capillary beds* in the lungs, and back to the left atrium of the heart.

a) Blood leaving the heart for the lungs is O_2 *poor* and CO_2 *rich*.

b) In the alveoli, CO_2 diffuses out of the capillaries and is expelled from the body during exhalation; O_2 diffuses from the alveoli to the capillaries to be carried back to the left ventricle and then through the systemic circuit once again.

3. Blood flow in veins and arteries occurs by different mechanisms.

i. *Veins* run through skeletal muscles which, when they contract and relax during normal body movements, assist the flow of blood through veins; valves in the veins keep the blood flowing in a one-way direction—toward the heart.

ii. On the other hand, blood flows through *arteries* as a result of pressure caused by the pumping action of the heart.

4. The *lymphatic system* involves the *one-way flow* of substances from the tissues to the heart via a network of lymph vessels, and has three main functions.

i. It picks up water and proteins, which have been forced out of the capillaries beds, and *returns* this *fluid* to the *cardiovascular system*.

        ii. It acts as part of the *immune system* by filtering out microorganisms and other foreign substances as lymph moves through the meshlike lymph nodes, and also produces and stores white blood cells called *lymphocytes*.

        iii. It carries *digested fats* from the small intestine—where they are picked up by lacteals—to the cardiovascular system.

D. *Summary* of *core concepts* of the human circulatory system.

1. The cardiovascular system of humans is a closed system.
2. The pulmonary circuit pumps blood from the heart to the capillary beds of the lungs and back to the heart.
3. The heart then pumps that blood through the systemic circuit to the capillary beds of the rest of the body and back to the heart.
4. The lymphatic system moves substances in one direction—from the tissues to the heart.
5. Nodes of specialized muscular tissue within the walls of the heart (one called a *pacemaker*), provide nervous impulses that cause both atria to contract simultaneously followed by the contraction of both ventricles.
6. Arteries have thicker walls than veins, because arteries carry blood away from the beating heart under higher pressure.
7. Veins are designed to move blood back to the heart under very low pressure.
8. O_2 is carried mainly by hemoglobin in red blood cells, whereas CO_2 is mainly carried in the blood plasma as bicarbonate ions.
9. The lymphatic system returns water and protein from body tissues, and digested fats from the small intestine, to the heart where they enter the cardiovascular system.

VI. The *excretory system* maintains water, salt, and pH balance, and removes *nitrogenous wastes* (*urea in humans*) from the body by filtering the circulating blood.

Figure 16.7 The Human Excretory System

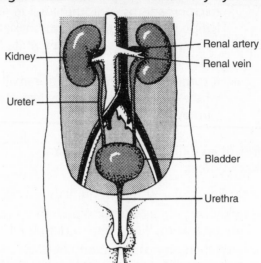

Kidney

Ureter

Renal artery

Renal vein

Bladder

Urethra

Table 16.4 Functions of the Components of the Human Excretory System

Component	Structure	Function
Renal Artery	(For structure of arteries, see Table 16.3.)	Carries unfiltered blood from the circulatory system to the kidneys for filtration
Renal Vein	(For structure of veins, see Table 16.3.)	Carries filtered blood from the kidneys back to circulatory system
Kidneys (Containing nephrons)	Contain about a million nephrons; some nephrons span cortex and medulla regions of kidney	Remove urea and toxins from blood; produce urine; maintain salt, pH and water balance of blood
Liver (role in excretion)	Cells with enzymes for making urea from ammonia and for detoxification of toxins	Synthesizes urea from ammonia; detoxifies other wastes
Ureters	Thin tubes	Carry urine from kidneys to bladder

(continued)

Table 16.4 (*continued*)

Component	Structure	Function
Bladder	Baglike, sphincter muscles near junction with urethra	Stores and eliminates urine from the body
Urethra	Thin tube, exterior opening	Carries urine from bladder to exterior of the body

Test Tip

Know the difference between the two similar-sounding terms, "ureter" and "urethra."

A. **Nephrons in the kidneys filter blood, removing wastes and returning vital substances to the circulatory system.**

1. The *functional units* of the kidneys are *nephrons*, which remove urea and toxins from the blood and return water, salts, glucose, and amino acids back to the blood as urine, which is concentrated before being sent to the bladder.

Figure 16.8 A Single Nephron

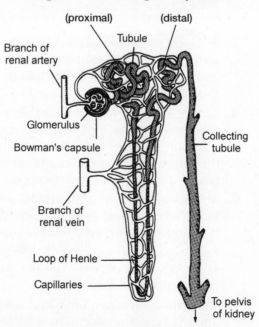

Table 16.5 Functions of the Components of a Nephron

Component	Structure	Function
Glomerulus	Tight ball of (arterial) capillaries surrounded by Bowman's capsule	Functions in filtration step by providing capillary blood supply under pressure
Bowman's Capsule	Closed, cup-shaped end of the nephron tubule that surrounds the glomerulus	Functions in filtration step by receiving water, urea, and salts (called *filtrate*) from the blood of glomerulus
Nephron tubule (proximal, loop of Henle, distal)	Thin, plasma membranes are selectively permeable	Functions in reabsorption of water and salt; functions in secretion
Collecting tubule	Branching tube	Reabsorption of water; collects urine from multiple nephrons and carries it to pelvis of each kidney from which the ureters arise
Capillaries (venous)	Surround nephron tubule	Take up reabsorbed substances

i. As blood enters the *glomerulus* under *high pressure*, water and small dissolved substances, including *urea* and other wastes, are forced into the Bowman's capsule of the nephron.

ii. As this *filtrate* travels through the rest of the tubule, *water, NaCl, glucose,* and *amino acids* are transported across the tubule membranes and into the surrounding capillaries and returned to the blood, a process called *reabsorption.*

iii. Additional toxins, wastes, and H^+ are *secreted* by the blood into the fluid in the folded parts of the tubule (the proximal and distal parts of tubule).

iv. *Reabsorption* and *secretion* of different amounts of selected substances maintain the *pH, water,* and *salt balance* of the blood.

v. The remaining water, urea, and other wastes flow into the collecting duct where additional water is reabsorbed, and the resulting *urine* passes to the ureters and eventually out of the body.

2. *Blood cells* and *large molecules*, such as proteins, are too large to pass from the glomerulus into the nephron tubule at the Bowman's capsule, and, thus, *remain in* the *blood* and are not part of the filtrate.

3. About 99% of the water and solutes in the filtrate is returned to the blood, allowing the body to *conserve water* and nutrients while clearing the blood of harmful wastes.

B. **Summary of core concepts of the human excretory system.**

1. The kidneys remove nitrogenous and other wastes from the blood and pass these wastes as urine to the bladder to be removed from the body.

2. The nephron is the functional unit of the kidney that filters the blood and reabsorbs water, salt, and other useful substances returning them to the blood.

3. Salt, water, and pH balance of the blood is maintained by the excretory system.

4. Urine is highly concentrated so that only a small percentage of the water that enters the nephrons actually leaves the body along with wastes.

 The *endocrine system* uses hormones as long distance cell-to-cell communication signals that allow different systems of the body to coordinate their activities to achieve a whole-body response to an event, or to maintain homeostasis.

A. **Communication between cells involving *chemical messengers* can be *local* or *long distance.***

1. *Local regulators* are secreted by cells and only affect the activity of nearby cells.

    i. Examples include *neurotransmitters* in the nervous system, *histamine* in the immune system, *growth factors* in development, and *prostaglandins* in the immune and reproductive systems.

      ii. Local regulators act quickly and do not enter the bloodstream.

  2. *Hormones* act over long distances because they enter the circulatory system and are transported around the body.

B. When a hormone comes in contact with a *target cell*, it either enters the cell or binds to receptors on the surface of the cell.

  1. Most chemical messengers, including most *protein-based hormones*, bind to *proteins* that act as *receptors* on the *plasma membrane* of target cells.

      i. The binding between a hormone and a receptor causes a physical change (usually involving movement) of the protein receptor, which sets in motion a message relay system inside the cell called a *signal transduction pathway.*

      ii. A series of *secondary messengers* carry the signal until it eventually results in a response by the cell.

      iii. Common signal transduction pathways include *protein phosphorylation*, activation of *G-proteins* and *cyclic AMP*, or increases in *calcium ion* levels.

  2. The *fat-soluble steroids* and *thyroid hormones* pass through the plasma membrane and bind to receptor proteins within the cytoplasm or the nucleus of cells.

      i. Hormone binding to a *cytoplasmic receptor* may trigger the response in the target cell.

      ii. Some steroids *enter* the *nucleus* bound to DNA regulatory proteins and *stimulate transcription* of specific genes.

C. The human body has exocrine and endocrine glands.

  1. *Exocrine glands* such as the salivary glands, deliver their secretions through *ducts*.

  2. Endocrine glands secrete their hormones directly into the interstitial fluid surrounding the gland, where they are picked up readily by the bloodstream.

  3. Some glands, such as the pancreas, have *both* endocrine and exocrine functions (e.g., the exocrine function of the pancreas in digestion, as well as release of the endocrine hormone, insulin).

4. Endocrine glands of the body produce a wide array of hormones with different functions throughout the body.

Figure 16.9 The Human Endocrine System

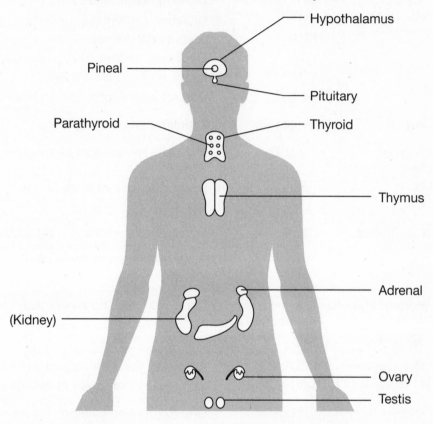

Table 16.6 Glands, Hormones, and Functions of the Human Endocrine System

Gland	Hormone	Function
Hypothalamus	Releasing and inhibiting factors	Regulates pituitary
Posterior Pituitary	Oxytocin	Uterine contractions and lactation
	ADH[1]	Water reabsorption in the kidneys

(continued)

Table 16.6 (*continued*)

Gland	Hormone	Function
Anterior Pituitary	GH[2]	Development of muscles and bones
	PRL[3]	Lactation (production of milk)
	FSH[4]	Gamete production
	LH[5]	Ovulation, testosterone production
	TSH[6]	Regulates thyroid hormones
	ACTH[7]	Cortisol and aldosterone secretion
Pineal	Melatonin	Regulates biorhythms; sleep
Thyroid	T_3[8] & T_4[9]	Stimulate metabolism by multiple effects
	calcitonin	Decreases calcium levels in the blood
Parathyroid	PTH[10]	Increases calcium levels in the blood
Thymus	Thymosin	T-cell development (immune system)
Adrenal Medulla	Adrenaline[11] and noradrenaline[12]	Stress response (fight or flight)
Adrenal Cortex	Glucocorticoids	Increase glucose levels in the blood
Pancreas (Islets of Langerhans)	Insulin	Decreases glucose levels in the blood
	Glucagon	Increases glucose levels in the blood
Ovaries (female)	Estrogens Progesterone	Growth of uterine lining; initiate and maintain secondary sex characteristics
Testis (male)	Androgens	Sperm formation; initiate and maintain secondary sex characteristics
(Lining of Small Intestine/ Stomach)	(Secretin/ gastrin)	Stimulate small intestine/stomach to release digestive enzymes

[1]antidiuretic hormone, [2]growth hormone, [3]prolactin, [4]follicle-stimulating hormone, [5]luteinizing hormone, [6]thyroid-stimulating hormone, [7]adrenocorticotropic hormone, [8]triiodothyronine, [9]thyroxine, [10]parathyroid hormone, [11]also called *epinephrine*; [12]also called *norepinephrine*

D. The interplay between the nervous system and between the glands of the endocrine system coordinate body functions in other organ systems.

1. The endocrine system works intimately with the nervous system.

   i. *Neurosecretory cells* receive signals from the nervous system, causing them to secrete hormones into the bloodstream. For example, neurosecretory cells in the *hypothalamus* receive signals from the nervous system, and, in response, the hypothalamus secretes hormones into the bloodstream that target the *anterior pituitary* gland.

   ii. Two types of hormones secreted by the hypothalamus are releasing hormones and inhibiting hormones.

      a) A *releasing hormone* stimulates the anterior pituitary to release one of its own specific hormones into the bloodstream.

      b) An *inhibiting hormone* stimulates the anterior pituitary to stop releasing one of its own specific hormones.

2. The *same hormone* can affect *different* types of *target cells* in different locations within the body.

   i. For example, *testosterone* produced in the testes acts during puberty to initiate sperm production in the testes, hair production in various locations, changes in muscular development, and changes affecting the voice box.

   ii. *Adrenaline* and *noradrenaline* secreted by the medulla region of the adrenal glands during stress has effects on heart rate, dilation of blood vessels, breakdown of glycogen in the liver, and release of glucose to the circulatory system.

3. Negative feedback loops regulate *homeostasis*—the maintenance of stable internal conditions—and positive feedback loops regulate events that require high levels of a hormone in order to occur.

   i. *Negative feedback* occurs when a stimulus produces a result, and the result inhibits further stimulation;

often two interacting negative feedback loops involving two *antagonistic hormones* are involved in homeostatic control.

a) For example, in one part of the negative feedback loop controlling calcium levels in the blood, when calcium levels decrease (the stimulus), the parathyroid secretes *PTH*, which *increases calcium levels* (the result); *high calcium levels inhibit* further *release of PTH*.

b) The other loop involves a second gland and an additional hormone: when calcium levels increase (the stimulus), the thyroid secretes *calcitonin*, which *decreases calcium levels* (the result), and these *low levels inhibit* further *release of calcitonin*.

c) A similar situation occurs for blood glucose levels where insulin made by beta cells of the pancreas decreases glucose levels, and glucagon made by alpha cells of the pancreas decreases blood glucose levels.

ii. *Positive feedback* occurs when a stimulus produces a result, and the result causes further stimulation, thereby triggering an event.

a) For example, when an infant nurses, it stimulates release of *oxytocin*, which causes mammary glands to secrete milk; this, in turn, stimulates infant nursing, which releases more oxytocin, eventually stimulating milk production.

b) In another example, *LH* causes production of *estrogen*, and estrogen further increases LH production, and so on; when LH levels rise high enough, ovulation occurs.

E. *Summary* of *core concepts* of the human *endocrine system*.

1. Local regulators only affect nearby cells.

2. Endocrine hormones are secreted by endocrine glands into the circulatory system and most act on cells distantly located from the gland.

3. Only certain target cells are affected by a particular hormone, because only target cells have receptor proteins that bind to the hormone.

4. Most hormones bind to receptor proteins on the surfaces of target cells, but some enter target cells and interact with receptors in the cytoplasm or nucleus.

5. Hormone binding to a receptor may set off a series of cellular events—called a *signal transduction pathway*—that relays the hormone signal to the proper cell component that will carry out the response.

6. The nervous system and the endocrine system interact closely.

7. The hypothalamus controls the pituitary by targeting it with its releasing and inhibiting factors.

8. The pituitary secretes many different types of hormones that target other endocrine glands and tissues.

9. The same hormone can have multiple effects if it targets more than one type of cell, tissue, or gland.

10. Homeostatic regulation often involves two negative feedback loops and two antagonist hormones.

11. Positive feedback in the endocrine system involves amplifying the production of a hormone until the hormone reaches sufficient levels to precipitate an event.

 VIII. **The *nervous system* receives input from internal and external sensors and relays that information to the brain where integration occurs; the brain sends out nervous signals to different parts of the body that carry out actions in response.**

A. The *functional units* of the nervous system are *nerve cells* (*neurons*).

Figure 16.10 A Typical Neuron

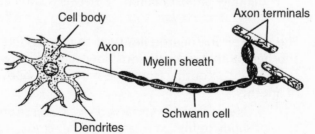

Table 16.7 Functions of Neuron Structures

Component	Structure	Function
Cell Body with Dendrites	Contains nucleus; many dendrites that contain plasma membrane receptor proteins for neurotransmitter binding, and Na^+ & K^+ channels that open when neurotransmitters bind to receptor proteins	Dendrites receive a chemical signal (neurotransmitters) sent from axons of other neurons and convert it to an electrical signal (action potential) as Na^+ rush into the cell, depolarizing its plasma membrane
Axon(s)	One or multiple long, thin extensions of the cell body	Transmit action potentials down their lengths
Myelin Sheath	Made of fat-containing Schwann cells	Insulate axon for faster action potential transmission
Schwann Cells	Flat cells; wrap around axon	Each is unit of myelin sheath
Nodes of Ranvier	Gaps between Schwann cells	Speed action potential by allowing it to jump from one node to the next
Axon Terminals	Ends of neuron; lie close to dendrites of next neuron; contain neurotransmitters in vesicles waiting to transmit signal across synaptic cleft	Convert action potential into chemical signal when an action potential triggers the release of its vesicles filled with neurotransmitters into the synaptic cleft
Synaptic Cleft	Narrow gap between axon of one neuron and dendrite of next neuron	Provides location for transmission of nerve signal between two neurons

1. The *axon* of one neuron lies next to the *dendrite* of another, so that a continuous flow called a *nerve impulse* can be sent smoothly from one part of the body or brain to another.

    i. Nerve signal *transmission within cells* (from the cell body to the axon terminal) is *electrical*.

      ii. Nerve signal *transmission between neurons* is usually *chemical* (but may also be electrical in some cases).

2. Electrical signals, called *action potentials*, are formed in the cell body and travel down the axon.

      i. Due largely to the action of the *Na^+–$K^{\pm}$ pump*, the inside of the plasma membrane is normally negatively charged compared to the outside of the cell. (See Chapter 2 for further information about the Na^+–K^+ pump.)

      ii. When a dendrite receives a chemical or electrical signal, *Na^+ channels* in the plasma membrane open up, flooding the cell suddenly with positive charge.

      iii. When a certain *threshold* of charge has been reached, an action potential occurs.

      iv. The action potential consists of a *rapidly moving* segment of charge reversal traveling down the axon membrane.

Figure 16.11 Action Potential in the Axon of a Neuron

Outside + + + + + + + + + --------------------- + + + + + + + + + + + + + + + +

                       (region of moving charge reversal)

Membrane _____ **Action potential** _____ Axon terminal

                       →   →   →

Inside   ------------------ + + + + + + + + + ------------------------------------

    a) The reason the region of charge reversal moves is because, as a new section of the axon membrane experiences the charge change, this stimulates Na^+ channels in the new section to open; Na^+ moves into the cell at that location, and the inside of that section becomes positive, and so on.

    b) The reason the action potential moves only in one direction is that, as quickly as the Na^+ channels open, they close again, and *K^+ channels* open causing K⁺ to flood out of the cell shunting positive charge once again to the outside of the axon membrane.

   v. The Na^+–K^+ pump then restores the normal charge pattern, which is called the *resting potential*.

  vi. As soon as the resting potential has been reestablished, another action potential can fire.

B. The nervous system is divided into the central nervous system and the peripheral nervous system.

  1. The *peripheral nervous system* consists of all the neurons outside the brain and spinal cord, and has two major divisions.

     i. The *sensory division* brings information from sense organs to the central nervous system via *afferent* (incoming) *neurons.*

    ii. The *motor division* brings information from the brain to the body by *efferent* (outgoing) *neurons,* and is divided into voluntary and involuntary systems.

      a) The *somatic nervous system* includes *voluntary responses* generally carried out by the movement of skeletal muscles.

      b) The *autonomic* nervous system controls the body's internal conditions by controlling smooth muscles throughout the circulatory system and other parts of the body and is usually *involuntary.*

        ▸ *The* parasympathetic division *generally functions to gain and conserve energy by shunting blood to the digestive system and related processes.*

        ▸ *The* sympathetic division *generally increases energy levels in anticipation of vigorous physical activity by inhibiting digestion, increasing glucose levels in the blood, accelerating heart rate, and shunting blood to skeletal muscles; the fight-or-flight response activates the sympathetic division.*

Figure 16.12 The Central and Peripheral Nervous Systems

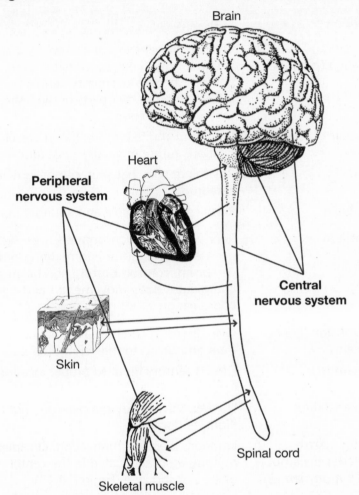

Brain

Heart

**Peripheral
nervous system**

**Central
nervous system**

Skin

Spinal cord

Skeletal muscle

2. The *central nervous system* consists of the brain and spinal cord.

    i. The *brain* can be divided into four main structural
       regions that have a variety of different functions, as
       shown in Table 16.8.

      a) Information coming from the right side of the
         body is often processed in the left side of the
         brain and vice versa.

      b) Regions of the cerebrum involved in processing
         different types of information are shown in
         Figure 16.13.

Table 16.8 Functions of the Region of the Brain

Region	Functions
Brainstem and Reticular Formation (hindbrain)	Overall: homeostasis of circulatory and respiratory systems; coordinates some complex body movements; sends information to other parts of the brain; filters sensory information
Medulla oblongata	Breathing and heart rate, blood vessel dilation, autonomous digestive functions
Pons	Breathing; relay between cerebellum and cerebrum
Midbrain	Relay center for visual and auditory input
Cerebellum	Receives information from muscles, skeleton, eyes, ears, and motor information from the cerebrum; controls posture and balance; coordinates body movement; hand–eye coordination
Diencephalon (upper brainstem)	Overall: relay center for information coming from and going to the cerebrum
Thalamus	Directs sensory input to proper location in cerebrum
Hypothalamus	Hunger, thirst, body temperature, fight or flight, endocrine
Limbic system (includes thalamus and hypothalamus)	Emotion, memory, motivation, circadian rhythm, arousal (located in the center of the brain, not shown in Figure 16.13)
Cerebrum (right and left cerebral hemispheres are divided by corpus callosum)	Overall: each hemisphere has four lobes (frontal, parietal, temporal, occipital); sensory processing (visual, auditory, olfactory, and body sensations converted to perceptions) motor responses, speech, language, memory

Figure 16.13 The Human Brain

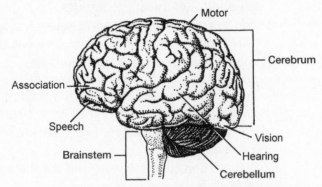

ii. The *spinal cord* has a *central canal* filled with *cerebrospinal fluid* that connects with fluid-filled spaces in the brain, called *ventricles*, and serves to cushion the spinal cord and brain.

iii. The major nerves of the peripheral nervous system branch from the central nervous system.

    a) Branching off from the spinal cord are *spinal nerves* that serve different parts of the body.

    b) *Cranial nerves* of the peripheral nervous system branch directly from the brain.

C. **Special types of neurons, called *sensory receptors*, detect *stimuli* and turn it into action potentials that travel to the proper region of the brain where the received *sensation* is processed to produce a *perception* (such as a visual image we might recognize as an apple or a banana).**

1. Action potentials sent from different sensory receptors are all the same; what makes them produce different perceptions is which part of the brain receives and interprets them.

2. Receptors vary in structure and in what type of stimuli they respond to.

    i. *Photoreceptors* in the eye respond to different intensities and wavelengths of light.

    ii. *Mechanoreceptors* in the ear (and some types in the skin) respond to differences in pressure.

    iii. *Chemoreceptors* in the nasal passages and the mouth respond to different types of chemicals.

    iv. *Thermoreceptors* in the skin and within the body respond to temperature changes.

    v. *Pain receptors* in the skin and elsewhere respond to extremes in heat, cold, pressure, or tissue damage.

3. A *visual image* is produced when *light* stimulates *photoreceptors* (*rods* and *cones*) in the *retina* of the eye causing them to send action potentials through the *optic nerve* to the *occipital lobe* of the *cerebrum* where they are interpreted.

    i. The locations of structures in the eye are shown in Figure 16.14.

    ii. The functions of these structures are shown in Table 16.9.

       a) Light passes through the *cornea* and into the eye through the *pupil*.

       b) As it passes through the *lens*, light is bent to allow it to be focused on the retina, which contains the photoreceptors—rods and cones.

       c) When rods and cones are stimulated by light, they send action potentials through the optic nerve, which includes positional information as to where on the retina light has fallen.

       d) The occipital lobe of the brain changes the sensations it receives from the rods and cones into a perception called a *visual image*.

Figure 16.14 Anatomy of the Human Eye

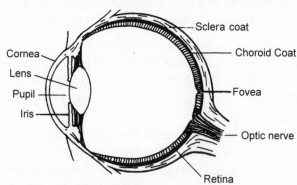

Table 16.9 Functions of the Structures of the Human Eye

Region	Functions
Cornea	Clear to allow light to pass into the eye, protects front of eye
Lens	Bends light to focus it on retina via attached muscles and ligaments
Pupil	Size-adjustable opening for light to pass into the eye
Iris	Dilates and contracts to control diameter of pupil
Sclera	Surrounds eye to protect it, becomes the cornea at front of the eye
Choroid	Middle layer, becomes iris at the front of the eye
Fovea	Center of visual field; high cone density; controls visual acuity
Optic Nerve	Transmits action potentials from photoreceptors to brain
Retina	Location of photoreceptors
Rods	Contain rhodopsin; light vs. dark; many more rods than cones
Cones	Three types with different variations of rhodopsin, each of which senses different wavelengths of light; responsible for color vision

4. *Sound* is detected when vibrations in the air of different frequencies stimulate *mechanoreceptors* (*hair cells*) in the *cochlea* of the inner ear causing them to send action potentials through the *auditory nerve* to the brainstem, the thalamus, and finally to the *auditory regions* of the *cerebrum* where they are interpreted.

    i. The locations of structures in the ear are shown in Figure 16.15.

    ii. The functions of these, and additional structures, are shown in Table 16.10.

    a) Sound waves vibrate the air, enter the *ear canal* causing the *eardrum* to vibrate, which causes the bones of the middle ear to vibrate, resulting in vibration of the oval membrane.

b) The fluid filled *organ of Corti,* within the *cochlea,* changes these vibrations into fluid-borne pressure waves causing the walls of the organ to shift the position of the *mechanoreceptor hairs.*

c) Movement of the receptor hairs causes action potentials to be sent through the auditory nerve to the auditory regions of the brain that interpret the action potentials into the perception of sound as pitch, volume, and rhythm.

iii. The inner ear also controls maintenance of *balance* by sensing the location of the head in three dimensions through other haired mechanoreceptors located within three *semicircular canals.*

Figure 16.15 Anatomy of the Human Ear

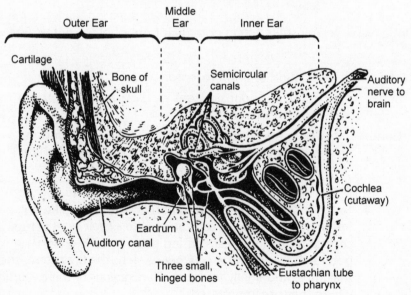

Table 16.10 Functions of the Structures of the Human Ear

Region	Functions
External Ear	Protects the middle and inner ear
Auditory Canal	Transmits sound waves from the outer ear to the middle ear
Eardrum (tympanic membrane)	Vibrates in response to sound waves, communicating these vibrations to the three bones of the middle ear
Bones (anvil, hammer, stirrup)	Vibrate in response to vibrations of eardrum, communicating these vibrations to the oval window, a membrane between the middle and inner ear (the stirrup is also called the *stapes*)
Eustachian Tube	Equalizes air pressure between the outer and inner ear during swallowing when there is a change in atmospheric pressure
Cochlea	Fluid-filled chamber; in inner ear; contains the organ of Corti
Organ of Corti	Site of mechanoreceptors (hair cells) in fluid-filled organ of Corti; hairs are stimulated due to vibrations of middle ear
Auditory Nerve	Transmits action potentials from mechanoreceptors to brain
Semicircular Canals	Three fluid-filled canals containing mechanoreceptors with hairs that bend in response to head movements; control balance

5. *Taste* and *odor* are detected by interaction between a *chemical* and its *receptor protein* located in the plasma membrane of a *chemoreceptor*.

   i. Taste is detected when chemicals dissolved in saliva in the mouth stimulate *chemoreceptors* in the *taste buds* of the tongue, causing them to send action potentials to the brainstem, the thalamus, and finally to the taste center in the sensory cortex of the cerebrum where they are perceived as combinations of salty, bitter, sweet, and sour tastes.

Figure 16.16 Anatomy of a Taste Bud

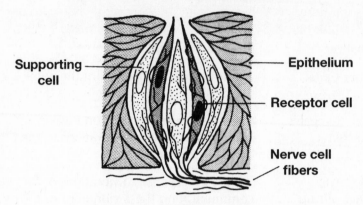

Supporting cell — — Epithelium

— Receptor cell

Nerve cell fibers

ii. Odor is detected when chemicals in the air stimulate *chemoreceptors* located in *olfactory epithelia* of the nasal passageway, causing them to send action potentials to the olfactory bulb and amygdala (parts of the limbic system), and then to the olfactory areas of the cerebrum where they are perceived as odors.

Figure 16.17 Location of Olfactory Chemoreceptors

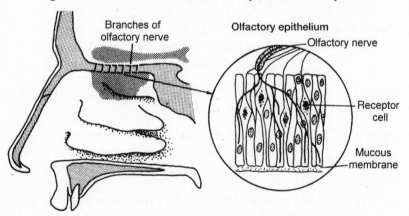

Branches of olfactory nerve

Olfactory epithelium

Olfactory nerve

Receptor cell

Mucous membrane

6. A combination of *touch* (*pressure*), *pain*, *heat*, and *cold* receptors in the dermis and epidermis of the *skin* send messages to the spinal cord and brain.

D. *Summary* of *core concepts* of the human *nervous system*.

1. Neurons are the functional units of the nervous system; they receive a nerve signal at their dendrites, convert it into an action

potential that travels down its axon, and generally causes the release of neurotransmitter molecules into the synaptic cleft.

2. The neurotransmitter travels across the synaptic cleft and binds to receptor proteins in the plasma membrane of the next neuron, generating an action potential in that neuron.

3. The general flow of signals along a neural circuit is electrical within a neuron and chemical (neurotransmitters) between one neuron and the next.

4. The Na^+–K^+ pump maintains a negative charge inside a neuron.

5. When a neuron is stimulated, this charge difference is reversed by the opening of ion channels in its plasma membrane, causing a rush of positive Na^+ into the cell, and is the source of the action potential, which is a wave of depolarization that travels along the axon's plasma membrane.

6. The human nervous system is divided into the central nervous system (the brain and spinal cord) and the peripheral nervous system (all nerves outside the central nervous system).

7. The peripheral nervous system has a sensory division (which collects stimuli from sense organs and structures) and a motor division (which controls responses of the body including movement of muscles).

8. Sense organs detect stimuli, convert it to action potentials, and send it to the brain for interpretation.
   i. Eyes sense differences in light intensity and wavelength using photoreceptors.
   ii. Ears sense differences in pressure using mechanoreceptors for hearing and balance.
   iii. The nasal passages and the mouth contain chemoreceptors that detect different types of chemicals.
   iv. Mechanoreceptors, heat and cold receptors, and pain receptors detect touch, temperature and tissue damage.

IX. The *skeletal, muscular,* and *nervous* systems coordinate the movement of body parts and the process of locomotion.

A. The *skeletal system* of humans is an endoskeleton composed of bones joined together at joints.

1. The skeleton is composed of two parts: the *axial skeleton* and the *appendicular skeleton*.

Figure 16.18 Bones of (a) Axial Skeleton and (b) Appendicular Skeleton

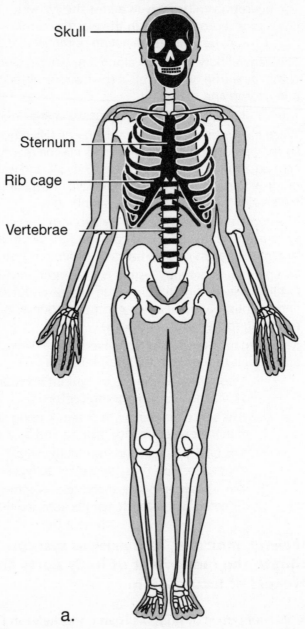

Skull

Sternum

Rib cage

Vertebrae

a.

Figure 16.18 (*continued*)

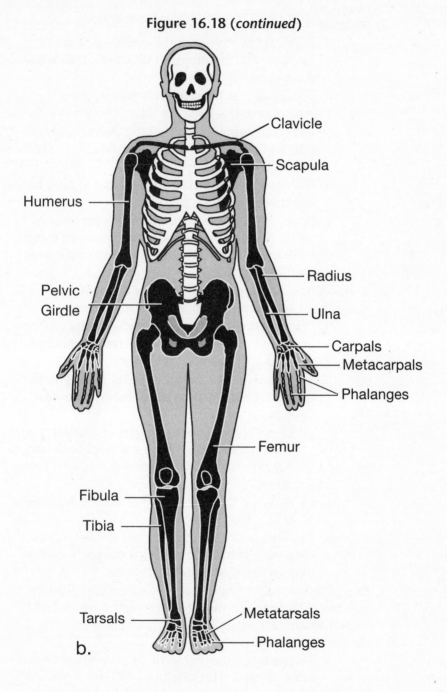

b.

2. Bones of the skeleton have a variety of *functions*.
    i. Bones act as *storage* sites for *minerals,* such as calcium and phosphorus, that can be released and redeposited as needed.
    ii. Bones, such as the skull and ribcage, provide *protection* and *support* for softer internal structures.
    iii. *Red bone marrow* in parts of the sternum, pelvis, ribs, and ends of the long bones produce *red blood cells* and *white blood cells.*
    iv. *Yellow bone marrow,* inside the shafts of long bones, stores energy in fat cells.
    v. Bones also provide *attachment sites* for *muscles* and provide a solid support against which muscle contraction acts to cause movement of different parts of the body.
3. Bones consist of three general layers of different types of living tissue and nonliving mineralized structures.
    i. The *periosteum* is the tough, living, outer covering of bones that contains blood vessels and nerves and protects and nourishes the bone.
    ii. A dense layer of *compact bone* lies directly under the periosteum, composed of many lamellae interspersed with osteocytes.
        a) *Lamellae* are cylindrical layers of mineral crystals and protein fibers; at the center of each lamella is a *Haversian canal* containing a *vein* and an *artery.*
        b) Between the many lamellae are the living bone cells, called *osteocytes.*
    iii. The *central cavity* contains a less dense, porous catacomb of hard bone, called *spongy bone* that may contain red or yellow marrow.
4. Except in the skull—where scattered osteocytes produce patches of bone that grow into bony plates—most bone begins as *cartilage* in the fetus and gradually becomes ossified up through early adolescence.
    i. *Ossification* is the replacement of cartilage with bone as osteocytes produce and release minerals into the surrounding cartilage.

ii. Bones are also capable of *elongation* during this period.

a) *Bone growth* occurs near the ends of long bones in a region called the *epiphyseal* plate.

b) In this area, *cartilage cells* arranged in columns divide pushing older cells to the center of the bone, where they become ossified.

c) The remaining cartilage cells located toward the ends of the bones continue to divide pushing the old cells inward, and causing the bone to lengthen along its long axis.

5. *Joints* are regions where bones are attached to each other by *ligaments* and their movements are facilitated by a lubricating substance called *synovial fluid*; the types, movement, and examples of joints are summarized in Table 16.11.

Table 16.11 Types of Skeletal Joints

Joint Type	Type of Motion	Example(s)
Fixed	None to very limited flexibility	In the skull between plates
Semimovable	Cartilage attachments allow some flexibility	Vertebral column, ribcage (bending, inhaling)
Movable	Greater flexibility	
Hinge	Back and forth	Elbow, knee, jaw
Ball and Socket	Complete rotation	Shoulder, hip
Pivot	Side to side	Between top two vertebrae
Saddle	Rotation	Base of thumb
Gliding	Bones slip over one another	Between small bones of feet

B. *Skeletal muscles*—attached to bones by *tendons*—cause *voluntary* body movements and locomotion in humans in response to *nerve impulses* when their functional units, called *sarcomeres*, contract and relax.

Figure 16.19 The Opposing Actions of a Flexor and an Extensor Muscle

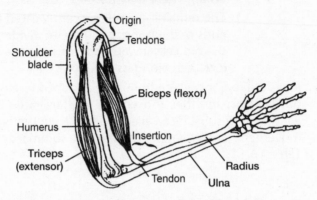

1. Skeletal muscles *span joints* and move limbs by *pulling bones*; this action often involves two muscles (a *flexor* and an *extensor*) that work in opposition.

    i. The biceps and triceps of the arm are an example of a flexor and extensor pair.

        a) The *biceps* is a *flexor* muscle attached across the elbow joint from its origin on the shoulder blade to its insertion point on the radius and ulna of the forearm.

        b) When the biceps contracts, it bends the elbow joint, moving the forearm toward the humerus.

        c) The *triceps*, on the other hand, is an *extensor*, and when it contracts it straightens the joint and the forearm extends.

        d) When a flexor contracts, the extensor must relax, and vice versa.

    ii. The *origin* of attachment of a muscle is on a bone that the muscle does not move (the shoulder blade for the biceps), and its point of *insertion* is on the bone(s) that it *moves* (the ulna and radius).

2. The *sarcomere* is the unit of muscle contraction; it contains alternating strands (filaments) of the proteins *actin* and *myosin*, which are attached to each other at multiple sites along their common area of contact.

   i. Contraction of a sarcomere involves the actin filaments being ratcheted along its myosin filaments.

      a) When a muscle is relaxed, the right and left actin strands in its sarcomeres are distant from one another.

      b) When a muscle receives a nerve signal directing it to contract, the actin filaments detach and reattach to the adjacent myosin filaments over and over again, and during each round of detachment and reattachment, the actin fibers are ratcheted a very short distance toward each other.

      c) The myosin remains stationary as the actin filaments gradually "slide" over them.

      d) When the muscle is fully contracted, the actin filaments have traveled so far that they overlap with one another.

Figure 16.20 Contraction of a Sarcomere

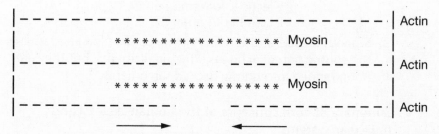

A sarcomere of a relaxed muscle

The same sacromere when the muscle is contracted

e) This contraction—that is, the contraction of many (microscopic) sarcomere units that are attached to each other end to end and span the length of a myofibril—causes the entire myofibril to contract.

f) Likewise, because many myofibrils are present in a muscle fiber (a large muscle cell with many nuclei), and many muscle fibers are bundled together to form a muscle, these contractions on a microscopic scale translate into the larger contraction of the entire muscle.

ii. ATP is required at each attachment site (between actin and myosin filaments) for each ratchet event.

a) When muscles are involved in vigorous activity, a large amount of ATP is used, which means a large amount of O_2 must be consumed by muscle cells in order to make the required ATP by cellular respiration.

b) Exercise causes an increase in heart rate and breathing rate to bring more O_2 to muscle tissue.

c) When circulating O_2 levels cannot keep up with the needs of exercising muscles, muscle cells use lactic acid fermentation, to provide ATP (as discussed in Chapter 5).

3. Smooth muscle and cardiac muscle contraction also requires the contraction of actin and myosin filaments, but they are not arranged into tightly packed sarcomeres.

C. **Summary of core concepts of the human skeletal and muscular systems.**

1. Humans have an endoskeleton with axial and appendicular bones.

2. Bones function in protection, as mineral reserves, production of red and white blood cells, and by providing a solid support for muscle action.

3. Bones are living tissues containing mineral deposits in specific arrangements interspersed with bone cells—osteocytes.

4. Most bones develop from cartilage that becomes ossified by mineral deposition as a child grows to adulthood.

5. Bones are joined to other bones by ligaments at joints, and muscles are joined to bones by tendons.

6. Pairs of opposing muscles—flexors and extensors—control the movement of limbs.

7. The sarcomere is the functional unit of skeletal muscle contraction, and contains alternating filaments of actin and myosin that require ATP to slide actin toward the center of the sarcomere.

8. The contraction of millions of sarcomeres within a muscle causes the whole muscle to contract.

9. Muscle contraction is controlled by nervous impulses.

X. The human body fights pathogens with nonspecific defenses as well as the specific defenses of the *immune system.*

A. *Pathogens* **are organisms that cause** *infectious disease* **including** *viruses, bacteria, protists, fungi,* **and** *small invertebrates.*

1. *Nonspecific defenses* are barriers or systems that attack all pathogens regardless of their type.

Table 16.12 Functions of the Components of Nonspecific Defense

Component	Function
Skin	Provides physical and chemical protection *Physical*: barrier between environment and interior of body *Chemical*: barrier created by sweat, oils, waxes, and lysozyme (lysozyme: enzyme that degrades bacterial cell walls)
Mucus	Traps pathogens that enter epithelia of systems that open to the exterior (e.g., trachea, bronchi, urethra, vagina)
Cilia	Sweep pathogens to exterior opening of respiratory tract

(continued)

Table 16.12 (*continued*)

Component	Function
Stomach Acid	Swallowed pathogens are destroyed by the low pH of stomach
Inflammatory Response	(1) Histamine is released from *basophils* and *mast cells*, (2) histamine causes increased blood flow to damaged area, (3) *neutrophils, macrophages,* and *natural killer cells* move to the site from capillaries and destroy pathogens and infected cells
Interferon	Inhibits reproduction of viruses
Fever	Suppresses bacterial growth, stimulates the immune system

2. The *organs* of the immune system include *bone marrow*, the *thymus, lymph nodes, tonsils, adenoids,* and the *spleen.*
   i. The bone marrow and the thymus are sites of white blood cell production and development.
   ii. White blood cells in the other structures are present in a mesh of fibers that filter the blood and lymph; when a pathogen is trapped, the white blood cells can then attack and destroy it.

Table 16.13 Functions of Selected White Blood Cells (Leukocytes)

Cell Type	Function
Phagocytes Neutrophils	Function in nonspecific defense; engulf and destroy pathogens
Macrophages	Function in nonspecific, humoral, and cell-mediated immune response; engulf and destroy pathogens and pathogen-infected cells; present antigens on their surface and secrete interleukin-1 to activate humoral and cell-mediated immune responses
Natural Killer Cells (NK)	Function in nonspecific defense; destroy virus-infected cells, and cancer cells; puncture cells, causing them to lyse (burst)

(continued)

Table 16.13 (*continued*)

Component	Function
Basophils Mast Cells	Function in nonspecific defense; release histamine to initiate the inflammatory response
Lymphocytes	B cells and T cells are made in bone (B) marrow, but T cells mature further in the thymus (T)
B cells	Function in humoral immunity; respond to interleukin-2; produce and secrete antibodies
B Memory Cells	Function in humoral immunity; mount fast response to second attack by the same pathogen
Helper T Cells	Function in humoral & cell-mediated immunity; respond to interleukin-1 and produce interleukin-2, which activates B cells and cytotoxic T cells
Cytotoxic T Cells	Function in cell-mediated immunity; destroy virus-infected cells and cancer cells; puncture cells, causing them to lyse

3. *Specific defenses*—those targeting specific pathogens—defend against pathogen attack, as well as cancerous cells, by recognizing *foreign substances* called *antigens* on the surface of pathogens; there are two specific immune responses in the human body.

    i. The *humoral immune response* involves the production of *antibodies* secreted into the blood by B cells.

        a) All specific immune responses start with a macrophage engulfing a pathogen, partially digesting it, and then presenting its antigens on the surface of the macrophage cells.

        b) This surface antigen signal is recognized by a *helper T cell* that causes the release of a cytokine called *interleukin-1* from the macrophage.

        c) Interleukin-1 activates helper T cells to release *interleukin-2*.

            ▶ *In response to interleukin-2, cells of the immune system, called* B cells, *secrete* antibodies *into the blood that recognize the antigens of pathogens and neutralize them.*

▸ *Antibodies can destroy pathogens by attaching to a pathogen's cell membrane; thereby blocking sites on its membrane, which it needs to infect healthy cells.*

▸ *Humoral defense has* primary *and* secondary responses.

▸ *In the primary response, when a pathogen infects the body for the first time, B cells, which recognize the pathogen, stimulate the production of more B cells of the same type.*

▸ *Once the infection is overcome,* memory B cells *are produced and continue to circulate in the bloodstream.*

▸ *In the secondary response, if the same pathogen is encountered* again, *the body mounts a* more rapid defense, *because memory B cells respond more quickly to the pathogen.*

d) *Vaccines*—medicines containing non-active pathogens—are used to inoculate a person against a pathogen.

▸ *In response to the vaccine, the body produces memory cells.*

▸ *These memory cells are used to mount a rapid defense—killing disease causing pathogens quickly—if the actual disease-causing pathogen is later encountered.*

Figure 16.21 Comparison of the Primary and Secondary Immune Responses

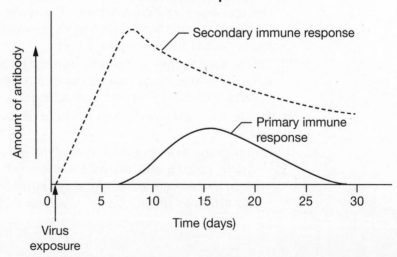

ii. The *cell-mediated immune response* involves the recruitment of *T cells* to help fight off a pathogen.

   a) When interleukin-2 (in the preceding step c), is secreted, it stimulates *cytotoxic T cells*.

   b) Cytotoxic T cells attack and destroy infected body cells by puncturing them.

iii. *Allergies* occur when the body overreacts to antigens, which are not associated with pathogens, by stimulating nonspecific defenses.

iv. *Autoimmune* diseases occur when the immune system attacks and destroys its own, normal cells.

v. *HIV* (human immunodeficiency virus) causes *AIDS* (acquired immune deficiency syndrome) by destroying helper T cells.

B. *Summary* of *core concepts* of the human *immune system.*

1. One defense strategy attacks all pathogens: the nonspecific defenses.

2. The other defense strategy attacks a specific pathogen by recognizing antigens on the pathogen and marshalling the humoral and/or cell-mediated defenses: specific defenses.

   i. The humoral immune response involves B cells, which attack pathogens with antibodies.

   ii. The cell-mediated immune response involves T cells, which attack pathogens, cells infected with pathogens, and cancer cells by lysing them.

XI. *Reproduction* in humans involves the production of *sperm* by *males* and *eggs* (*ova*) by *females*, and their *union* to form a *zygote*, which develops into a fetus in the female's uterus.

A. Sperm are produced in the testes of the *male reproductive system.*

Figure 16.22 The Male Reproductive System

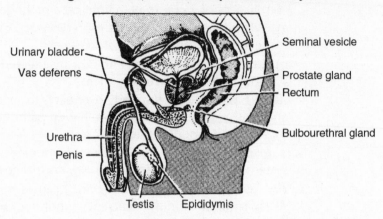

Urinary bladder
Vas deferens
Urethra
Penis
Testis   Epididymis
Seminal vesicle
Prostate gland
Rectum
Bulbourethral gland

Table 16.14 Functions of Male Reproductive System Components

Component	Function
Scrotum	Holds testes and epididymis outside body at the lower temperature required for sperm production
Testes (sing. *testis*)	Produce testosterone (an endocrine hormone) and sperm
Seminiferous Tubules	Site of sperm production within testes
Epididymis	Site of sperm maturation and storage in scrotum
Vas Deferens	Tube that carries sperm to urethra
Exocrine Glands (seminal vesicles, bulbourethral glands, prostate gland)	Secrete fluids, which, together with sperm, constitute semen; secretions include: *Fructose and citric acid*: nutrition for sperm *Alkaline fluid*: neutralizes acid pH of female reproductive tract *Prostaglandins*: cause contractions of smooth muscles of the female reproductive tract
Penis	Delivers sperm to female reproductive tract
Urethra	Carries semen from the vas deferens to the exterior

1. *Spermatogenesis*—the production of sperm—is stimulated by the hormone *testosterone*, and occurs in the *seminiferous tubules* of the *testes*, which are located in the *scrotum*.

2. Sperm then move to the *epididymis* where they *mature* and are stored until ejaculation.

3. During *ejaculation*, sperm travel from the epididymis through the *vas deferens* to the *urethra* and exit the *penis*.

4. As sperm travel through the vas deferens, nutritive and protective secretions from the *seminal vesicles* and the *bulbourethral*, and *prostate, glands* are combined with sperm to produce *semen*.

B. Spermatogenesis and *oogenesis* (the production of ova) differ in three significant ways.

1. Spermatogenesis produces *four sperm* during each meiosis, while oogenesis produces only *one* large *egg* cell per meiosis: the other three cells, called *polar bodies*, degenerate in humans.

2. The cells that give rise to sperm are continually produced from *puberty* (sexual maturation) onward, whereas a female is born with a defined number of cells that produce ova from puberty until *menopause*, which occurs around 50 years of age in females.

3. Egg cells begin meiosis, but are *arrested* in *prophase I* until one egg per menstrual cycle is stimulated to complete meiosis by the hormone, FSH; meiosis then stops again and the ova does not undergo *meiosis II* until after fertilization. In males, meiosis occurs in an uninterrupted sequence.

Figure 16.23 Comparison of the Formation of Sperm and Eggs

Spermatogenesis   Oögenesis

Spermatogonia in testis and oögonia in ovary divide many times by mitosis

A spermatogonium grows into a   An oögonium grows into a

Diploid: Primary Spermatocyte   Primary Oöcyte

First meiotic division

Haploid: Secondary Spermatocyte   Secondary Oöcyte   First polar body

Second meiotic division

Haploid: Spermatid   Egg   Second polar body

Sperm

Diploid:

Zygote

C. In the *female reproductive system*, one egg cell matures each month in one of two ovaries.

Figure 16.24 The Female Reproductive System

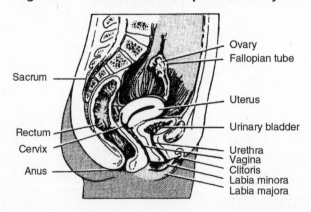

Sacrum

Rectum
Cervix
Anus

Ovary
Fallopian tube

Uterus

Urinary bladder

Urethra
Vagina
Clitoris
Labia minora
Labia majora

Table 16.15 Functions of Female Reproductive System Components

Component	Function
Ovaries	Produce progesterone and estrogen, which are endocrine hormones, and egg cells
Follicle	Protective tissue surrounding a developing egg cell
Corpus Luteum	Produces progesterone and estrogen (see Menstrual Cycle)
Fallopian Tubes	Tubes that carry ova to uterus; site of fertilization event
Uterus	Site of development of fetus
Uterine Lining	Site of implantation of fertilized egg
Uterine Wall	Smooth muscles that contract during labor to expel fetus
Cervix	Opening between uterus and vagina, contains sphincter muscle
Vagina	Site of sperm deposition; passageway of fetus during birth
Vulva	External structures of the reproductive tract
Labia	Protect vaginal opening

1. Under the control of four *endocrine hormones*—LH, FSH, estrogen, and progesterone—one of two ovaries releases one egg cell per *menstrual cycle*, which has two phases: the *follicular phase* (including *menstruation*) and the *luteal phase*. *Ovulation*—the release of an egg from an ovary—occurs between the follicular and luteal phases.
    i. *LH* (luteinizing hormone) and *FSH* (follicle stimulating hormone) are made by the *anterior pituitary*.
    ii. *Estrogen* and *progesterone* are made in the *ovaries*.

Table 16.16 Hormonal Control of the Menstrual Cycle

Stage	Hormonal Control of Events
Follicular Phase (approx. 14 days) Menstruation (1st 5 days)	At the start of the cycle, menstruation is occurring and levels of all four hormones are low, then three of the hormone levels increase. *FSH*: causes an egg cell to complete meiosis I and stimulates mitosis in follicular cells surrounding and nourishing the egg cell *Estrogen*: causes cell division in the uterine lining and stimulates release of LH *LH*: when LH levels spike, the follicle bursts, releasing the egg
Ovulation	The egg is released into the abdominal cavity; it is swept into a fallopian tube by cilia at the end of the tube and begins to travel through the fallopian tube toward the uterus
Luteal Phase (approx. 14 days)	Ruptured follicle left in the ovary develops into corpus luteum; corpus luteum secretes high levels of progesterone and estrogen *Progesterone*: causes blood vessel growth in uterine lining *Estrogen* and *progesterone*: cause LH and FSH levels to fall
If Fertilization Does Not Occur	The corpus luteum stops producing estrogen and progesterone, causing menstruation to occur (and cycle repeats)

2. *Menstruation* is the monthly loss of the uterine lining and its blood vessels through the vagina if fertilization of an egg has not occurred.

D. If an egg is fertilized by a sperm, a zygote is formed.

1. When semen is ejaculated into the *vagina*, sperm swim through the *cervix* and down each *fallopian tube*.

i. The structure of sperm is important to how they function.

a) The *head* of a sperm cell contains the nucleus carrying its 23 chromosomes.

b) At the front of the head is an area containing digestive enzymes that are used to digest the layer of cells surrounding the egg.

c) Immediately below the head is the *midpiece*, which contains the many mitochondria it uses to make ATP to power its flagellum.

d) Each sperm has a single *flagellum*, which moves to propel the sperm forward.

Figure 16.25 Structure of a Sperm Cell

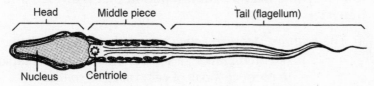

ii. About 300 to 400 million sperm are produced per ejaculation, but most do not survive to reach an egg.

iii. Sperm contact the egg with their heads, and release their enzymes; when one sperm reaches the egg plasma membrane, it fuses with it.

iv. The flagellum detaches, and only the head and midpiece enter the egg.

v. Usually only one sperm enters an egg, because when it fuses with the egg, the egg rapidly blocks any remaining sperm from entering.

2. Fertilization usually occurs in the fallopian tubes, and the fertilized egg begins to divide by mitosis as it moves to the uterus, where it then attaches to the uterine lining and finishes embryonic and fetal development.

Figure 16.26 Unfertilized Egg cell

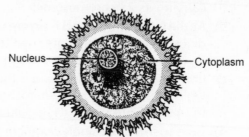

Nucleus—|—Cytoplasm

E. **During *gestation* (pregnancy), a human fetus develops from a zygote over a 9-month period that is divided into trimesters.**

   1. The *first trimester* is an active period of organ formation.

      i. After fertilization, a series of mitoses occurs rapidly, to produce a ball of cells called a *morula*.

      ii. From the morula, a *blastocyst* forms that contains a fluid-filled cavity.

      iii. The blastocyst implants within the wall of the uterus, and a *placenta* and *umbilical cord* form to provide nutrition to the embryo and to remove its waste products.

      iv. *HCG (human chorionic gonadotropin)* serves to maintain high levels of estrogen and progesterone, which help maintain the pregnancy.

      v. A group of four embryonic membranes form exterior to the embryo and have different functions in different animal groups.

        a) A protective membrane, called the *amnion*, forms around the embryo and is filled with *amniotic fluid*, which helps to *cushion* and *protect* the embryo.

        b) The *yolk sac* surrounds the *yolk*, which is present in the eggs of some vertebrates (such as *birds* and *frogs*) and is digested as the embryo grows; in *humans* the yolk sac does not contain yolk, but is the site of early *blood cell formation*.

        c) The *allantois* forms from within the embryo's gut and is the site of *waste removal* and *gas exchange* in shelled eggs; the allantois becomes part of the umbilical cord in humans, where it is involved in the formation of blood vessels that deliver *oxygen* and remove *carbon dioxide* and *nitrogenous waste*.

d) The *chorion* surrounds all the other membranes, and functions, like the amnion, to cushion and protect the embryo.

vi. The developing *embryo* progresses through a period of organ formation, called *organogenesis*, to produce a *fetus* in the eighth week of pregnancy.

2. In the *second trimester*, the fetus grows from about 2 inches long to 12–13 inches long, and its organs and organ systems continue to mature.

3. At the end of the *third trimester*, the fetus has generally grown to around 20 inches long, and its organ systems become ready to function on their own.

F. **Labor pains signal the onset of *parturition* (birth).**

1. Prostaglandins, estrogen, and oxytocin levels rise, causing rhythmic *uterine contractions*.

2. The *cervix* gradually opens, and when it is completely open the mother feels a strong urge to push the baby through the vagina.

3. After the baby is born, the umbilical cord is cut, and the baby's circulation is altered so that it becomes a closed, independent circulatory system.

4. Shortly after birth, the placenta is pushed from the body by additional uterine contractions.

G. ***Summary* of *core concepts* of the human *reproductive system*.**

1. Meiosis in the testes and ovaries produces gametes.

2. Males produce four sperm per meiosis, whereas females produce one egg cell per meiosis.

3. Males produce sperm from puberty onward, whereas females are born with a defined number of reproductive cells, and start releasing egg cells from their ovaries once per month from puberty until menopause.

4. Testosterone controls sperm production in males, and the interplay of four hormones—LH, FSH, estrogen, and progesterone—control monthly egg maturation and release in females.

5. Fertilization usually occurs in the fallopian tubes of the female reproductive tract, where the head and midpiece of one sperm usually combines with one egg.

6. After implantation of a fertilized egg, pregnancy ensues and a placenta is formed to provide nutrition from the mother to the developing fetus through the umbilical cord without the mixing of maternal and fetal blood.

7. Rapid organogenesis occurs in the fetus during the first trimester of pregnancy, making it especially important to protect the fetus from damaging substances that may harm it.

8. Labor produces strong contractions of the smooth muscles of the uterus, the cervix dilates, and the baby is pushed out through the vagina.

 XII. *Development* **in humans shows similarities to development in other organisms.**

A. Development in all multicellular organisms involves the expression of different genes in different cells to produce cells of different types—a process called *cell differentiation*.

1. *Morphogenesis* is the development of an organism's characteristic form.

    i. *Homeotic genes* regulate the expression of genes during development in most organisms, and these genes contain a specific DNA sequence called a *homeobox*.

    ii. Homeotic genes code for *regulatory proteins* that control which genes will be turned on in which cells during development, leading to cell differentiation.

    iii. Most eukaryotic organisms have genes containing homeobox sequences, and some of these genes appear to control morphogenesis in many animals.

B. Morphogenesis in animals, unlike in plants, involves the *movement of cells* within the embryo to form a distinct arrangement of three tissue layers.

  1. As in humans, vertebrate development starts with a zygote that divides many times by mitosis without cell growth in between the mitoses—a process called *cleavage*—which produces a ball of cells not much bigger than the original fertilized egg.

  2. The hollow ball of cells that results is called a *blastula*, and the space in the center is called the *blastocoel*.

  3. The cells of the blastula are rearranged, during a process called *gastrulation*, to form a *gastrula* with three distinct layers of cells.

    i. At one side of the blastula, the cells push inward to form a region called the *blastopore*.

    ii. Some cells from the blastopore detach and migrate inward; these cells will become the middle tissue layer (mesoderm).

    iii. The cells of the blastopore push further inward, creating an in-folding called the *archenteron* that will form the gut (digestive tract) of the organism.

    iv. The resulting gastrula has three distinct tissue layers.

      a) *Ectoderm* is the tissue layer surrounding the embryo.

      b) *Mesoderm* is the tissue layer lying between the ectoderm and the endoderm.

      c) *Endoderm* is the tissue layer lining the inside of the archenteron.

Figure 16.27 Gastrulation

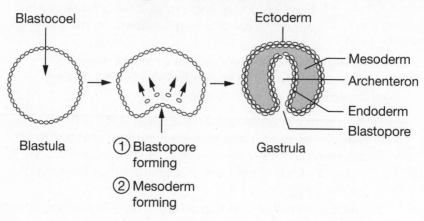

Table 16.17 The Three Tissue Layers Become Different Structures in Multicellular Organisms

Tissue Layer	Structures in Adult
Ectoderm	Nervous system, epidermis (skin, hair, nails), epithelia of mouth and rectum, parts of the eye
Mesoderm	Notochord (disks between vertebrae in humans), bones, muscles, circulatory, lymphatic, excretory, dermal layer of skin
Endoderm	Liver, pancreas, thyroid, parathyroid, thymus, bladder

4. Humans are *deuterostomes* and exhibit both *radial* and *indeterminate cleavage*.

   i. In most animals, further development of the gastrula results in the formation of a gut with one opening called a *mouth*, and another opening called an *anus*.

   a) The archenteron eventually fuses with the opposite side of the embryo to create the second opening.

   b) In humans, and other deuterostomes, this opening becomes the mouth, and the blastopore becomes the anus.

   c) In *protostomes*, the first opening (the blastopore) is the mouth, and the second opening is the anus.

Figure 16.28 Protostome vs. Deuterostome Development

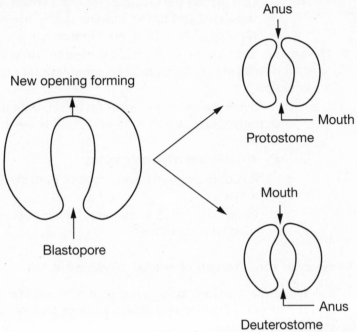

"*Proto" means "first," so the first (blastopore) opening in protostomes is the mouth; and "deuteron" means "second," so the second opening in deuterostomes is the mouth. "Stoma" means "mouth."*

ii. Many protostome embryos undergo *spiral cleavage* (in which early cell divisions are skewed around a central axis), whereas deuterostome embryos, such as in humans, undergo *radial cleavage* (in which early cell divisions cut cells in half along longitudinal or latitudinal lines).

iii. Animals differ in how early the cells of the embryo specialize.

    a) Animals with *indeterminate cleavage* produce cells during the first few cleavages which, when separated and grown independently, can produce an entire organism.

      b) Animals with *determinate cleavage* produce cells during the first few cleavages which, when separated and grown independently, are not capable of producing an entire organism.

5. The type of *body cavities* an animal has depends on whether or not it develops a coelom, and if so, what layer of cells line the coelom.

      i. A *coelom* is a second internal cavity separate from the digestive tract, which *holds* and *protects* the internal organs.

      a) *Acoelomates* have no coelom.

      b) *Pseudocoelomates* have a coelom partially lined by mesoderm.

      c) *Coelomates*, such as humans, have a coelom fully lined with mesoderm.

C. *Summary* of *core concepts* of animal *development*.

1. Cell types in a multicellular organism are different from one another because they express different genes present in their identical genomes.

2. Developmental genes, such as the homeotic genes, generally code for proteins that regulate differential gene expression.

3. Development in animals involves cell division, cell differentiation, and movement of cells in the developing embryo.

4. Embryonic development in most vertebrates starts with a zygote that develops into a blastula and then a gastrula.

5. Most animals have three embryonic tissue layers: ectoderm, mesoderm, and endoderm.

6. Cells from animals with indeterminate cleavage can be separated from each other within the first few mitotic divisions, and each cell can then generally go on to form an entire organism.

7. The digestive tract of most animals develops from the archenteron and has two openings.

8. The coelom is a second internal compartment in many animals that cushions and protects internal organs.

Much of what we know about *animal behavior* comes from studying model animals as diverse as bees, fish, birds, and mammals.

A. Both *heredity* and *environment* influence behavior.

1. Like all phenotypes, the basis for behavior is genetic.

2. All behaviors require interaction with the environment, because they are defined as a response to environmental stimuli.

3. Environment plays a large role in shaping the expression of most behaviors, and, as a result, the same *genotype* often results in a wide range of varying *phenotypes*.

B. *Innate behavior* is behavior that is *not learned*.

1. In response to a stimulus, called a *sign stimulus*, an organism may behave in a predictable fashion that does not need to be learned in order to occur.

    a) For example, males of many species demonstrate aggressive behavior or sexual behavior in response to the sign stimulus of red color.

    b) Infants, when presented with even the simplest resemblance of a human face, smile.

    c) Some hatchlings lift their heads and open their mouths toward the sky in response to any motion in their vicinity.

2. *Kinesis* is a type of innate behavior in which an organism lowers or raises its activity level depending on environmental conditions.

    i. For example, pillbugs move around less in dark areas as opposed to light areas.

    ii. The bug's movements are random, but the differences in activity levels make it more likely that the bug will find a dark location and stay there.

3. *Taxis* is the innate movement toward or away from a stimulus.

    i. For example, when moths move toward light it is called *phototaxis*; when mosquitoes move away from a repellant, it is called *chemotaxis*.

      ii. Movement toward a stimulus is a *positive taxis* (e.g., movement toward light is called positive phototaxis), and movement away from a stimulus is a *negative taxis* (e.g., movement away from light is called negative phototaxis).

C. *Learned behavior* involves modification of a behavior in response to experience.

    1. *Habituation* is a learned behavior involving the loss of responsiveness to a stimulus that occurs repeatedly without resulting in harm.

        i. An example is learning to be able to sleep with nonthreatening background noise, even though another set of noises result in waking.

        ii. Another example is when birds learn to ignore warning calls of members of their own species if those calls are repeated without being connected to a consequent threat.

    2. *Imprinting* is innate behavior that has a learning component that only occurs during a *critical period*—a specific time period, usually early in development, when the behavior is learned; the behavior is usually irreversible.

        i. For example, bonding between parents and offspring involves some type of recognition between the two that generally only occurs shortly after birth or hatching, such as when goslings bond with their mother in the first few hours of life and, thereafter, follow her around as opposed to any other adult bird.

        ii. If the behavior is not learned during the critical period, the behavior is usually *absent or aberrant* (different), such as when young birds do not hear their species' song during the critical developmental period, and thus fail to be able to learn to sing the song later in life.

    3. *Associative learning* is learning to associate one stimulus with another.

        i. *Classical conditioning* is when an animal learns to associate an arbitrary stimulus with a reward or punishment.

a) For example, a dog may learn to salivate in response to an unrelated stimulus, such as the ringing of a bell, if the ringing of a bell is always followed by a treat.

b) Or a cat may learn to jump off the table when it hears a clapping sound, if the clapping sound has been associated previously with a punishment such as being sprayed with water.

ii. *Operant conditioning* is closely related, but involves an animal associating one of its own behaviors with a reward or punishment through *trial-and-error learning.*

a) For example, a rat may learn to push one lever of a particular type that delivers a reward, while ignoring other levers that do not result in a reward by trial and error.

b) Or a dog may learn to avoid all skunks after being sprayed by one.

D. *Cognition* is the ability of a nervous system to perceive, store, process, and respond to information obtained by the senses.

1. A *cognitive map* is an internal representation or code of the spatial relationships among objects in an organism's environment.

    i. Migration may involve cognitive mapping.

    ii. Bees use cognitive mapping to remember and communicate the locations of food sources.

2. *Consciousness* (awareness of self and environment) involves cognition.

E. *Social behavior* is the interaction between members of the same species (or, sometimes, members of different species), and includes aggression, courtship, cooperation, and deception.

1. *Agonistic behavior* may occur when two members of the same species are competing for the same resource and includes *ritual threatening* and ritual *submission* or, less often, actual fighting involving injury or death.

        i. Agonistic behavior can be the basis of *dominance hierarchies* where each member of a social group has a ranking within the group.

        ii. *Territories*—physical space partitions within a species' home range—are usually defended by agonistic behavior.

2. *Courtship* is another type of ritual behavior occurring before two members of the same species mate, and may involved agonistic behavior and/or assessment behavior.

        i. Agonistic behavior between males may be involved: a situation in which a competition determines which male will mate with female(s).

        ii. *Assessment behavior* of females may be involved: a situation in which females chose between males displaying specific physical or behavioral characteristics highlighting their health or parenting abilities.

        iii. Mating systems can be *promiscuous* (no pair bonding), *monogamous* (one female and one male), *polygamous* (one male and multiple females), or *polyandrous* (one female and multiple males).

           a) The amount of *parental care* required may influence the type of mating system of a species.

           b) *Certainty of paternity* may influence the type of mating system as far as the investment of paternal parental care is concerned.

3. *Communication* is a feature of social behavior within a species that usually facilitates cooperation.

        i. Types of communication include *auditory* (vocalizations, or other sounds), *visual* (e.g., displays, dances, light flashes), and *olfactory* (e.g., *pheromones*).

        ii. The purpose of some communication may be *deception*, such as when certain fireflies flash the signals of other species and then eat the other species' members that respond to the signal.

4. *Altruistic behavior* may be the result of *inclusive fitness*; for example, an animal may behave in a way that decreases its own fitness in order to increase the fitness of a *kinship group* that carries a large percentage of genes similar to its own.

      i. For example, a bird or mammal may give a warning call that directs the attention of a predator to itself, placing it in danger, but allowing related individuals to protect themselves.

     ii. Altruistic behavior may be influenced by the *coefficient of relatedness* —the proportion of genes an individual shares with a particular member of its species—such that the more genes an animal shares with another member of the group, the more likely altruistic behavior is to occur.

        a) The coefficient of relatedness is 50% between a mother or father and his or her offspring, and also between full siblings.

        b) The coefficient of relatedness is 25% between an individual and his or her full blood-related aunts, uncles, nieces and nephews; and 12.5% between cousins.

        c) The coefficient of relatedness between all (female) worker bees within a hive is 50%.

    iii. *Kin selection*—the evolutionary selection of behaviors that increase the likelihood of preserving a group of related individuals—is the hypothesized mechanism of inclusive fitness.

F. *Summary* of *core concepts* of animal *behavior.*

1. Heredity and environment contribute to most behaviors.
2. Behaviors can be innate or learned, or a combination of both.
3. Behavior between members of the same species involves communication of some sort.
4. Agonistic behaviors are used to settle disputes over resource partitioning between members of a species.
5. Courtship behaviors serve to bring two members of the same species together for sexual reproduction and may serve to maximize fitness of offspring.
6. Inclusive fitness may explain altruistic behavior among members of a kinship group.

Questions on the test involving animal systems can be specific—such as identifying the functions of specific hormones, behaviors, or parts of an organ—or can be general—such as understanding the concept that increasing surface areas of key parts of systems is a common structural feature that allows a lot of an activity to take place within a compact space. For this reason—although not every system will be covered in detail or every concept covered in any particular test year—it is important to be familiar with both the specifics and concepts for all the systems in order to do well on the animal systems questions.

PLANT STRUCTURE, FUNCTION, REPRODUCTION, INTERNAL REGULATION, AND RESPONSE TO THE ENVIRONMENT

I. Key Concepts

A. Plants are multicellular, eukaryotic, autotrophic organisms organized into three main types of tissue systems—dermal, ground, and vascular.

B. Tissue systems may contain one or several fundamental cell types—parenchyma, collenchyma, and sclerenchyma—and within each cell type there are specialized cells with features designed for different functions.

C. Each of the plant organs—roots, leaves, and stems—contain different structural arrangements of each tissue system.

D. Plants have primary meristematic cells that allow them to continually produce new shoots and roots.

E. Woody plants have secondary meristems, as well, that allow their stems and roots to grow dramatically in circumference from year to year.

F. Two types of vascular tissue are responsible for movement of substances in plants: xylem transports water and dissolved minerals from roots to leaves, and phloem transports organic nutrients (sucrose) from sources (such as leaves) to sinks (such as growing or storage regions of the plant).

G. All plants are capable of sexual reproduction, but many have asexual (vegetative) methods for reproducing, as well.

H. The sexual life cycle of plants is alternation of generations in which the plant alternates between a multicellular diploid form and a multicellular haploid form.

I. The multicellular haploid form—the gametophyte— is dominant in bryophytes such as mosses, while the multicellular diploid form—the sporophyte—is dominant in ferns, gymnosperms, and angiosperms.

J. Gymnosperms and angiosperms have very small gametophytes that are dependent on the sporophyte and develop within cones in gymnosperms and flowers in angiosperms.

K. Plants grow and develop in response to five main types of hormones: auxin, cytokinins, ethylene, abscisic acid, and gibberellins.

L. Plants are capable of sensing and responding to various stimuli such as light, gravity, touch, temperature, stressors (such as lack of water and high salt concentrations), as well as pathogens (viruses, bacteria, and fungi).

II. *Plants* **are** *multicellular* **organisms composed of** *eukaryotic* **cells of different types that are organized into tissues that, in turn, make up the organs of the plant: roots, stems, leaves, and flowers.**

A. *Plant cells* have some features that are different from animal cells.

1. Plant cells are surrounded by a rigid *cell wall* made up of the polysaccharide *cellulose.*
2. *Plastids* of different types, including *chloroplasts*, are found in many types of plant cells.
3. Many plant cells also have a *large*, centrally located, fluid-filled *vacuole*, which, along with their rigid cell walls,

provides the turgor pressure necessary for physical support in herbaceous (nonwoody) plants.

4. Plant cells also have *plasmodesmata*—cytoplasmic connections between cells—through which small and large molecules can move freely.

Test Tip

Know the differences between plant and animal cells.

B. **Three types of cells—*parenchyma, collenchyma*, and *sclerenchyma*—are found throughout the plant in different tissues, and have different functions consistent with their structures.**

Table 17.1 Basic Plant Cell Types

Type of Cell	Structure	Functions/Examples
Parenchyma	Thin cell walls, large central vacuole	Storage; photosynthesis; protection; transport/storage cells in stem and root, mesophyll cells in leaf (photosynthesis); epidermis; phloem cells
Collenchyma	Thick, flexible cell walls	Support growing parts of plant/growing regions of the stem
Sclerenchyma	Thick, rigid cell walls often containing *lignin*[1]; often dead when mature	Support nongrowing parts of plant; transport/fibers; "wood": tracheids and vessels of vascular tissue

[1]lignin—hard substance secreted into the cell wall to strengthen it

C. **The plant body has three types of** *tissue systems* **that are present in all organs throughout the plant: dermal tissue, ground tissue, and vascular tissue.**

Table 17.2 Basic Plant Tissue Types

Type of Tissue	Location	Functions/Examples
Dermal	Exterior of plant body	Protection; gas exchange; mineral and water absorption/epidermal cells; guard cells of stomata; root hair cells
Ground	Interior body of plant	Support; storage; photosynthesis/ fibers, storage cells in root, mesophyll cells in leaf
Vascular	Embedded in ground tissue throughout the plant body	Transport water; transport products of photosynthesis/ xylem tracheids and vessels; phloem sieve tubes

1. The *dermal tissue system* is the outermost layer of all parts of the plant and consists of the epidermis and related structures.
   i. The *epidermis* consists of one or two layers of parenchyma cells covered with a *cuticle* made of wax for protection and to reduce water loss.
   ii. *Guard cells* in leaves create openings called *stomata* that allow gas exchange between the atmosphere and the interior of the leaf.
   iii. *Cork* replaces the epidermis in some woody plants, such as trees.
2. The *ground tissue system*—comprising the bulk of plant roots, stems, and leaves—consists of specialized parenchyma, collenchyma, and sclerenchyma cells.
   i. Ground tissue in roots and stems provide physical support and storage of water, nutrients, and other substances.
   ii. Ground tissue in leaves contain chloroplasts that carry out photosynthesis.

3. The *vascular tissue system* contains cells specialized for transport that are bundled into groups and are embedded in ground tissue.

    i. *Xylem* transports water from the roots, through the stem, and to the leaves where it exits the leaf through stomata: a process called *transpiration*.

        a) Xylem contains two main types of nonliving cells that lack cytoplasm and are designed to transport water.

- Tracheids *are long, tapered cells stacked end to end to form tubes—a group of which are bundled together.*
- Vessel elements *are stouter cells arranged in a similar manner to form wider tubes called* vessels.

        b) Holes in the cell walls, called *pits*—present between individual tracheids in a bundle, or between vessels in a bundle—allow water to move laterally from tube to tube as it is carried upward in the stem.

    ii. *Phloem* transports nutrients and hormones from sources to sinks within living cells.

        a) Phloem consists of two main types of living parenchyma cells.

- Sieve tube members *are the conducting cells of phloem and are connected end to end to form* sieve tubes.
  - Openings in the *sieve plates* separating sieve tube members in a tube allow for movement of substances from cell to cell through the tubes.
  - Sieve tube members contain cytoplasm, but lack ribosomes and nuclei.
- *Lying alongside sieve tube members are* companion cells *that do have nuclei and ribosomes.*
  - Companion cells have numerous plasmodesmata connections with sieve tube members through which substances can be transported.

- Companion cells may provide proteins to sieve tube members and can assist in transporting sugars from surrounding tissues into sieve tubes.

b) *Fibers*, consisting of long *sclerenchyma* cells, function to protect and support sieve tubes and companion cells.

A common question about plants on the test is the function of different cell types, including vascular cell types.

D. Another important tissue in plants is *meristematic tissue,* which contains cells capable of dividing to produce new tissues throughout the life of the plant.

Figure 17.1 Location of Tissue Systems and Meristems in a Woody Dicot Seedling

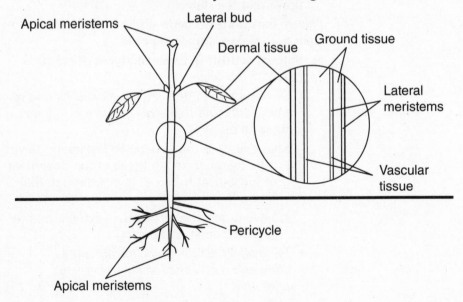

1. *Apical meristems*, generally present at the tips of roots and shoots, result in primary growth, which increase the *length* of the plant body.
    i. *Lateral shoot buds,* located in the junctions between stems and leaves, also contain meristematic tissue that can give rise to new shoots.
    ii. Roots contain an additional meristematic tissue, called the *pericycle,* that gives rise to new roots that branch off from the main root.
2. *Lateral meristems*, present in woody plants along the lengths of their shoots and roots, are responsible for secondary growth that increases their girth (diameters), and are of two types.
    i. *Vascular cambium*, located between phloem and xylem, gives rise to new phloem and xylem cells.
    ii. *Cork cambium*, located exterior to phloem, produces nonliving cork cells that replace the epidermis in woody dicots such as angiosperm hardwood trees (e.g., maple, oak, beech), and in gymnosperm softwood trees (e.g., pines, fir, spruce).
3. Special types of meristems, called *intercalary meristems*, are present at the bases of leaves and the nodes of stems in a division of angiosperms known as *monocots* (which include corn and grasses), and result in primary growth.

 III. The *organs* of plants are collections of cooperating tissues, and include leaves, roots, and stems.

A. The primary *function* of most *leaves* is to provide nutrition by carrying out photosynthesis, but some plants also have modified leaves adapted for a variety of functions.

1. *Photosynthetic leaves* of angiosperms and gymnosperms have different morphologies, but both are well adapted for photosynthesis, gas exchange, and controlling transpiration.
    i. *Gymnosperms* have *compact* needle-shaped or scale-like *leaves*, with stomata sunken into the epidermis: adaptations that reduce exposure to the

atmosphere in cold, dry climates, allowing them to conserve water (and avoid freezing) while carrying out photosynthesis year round.

   ii. *Angiosperm leaves* come in different sizes and shapes, but are usually broad, flat, and thin with many stomata, increasing exposure to sunlight and the atmosphere in temperate climates.

     a) *Simple leaves* have two main parts.

       ▸ *A single leaf is attached to the stem by a stalk called a* petiole.

       ▸ *Attached to the petiole is a single leaf* blade *that varies in shape from plant to plant.*

     b) Other angiosperms have *compound leaves* in which the blade is divided into smaller *leaflets.*

Figure 17.2 Cross-section of a Typical Angiosperm Leaf

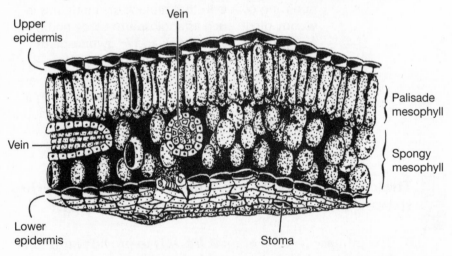

2. The *structure of a* typical angiosperm *leaf* makes it an efficient organ for light capture and gas exchange required for photosynthesis.

   i. The epidermis is covered with a waxy cuticle to protect it from pathogens and water loss, but contains stomatal pores to allow for controlled gas exchange.

a) Hairs are present on many leaves and function in protection and reducing air flow, which reduces evaporation.

b) *Stomata* (sing. *stoma*)—pores in the epidermis—are often more numerous on the lower side of the leaf: an arrangement that limits evaporation of water while allowing the plant to obtain CO_2 and release O_2 during photosynthesis.

c) The opening and closing of stomata occurs by the *osmosis* of water into and out of its two surrounding guard cells.

Figure 17.3 Guard Cells Control the Opening and Closing of Stomata

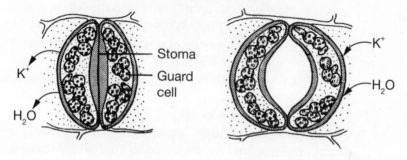

Stoma

Guard cell

K^+

H_2O

K^+

H_2O

▸ *A stoma* opens *when K^+ is pumped into the* guard cells *by surrounding epidermal cells followed by the* osmotic uptake of water; *this causes the guard cells to become* turgid, *inflating to form a pore.*

▸ *Stomata* close *when K^+ is transported* out of guard cells, *followed by* water, *causing the guard cells to* shrink, *closing the pore.*

d) Under *dry conditions*, a plant may close its stomata to reduce water loss—a situation that also cuts off its supply of CO_2 for photosynthesis—but when water is abundant, open stomata contribute to transpiration, which brings a constant supply of water and minerals to the leaves from the soil.

ii. The ground tissue consists of two layers of parenchyma cells—called *mesophyll*—that contain abundant *chloroplasts*.

    a) A dense layer of *palisade mesophyll* immediately under the upper epidermis provides a broad surface for capturing light.

    b) The more loosely packed layer of *spongy mesophyll* below the palisade is surrounded by *air spaces* in contact with the atmosphere through stomata, facilitating exchange of CO_2 and O_2.

iii. Running throughout the ground tissue are the *veins* consisting of bundles of xylem and phloem that are connected to the vascular system of the rest of the plant and transport water into the leaves and the products of photosynthesis out of the leaves.

    a) Veins in *monocots* run *parallel* from the stem to the tip of the leaf.

    b) Veins in *dicots* are arranged in a *net* pattern with larger veins, called *ribs*, that are more prominent than smaller veins.

3. Leaves have no secondary growth: those of deciduous trees (most angiosperms) are shed during cold or dry seasons, while those of evergreens (most gymnosperms) are present year long.

4. Leaves in some plants are *modified* for functions other than photosynthesis.

    i. The *tendrils* of peas and squash are modified leaves providing support to the plant as they wind around objects they come in contact with.

    ii. In some cacti, leaves are modified as *spines* for protection, and photosynthesis is carried out by cells in the fleshy, green stems.

    iii. In some plants, such as poinsettia, groups of leaves surrounding inconspicuous flowers are *brightly colored* to attract pollinators.

    iv. Carnivorous plants have leaves modified as *traps* to capture small insects.

B. The primary *functions* of *roots* are to anchor the plant, to absorb water and mineral nutrients, and to store carbohydrates.

1. The carbon in plants comes from the atmosphere as CO_2, and most of the hydrogen and oxygen come from water; other nutrients needed by plants are actively absorbed by the roots as ions.

   i. *Macronutrients* needed by plants in relatively large quantities are *nitrogen*, *phosphorus*, and *potassium*, and to a lesser extent, calcium, magnesium, and sulfur.

      a) Plants can absorb nitrates and ammonium directly from the soil, but some plants, such as legumes, obtain *nitrogen* from *symbiotic bacteria* that live in special *root nodules* that develop in their roots for that purpose (see the Nitrogen Cycle in Chapter 9).

      b) Most plants also associate with *fungi* in a *symbiotic relationship* called *mycorrhizae* in which the plant provides carbohydrates to the fungus, and the fungus provides *phosphorus* to the plant, as well as an additional filamentous network (their bodies) for collecting *water*.

   ii. *Micronutrients*, needed in even *smaller amounts*, include iron, manganese, boron, chlorine, zinc, copper, and molybdenum.

2. There are two main types of *root systems*.

   i. A *taproot system*, common in *dicots*, consists of one large, central root with many branching lateral roots.

      a) The *taproot* and larger *lateral roots* function to anchor the plant in the soil.

      b) The uptake of water and nutrients occurs at the tips of roots.

   ii. *Fibrous root systems*, common in *monocots*, have many branching roots of similar size, all generally derived from the stem instead of from one main root.

3. The *structure of roots* makes them efficient at collecting water and minerals from the soil for transport to the plant shoot (stems, leaves, and flowers).

    i. Roots extend lengthwise at their tips by the division of cells in their many apical meristems.

        a) The *root cap* consists of cells that lubricate and protect the tip of the root as it grows through the soil.

        b) Cells in the *meristematic region* continually divide to produce new cells that either replace root cap cells or elongate and differentiate behind the meristematic region.

        c) As cells in the *elongation region* grow longer, the root tip is pushed further into the soil.

        d) The *maturation region* is the part of the root tip where the recently elongated cells are differentiating into dermal, ground, and vascular cells.

Figure 17.4 Structure of a Root Tip

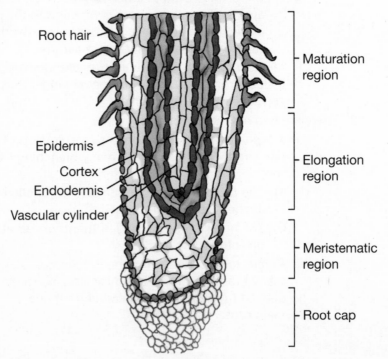

Root hair

Maturation region

Epidermis

Cortex

Endodermis

Vascular cylinder

Elongation region

Meristematic region

Root cap

ii. Throughout the rest of the root, the arrangement of tissues is uniform.

    a) Many epidermal cells have extensions called *root hairs* that provide a large surface area for water and nutrient uptake.

    b) Immediately inside the epidermis are the parenchyma cells of the cortex ground tissue, which specialize in storage.

    c) The vascular tissue is generally found in a bundle at or near the center of the root, and is called a *vascular cylinder*, or *stele*.

    d) *Monocot* roots often have a second type of ground tissue, called *pith*, in the very center of their roots.

iii. Just outside the stele is a special layer of cells called the *endodermis* that controls what substances will pass into the vascular bundle for transport to the rest of the plant.

iv. Between the endodermis and the vascular bundle is a layer of cells called the *pericycle* from which *lateral roots* develop.

v. Roots of *woody plants* have *secondary growth* that produces additional vascular tissue from vascular cambium lying between phloem and xylem cells, and cork from cork cambium, which develops from the pericycle.

vi. Some roots are *specialized* for other functions, or to provide support in other ways.

    a) The *prop roots* of corn plants, radiating from the lower stem, are a type of *adventitious root* (one arising directly from the stem or from leaves) used to support the top-heavy plant.

    b) The roots of some trees that grow in water-logged soil push above ground and are specialized to *obtain oxygen* for the rest of the root system.

    c) The roots of some plants are specialized for *attachment* during *climbing* or even for *obtaining water* and *minerals from* the *air*.

C. **The primary** *functions* **of** *stems* **are to support the shoot and to transport water and sugar.**

    1. Some stems are specialized for storage or other functions.

        i. *Tubers* are special stems of some plants, such as white potatoes, which store starch in the plastids of their cells.

        ii. *Bulbs* are stems with modified swollen leaves surrounding them.

        iii. The *tendrils* of grape vines are stems modified for attachment.

        iv. Strawberry plants have modified horizontal stems, called *stolens*, which branch out to produce new plants—a type of vegetative reproduction.

        v. Many *cacti* have very thick fleshy stems that contain large stores of water that are also their photosynthetic organs.

    2. The *structural* arrangement of dermal, ground, and vascular tissue in *stems* helps them support the plant shoot and transport substances.

        i. The *shoot* often has a *terminal bud* at the tip, and the rest of the shoot below it is divided into short lengths of stem called *internodes*, separated by *nodes*.

            a) Nodes are the attachment sites of leaves.

            b) Each node also has an *axial lateral bud* containing meristematic tissue protected by modified leaves called *bud scales*.

            c) In woody plants, when the bud grows out into a new shoot, the bud scales fall off leaving a *bud scar*.

        ii. All three tissue systems are found in the stem.

            a) The *epidermis* is the outer layer of dermal tissue in herbaceous plants that protects the stem; many stems also contain stomata for gas exchange.

b) Ground tissue consists of *cortex* and *pith* parenchyma cells for storage, as well as collenchyma cells that provide support to the growing parts of the stem.

c) Vascular tissue occurs in bundles of different arrangements in monocots and dicots: *vascular bundles* are more or less *evenly distributed* throughout the cortex *in monocots,* and are generally arranged in a *ring* around the stem near the epidermis in *dicots.*

iii. *Secondary growth* in dicots and gymnosperms widens the stem and forms the *wood* of *tree trunks.*

a) Cells in the *vascular cambium* divide to produce *phloem* facing the epidermis and *xylem* facing inward.

b) Cells in the *cork cambium* divide to produce *cork cells* to the exterior of the phloem, which, along with *dead phloem cells,* comprise the *bark* of the tree.

c) Layers of xylem are laid down each year in temperate climates, with the vessels produced in the summer being larger than those produced in the spring—this creates *annual rings* that can be used to determine the age of a tree.

d) Xylem toward the center of the tree, comprising the *heartwood,* becomes nonfunctional over time and is generally darker in color than the living xylem, called *sapwood,* which surrounds the heartwood.

Test Tip

Questions on the test dealing with plant organs may include identifying structures and their functions based on a diagram of a root, leaf, or stem.

IV. *Water transport* in the *xylem tracheids* and *vessels* moves water, and the mineral nutrients dissolved in it—called *xylem sap*—from the soil into the vascular bundles of the root, stem, and leaves in a continuous flow.

A. The difference in water potential between the atmosphere and the soil (the *atmosphere* generally being *drier* than the soil) is the driving force for the *bulk flow* of water through xylem tubes.

1. Cohesion and adhesion create a tightly bound column of water molecules that extends from the root tips to the air spaces of each leaf.

    i. *Cohesion*—the attraction of water molecules to each other achieved by hydrogen bonds between the water molecules—is responsible for the continuity of the *water column* (as if each water molecule were holding hands with the one in front of it and the one behind it).

    ii. *Adhesion*—the attraction of water molecules to the cellulose of the (drier) xylem walls—is responsible for momentarily keeping the water column in place so it does not succumb to gravity and fall back to the soil (as if each water molecule were placing its head and feet against the sides of the xylem tube).

2. When water molecules *evaporate* from the leaf spaces that are in contact with the air through open stomata, they pull the water molecules, below them in the leaf vein xylem, into the leaf spaces.

    i. A chain effect occurs in which the whole column of water molecules in the rest of the xylem tube is pulled up a little farther as well.

    ii. Since the water column is in contact with the soil, additional water molecules are pulled in by the root hair cells to replace those lost in the leaves.

B. **The flow of water from the soil, through the xylem of the plant, and into the atmosphere through stomata is called** *transpiration.*

    i. Most of the water taken up by a plant's roots is lost through transpiration.

    ii. The rest of the water, along with the mineral nutrients dissolved in it, is taken up by cells along the way to be used in metabolism, or is stored in parenchyma cells in the stem for later use.

V. *Translocation*—**transport in the** *phloem sieve tubes*—**moves** *organic nutrients* **and** *hormones* **from sources to sinks by pressure-driven bulk flow.**

A. **Sugars that are made in the chloroplasts of leaves are converted to** *sucrose* **before transport.**

1. *Sources* are regions of the plant that are actively photosynthesizing, mainly mature leaves, or sites where sugars made previously in leaves are being stored as starch, such as roots or tubers.

2. *Sinks* are regions of the plant that are actively growing—such as new shoots, roots, and flowers—or sites where new sugars are to be stored, such as roots, tubers, and developing fruit.

3. Some hormones are also transported through the phloem.

B. **Movement of phloem sap occurs by a** *pressure flow* **mechanism as sucrose is loaded into a sieve tube at a source and unloaded at a sink.**

1. Sucrose produced or released from storage in a sink is *loaded* into the sieve tube from parenchyma cells by *active transport* in some species, or through *plasmodesmata* connections between parenchyma, companion cells, and sieve tube members in other species.

    i. As sucrose moves into the *sieve tube*, the phloem sap becomes *hypertonic compared to* the *cytoplasm* of surrounding cells.

ii. Therefore, water moves by *osmosis* from surrounding cells into the sieve tube, creating *positive hydrostatic pressure* at the *source* end of the tube.

iii. This positive pressure forces the phloem sap down the sieve tube.

2. As sucrose is *unloaded* into parenchyma cells at a *sink*, water, again, follows the sucrose by osmosis: this creates an area of *negative pressure* in the *sink* end of the sieve tube that pulls the phloem sap toward the sink.

3. Thus, positive pressure at the source end of the tube and negative pressure at the sink end keeps the phloem sap flowing from sources to sinks.

Figure 17.5 Pressure Flow in Phloem Sieve Tube

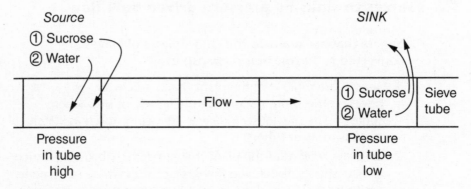

VI. ***Sexual reproduction* in plants varies from group to group, but all plants have a sexual life cycle called *alternation of generations*.**

A. Unlike animals, in which the diploid organism is the only multicellular form, in plants there are *two multicellular forms*: the gametophyte and the sporophyte.

1. The *gametophyte* is the *haploid multicellular* generation of a plant and produces *haploid gametes* by *mitosis*.

2. The *gametes,* a sperm and an egg, fuse during *fertilization* to form a *diploid zygote* that divides by *mitosis* to become the sporophyte.
3. The *sporophyte* is the *diploid multicellular* generation and produces *haploid spores* by *meiosis.*
4. The *spores* divide by *mitosis* to become the haploid gametophyte, and so on. (See Chapter 12, Figure 12.2 for additional information.)
     i. In bryophytes, such as mosses, the gametophyte is the dominant of the two forms.

B. In *bryophytes*—which include *mosses, liverworts,* and *hornworts*—the *dominant* (larger and longer-lived) generation is the *gametophyte.*

1. The familiar, low-growing, leafy green moss consists of separate male and female gametophytes (*n*).
     i. The male gametophytes form reproductive structures called *antheridia* (sing. *antheridium*) that produce *sperm* (*n*).
     ii. The female gametophytes produce an *egg* (*n*) in an *archegonium* (pl. *archegonia*).
     iii. The sperm are *flagellated,* and, during moist weather, a sperm swims to an archegonium and fertilizes the egg to form a zygote (*2n*).
2. The zygote divides by mitosis within the archegonium to produce a small stalklike sporophyte (*2n*) that grows out of the archegonium and forms a *capsule* at its tip.
     i. The small sporophyte (*2n*) depends on the female gametophyte for its nutrition and does not detach from it.
     ii. Meiosis occurs in the capsule to produce spores (*n*) that are dispersed by wind and develop into a *protonema* (*n*) that grows to produce new male and female gametophytes (*n*).

Figure 17.6 Moss Life Cycle

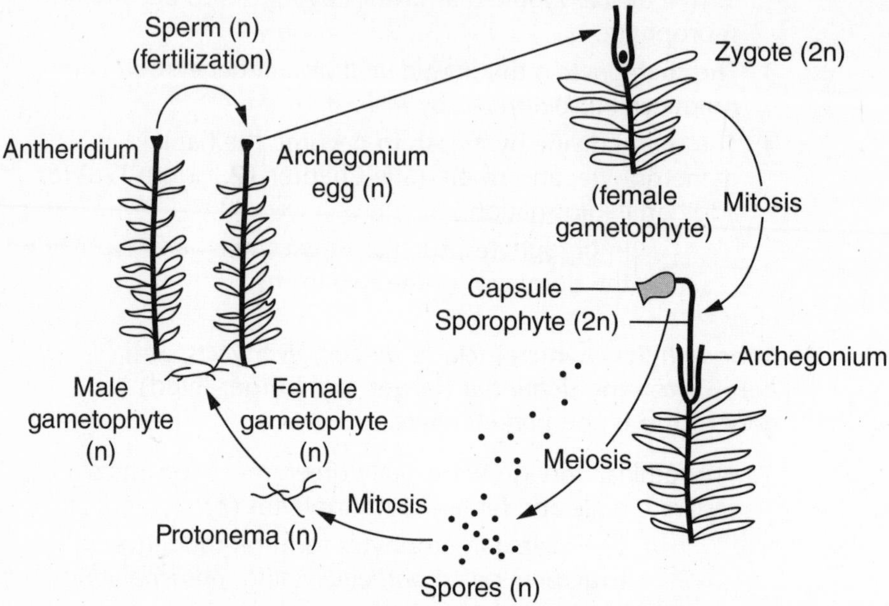

C. In most other plants species—including *ferns, gymnosperms,* and *angiosperms*—the *sporophyte* is the *dominant* generation.

    1. In ferns, the gametophyte (*n*) is very small and produces both antheridia and archegonia on its underside.

        i. The sperm (*n*) produced by the antheridia are flagellated and swim to an archegonia and fertilize its egg (*n*) to produce a zygote (2*n*).

        ii. The zygote becomes the sporophyte (2*n*) and produces *sporangia* in clusters called *sori* on the underside of its leaves (*fronds*) in which meiosis occurs to produce spores (*n*).

        iii. The spores are dispersed by wind and grow into a young gametophyte called a *prothallus* and then into the mature gametophyte (*n*).

Figure 17.7 Fern Life Cycle

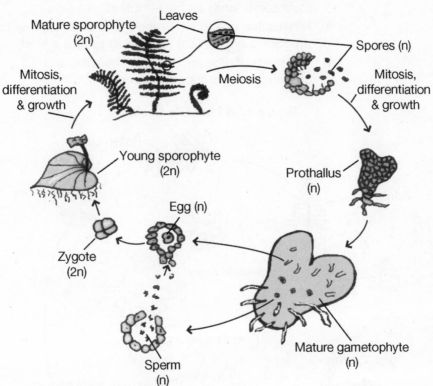

2. In gymnosperms and angiosperms, the gametophyte is very reduced in size and develops within reproductive structures of the sporophyte.

   i. In *gymnosperms*, such as pine trees, the sporophyte (the pine tree—2n) produces male gametophytes within male cones and female gametophytes within female cones.

   a) Microsporangia (2n) within the male cones produce microspores (n) by meiosis that develop into small male gametophytes (n) called pollen grains that produce sperm (n) by mitosis.

   b) Megasporangia (2n) within the female cones produce megaspores (n) by meiosis that develop into small female gametophytes (n) (housed within ovules) that produce eggs (n) by mitosis.

ii. Pollination occurs when wind-blown pollen from male cones lands on female cones.

iii. Fertilization occurs when the sperm and egg fuse to produce a zygote (2*n*) that develops into a seed.

iv. The seeds of pine are dispersed by wind and germinate to produce sporophytes (2*n*).

Figure 17.8 Pine Life Cycle

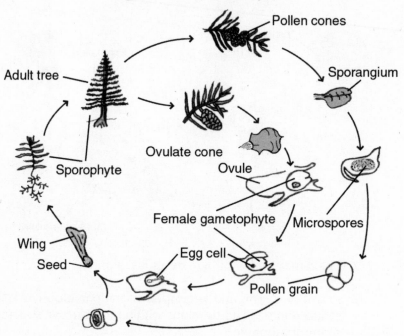

D. **Angiosperms have a dominant sporophyte generation with very reduced gametophytes, double fertilization, and seeds that develop within an ovary.**

1. The *reproductive structures* of *angiosperms* are *flowers* that contain *four whorls* of *modified leaves.*

i. The outermost whorl consists of *sepals* that serve to protect the flower bud before the flower blooms.

ii. The next whorl consist of *petals* that are brightly colored if pollinated by animals, but are often small and white in plants with flowers that are wind pollinated.

iii. The *stamen* (male reproductive structures) comprise the next whorl, and each consists of a *filament* and an *anther*.

iv. In the center of the flower is the *carpel* (female reproductive structure), which may contain more than one pistil; each *pistil* consists of a *stigma*, a *style*, and an *ovary*.

Figure 17.9 Structure of a Flower

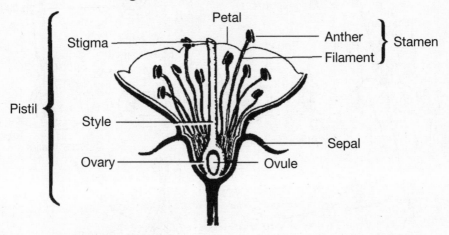

2. The female gametophyte develops within an *ovule* in the ovary of a flower.

   i. A large diploid cell, called a *megaspore mother cell*, undergoes *meiosis* to produce *megaspores*.

   ii. One megaspore divides three times to produce the female gametophyte (called an *embryo sac*) that contains an unfertilized egg.

   iii. An opening, called a *micropyle*, is present at the base of the embryo sac.

3. The male gametophyte develops within the anther of a stamen.

   i. The anther contains *microsporangia* that produce many diploid cells, called *microspore mother cells*.

   ii. Each microspore mother cell divides by *meiosis* to produce four *microspores*, each of which develops into the *male gametophyte* (called a *pollen grain*).

iii. Each pollen grain consists of a *tube cell* and a *generative cell*; the generative cell will divide by mitosis to produce *two sperm nuclei*.

Figure 17.10 The Angiosperm Life Cycle

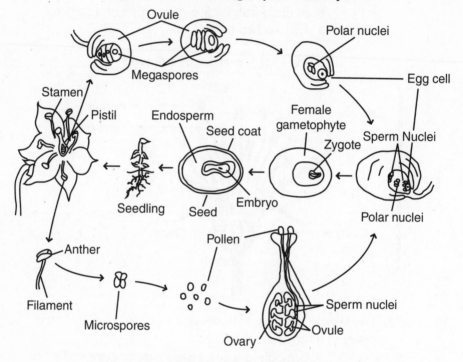

4. *Pollination*—the contact of pollen with a stigma—can occur in many different ways, but is usually specific for a species.

   i. In many species, wind carries pollen from one flower, or plant, to another.

   ii. Other flowers have showy petals, strong odors, or nectar that attract specific animal pollinators such as bees, beetles, birds, bats, butterflies, or mammals.

5. *Double fertilization* occurs in angiosperms.

   i. When a pollen grain lands on a stigma, it germinates and its *pollen tube* grows down through the style to the ovary and enters the egg sac through the micropyle.

   ii. One sperm fuses with the egg and the other fuses with two other cells of the female gametophyte, called *polar nuclei*.

      a) The fusion of a *sperm* and *egg* results in a *zygote*.

Figure 17.11 Double Fertilization in Angiosperms

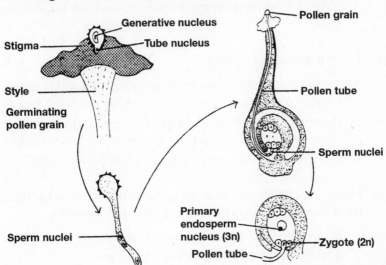

b) The fusion of the other *sperm* with the *two polar nuclei* produces a *3n* cell that goes on to form a *nutritive tissue* in the developing seed called *endosperm*.

c) The resulting *ovule* then develops into a *seed* within the ovary.

Figure 17.12 Development of an Ovule Into a Seed

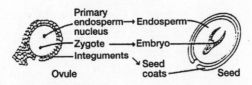

E. Because plants, unlike animals, are not capable of locomotion, *seed* and *fruit dispersal* are the main ways plants can *migrate* from one location to another.

1. Some seeds, such as the winged seeds of maple and the fluffy seeds of dandelions and milkweed, are dispersed by *wind*.

2. Other seeds are surrounded by *burrs* that are dispersed by attaching to the fur of mammals.

3. Some plants have seeds surrounded by a *fruit* that, when eaten and eliminated by animals, can widely disperse their seeds.

F. **Fruits are *ripened ovaries*.**

1. *Simple fruits* are formed from one pistil of a single flower and include peas, beans, grains, cherries, apples, and grapes.
2. *Aggregate fruits* are formed from several pistils of a single flower, including raspberries, blackberries, and strawberries.
3. *Multiple fruits*, such as pineapple, form from several flowers.

G. **Monocot and dicot seeds have different structures, but both have similar, basic requirements for germination.**

1. A *seed* contains an *embryo* and a *food supply* surrounded by a tough outer covering called a *seed coat*.
    i. Monocots and dicot differ in the number of their cotyledons and whether or not they contain endosperm when they are mature.
        a) A *monocot* has *one cotyledon* and it is composed of *3n endosperm* tissue.
        b) A *dicot* has *two cotyledons*; some dicot seeds contain endosperm, but others have already digested all of their endosperm and have transferred it to the cotyledons by the time the seed is mature.
    ii. The *embryo* of the seed has four main parts.
        a) The *radicle*, which is the embryonic root
        b) The *hypocotyl*, which is the stem from the radicle to the cotyledons
        c) The *epicotyl*, which is the stem above the cotyledons
        d) And the *plumule*, which is a small group of *embryonic leaves*
2. *Seed germination* occurs when several conditions have been met.

    i. All seeds need *sufficient water* before they will
      germinate, ensuring that there will be enough water
      for the developing seedling to survive.

      a) Because seeds are dehydrated, they readily take
         up water by osmosis.

      b) When seeds take up water, they swell, breaking
         the seed coat.

      c) When the seed coat is broken, the cotyledons can
         expand and take in sufficient water to support
         metabolism, which includes the breakdown of
         stored carbohydrate or fat reserves.

    ii. The seeds of many plants adapted to temperate
      climates do not germinate until they have
      experienced a *cold* period of a specific duration.

    iii. Some seeds require *light* to germinate, ensuring that
      seeds buried too far under ground will not germinate
      if they are too far away from the surface to survive.

    iv. Seeds also require *oxygen* for cellular respiration:
      when the seed coat has opened, and if the seed is
      close enough to the surface, it can obtain enough
      oxygen to germinate.

 VII. **Although all plants can reproduce sexually,
many types of *asexual reproduction*—or *vegetative
propagation*—are also common in plants.**

A. **Parts of plants, such as the leaves (of jade plants), the roots
(of grasses), the shoots (of philodendrons), and tubers
(of potatoes) can grow to produce entire plants.**

B. **Ginger, sugar cane, and irises have underground stems,
called *rhizomes*, that produce new plants from each node.**

C. ***Bulbs* of tulips, daffodils, onions, and garlic divide to produce
new plants.**

D. **Strawberry and raspberry plants send out lateral stems that
can root to form new plants.**

E. Many plant cells are *totipotent*—they retain the ability to regenerate an entire plant from a single cell, or groups of cells, that has already differentiated into dermal, ground, or vascular tissue.

    1. Cells that are differentiated have gone down a developmental path that causes them to produce specific proteins that allow them to function in one particular way—such as guard cells or a phloem cell.

    2. Plant cells can be deprogrammed—returned to their original meristematic state—in tissue culture, and then redifferentiated into shoots and roots of a new plant.

VIII. Plants *sense* and *respond* to changing conditions in the *environment* and exert *internal regulation* over growth and development through the action of *hormones* (sometimes called *growth regulators* in plants).

Test Tip  *Probably one plant hormone or one plant response to an environmental stimulus will be featured in an application-type question on the test.*

A. Plant hormones are similar to animal hormones in important ways, and a single plant hormone can have different effects depending on a number of factors.

    1. Plant hormones have some similarities and differences compared to animal hormones.

        i. Both types of hormones act at *very low concentrations*, and stimulate cells through *signal transduction pathways* that lead to a cellular response that sometimes involves turning on the expression of a gene or a set of genes.

        ii. Some plant hormones, such as auxin, travel from cell to cell, and others are transported in xylem or phloem.

        iii. One plant hormone, ethylene, is a gas, and like the gas regulator in animals, *nitric oxide*, it is produced and acts locally on nearby cells.

        iv. While many receptors for animal hormones are proteins present on the plasma membrane of cells and have been isolated and characterized, plant cell receptors have not been isolated and characterized.

2. The effects of a plant hormone depend on a number of factors.

        i. The *concentration* of a hormone, and its *interaction* with other hormones, influences the type of effect it will have.

        ii. Hormones often have different effects in different *types of tissues*.

        iii. The *stage of development* of a plant, or a plant tissue or organ, often determines whether and how it will react to a hormone.

Table 17.3 Synthesis, Transport, and Functions of Major Plant Hormones

Hormone	Synthesis/Transport	Main Functions
Auxin (IAA) (one naturally occurring compound)	Leaf buds; developing leaves and seeds/ from cell to cell	Apical dominance; tropisms; promotes ethylene synthesis and growth of vascular tissue, roots, fruit; inhibits leaf and fruit abscission
Cytokinins (zeatin) (several naturally occurring compounds)	Root tips/xylem	Inhibits apical dominance; promotes cell division and germination; delays aging in leaves
Ethylene (a gas: $CH_2=CH_2$ synthesized from methionine)	Most tissues/diffusion	Promotes fruit ripening, and leaf and fruit abscission; promotes or inhibits growth depending on species

(continued)

Table 17.3 (*continued*)

Hormone	Synthesis/Transport	Main Functions
Abscisic acid (ABA) (one compound)	Mature leaves and seeds/phloem	Causes stomatal closure; promotes *dormancy* (inhibits growth) in seeds and buds
Gibberellins (GA$_1$) (many types)	Developing shoots and seeds/xylem and phloem	Promote cell division and cell elongation in stems and leaves; promote seed germination

B. The five major types of hormones are auxin, cytokinins, ethylene, abscisic acid, and gibberellins.

1. *Indoleacetic acid (IAA)* is the only naturally occurring *auxin*, although synthetic versions have been produced for commercial use.

   i. Auxin, produced by the apical meristem (terminal bud) of a shoot, *inhibits growth* of *lateral buds*, a situation known as *apical dominance*.

      a) If the apical meristem of a plant is removed, new shoots develop from the lateral buds.

      b) If auxin is applied to the site of removal, lateral buds remain dormant.

   ii. Auxin moves downward from the apical meristem and *promotes elongation* of *stem cells* below the meristem.

      a) Auxin movement is *polar* (in only one direction), and it travels through parenchyma cells from shoot tips downward.

      b) When it reaches the elongation region of the stem, auxin causes H^+ to be pumped from the cells into the *cell wall*.

      c) This *acidification* of the cell wall *loosens cellulose bundles* in the wall, allowing the wall to *stretch*, which allows the cell to lengthen.

       iii. Auxin produced in developing seeds, along with gibberellins, *promotes fruit growth.*

       iv. Auxin *stimulates root growth*, and is often used to cause shoot cuttings to form roots during vegetative propagation.

       v. In higher concentrations, auxin *promotes leaf abscission* (detachment of leaves from the plant), and synthetic auxins are commonly used as *defoliants.*

2. *Cytokinins* are a small group of hormones that stimulate cell division and are used, along with auxin, to stimulate the production of whole plants from cells in tissue culture.

       i. Cytokinins are important in plant growth by *promoting cell division* in growing leaves, stems, roots, seeds, and fruits.

       ii. Plant cells can be induced to dedifferentiate and then differentiate again to produce new plants in tissue culture.

          a) Dedifferentiated cells given *low* concentrations of *auxin* and *high* concentrations of *cytokinins* produce *shoots.*

          b) The tissue can then be treated with *high* concentrations of *auxin* and *low* concentrations of *cytokinins* to stimulate the formation of *roots.*

       iii. Cytokinins applied to lateral buds can *overcome apical dominance*, causing the buds to shoot.

       iv. When applied to mature leaves, they *prevent* them from *aging.*

3. *Ethylene* is a *gas* (see chart) produced from the amino acid, *methionine*, in plants, and is important in fruit ripening and leaf and fruit abscission.

       i. Ethylene is made in the plant where it is going to be used and moves by simple *diffusion* to surrounding tissue.

       ii. The production of a small amount of ethylene causes more ethylene to be produced by a *positive feedback* mechanism.

       iii. Ethylene is used commercially to *ripen fruit* that is picked while unripe to minimize damage during shipping.

iv. *Decreasing auxin* levels and *increasing ethylene* levels promote aging in leaves (senescence) and *defoliation*—the loss of leaves from trees in temperate climates during the fall.

4. *Abscisic acid (ABA)* is a hormone responsible for stomatal closure and also dormancy in buds and seeds.

    i. When a plant is subjected to *water stress*—lack of sufficient water—it begins to *wilt*, which causes *increased ABA* levels in the leaves. This, in turn, triggers the release of K^+ and water from guard cells, thereby *closing stomata* to reduce water loss.

    ii. At the onset of winter, ABA levels increase in primary and secondary *meristems, inhibiting* their *growth* and causing production of *bud scales* that cover and *protect buds* during cold weather.

    iii. High levels of ABA in the *seeds* of some species keep them *dormant* until heavy rains wash away the ABA, breaking their dormancy and allowing them to germinate.

5. More than 78 structurally related *gibberellins* have been isolated from different plants; their primary role is to stimulate growth, but they are also responsible for breaking seed dormancy in some plants.

    i. Gibberellins *promote stem elongation*—presumably in conjunction with auxin—by *increasing* both *cell division* and *cell elongation*.

        a) Many *dwarf plants* are deficient in gibberellin synthesis and can be induced to grow to normal size by spraying them with gibberellin.

        b) *Bolting*—the rapid growth of a floral stem from a condensed rosette of leaves with very short internodes—occurs due to a rapid increase in gibberellin concentration in the stem.

    ii. Gibberellins *promote seed germination* in some species and the *mobilization* of *food reserves* for the developing embryo in others.

        a) Gibberellins are required by some seeds to *break dormancy* and initiate germination.

        b) Gibberellins regulate the expression of genes coding for *enzymes* that *digest* nutrients in the *endosperm* of the seeds of cereals, such as barley.

      iii. Gibberellins also *promote fruit growth* and are used commercially to enhance the growth of seedless grapes.

C. *Plant movements* **are one way a plant responds to its environment and can be the slow result of changing growth patterns or rapid movements that involve reversible changes in specific cells.**

    1. A *tropism* changes the *growth pattern* of part of a plant, so that it moves toward (positive) or away from (negative) a specific stimulus.

        i. The *shoots* of plants exhibit *positive phototropism.*

           a) When light is shining on a plant mainly from one direction, the cells on the *shaded side* of the plant *elongate more* than those on the lighted side.

           b) This causes the stem to bend so that the shoot grows toward the light.

           c) The reception of light occurs in the tip of the shoot.

           d) Bending of the stems of grass seedlings toward light occurs because *auxin* is transported from the tip to only the shaded side of the stem, stimulating cell elongation on the shaded side below the tip.

           e) In contrast, the bending of other types of stems toward light may involve an *inhibitor* of cell elongation that accumulates on the lighted side of the stem.

           f) *Solar tracking,* such as when sunflowers orient toward the sun, following it as it travels across the sky, is another example of positive phototropism.

           g) *Blue light receptors,* called *cryptochromes,* are involved in light sensing in some phototropic responses.

        ii. *Roots* exhibit *positive gravitropism,* and *shoots* exhibit *negative gravitropism.*

           a) The exact *mechanism* of gravity reception is *not known,* but *plastids* (called *statoliths*) containing *starch granules* that fall to the "bottom" of cells are one possible candidate.

       b) Regardless of how plants sense gravity, *auxin accumulates* on the sides of roots and stems that are *closest* to the *ground*.

       c) The high concentrations of auxin stimulate elongation of cells on the lower side of the shoot, causing it to bend upward.

       d) In contrast, the same high concentrations of auxin on the lower side of a root inhibits cell elongation, causing the cells on the upper side of the root to grow faster than those on the bottom, which causes the root to bend downward.

    iii. Leaves and stems modified as tendrils exhibit *thigmotropism*, which causes them to grow around an object (including another plant) that they *touch* and allows them to better position themselves to absorb light for photosynthesis.

    iv. Pollen tubes exhibit positive *chemotropism* when they grow down a style toward the ovary in response to chemicals produced by the ovule.

2. *Nastic movements* are a response to external stimuli that occur when specialized cells lose *turgor pressure* similar to the guard cells of stomata.

    i. *Thigmonastic* movements occur in response to *touch*, such as the closing of the *Venus' flytrap* leaf, and the closing of *leaflets* in *mimosa* (*sensitive*) plants.

       a) An *electrical signal*, called an *action potential*—which is much *slower* than the action potentials that travel along axons in animal nerve cells—travels from the *hairs* inside the Venus' flytrap leaf to cells under the leaf.

       b) In response, the cells become *turgid* (fill with water), pushing the two sides of the leaf together.

       c) Another thigmonastic response occurs in the sensitive plant when cells at the base of its leaflets and petioles quickly pump out K^+, and water follows by *osmosis*.

       d) The rapid loss of turgidity of these cells pushes the two sides of the leaflet together.

e) One by one, leaves along the length of the stem also close their leaves as a traveling action potential reaches them.

f) Nastic movements do not involve extended periods of growth as tropisms do, and they are *reversible*—i.e., the cells can lose or gain water to reverse the movement.

ii. *Nyctinastic movements* (also called *sleep movements*) follow a *circadian rhythm*—a repeated daily cycle of activity lasting about 24 hours.

a) During the *day*, the leaves of most plants are *horizontal* to capture as much light as possible.

b) Every *evening* as the sun sets, the leaves of some plants move up or down to a *vertical* orientation.

c) The mechanism of movement is the same as for thigmonasty, except the changes in turgor pressure of the appropriate cells occur over a longer period of time.

D. Plants respond to *seasonal changes* by sensing photoperiod, temperature, or a combination of the two.

1. *Photoperiodism* is the response of plants to increasing and decreasing amounts of dark and light throughout the year.

   i. In some plants, *flowering* is controlled by the *length of nights* (the length of the *dark period*).

   a) Flowering in some plants occurs only when *nights* are *shorter than* some *critical length*.

   Plants that require short nights to flower are called long-day plants, and usually flower in the summer when nights are short.

   For example, when nights are longer than 10 hours, wheat plants will not flower, but, as summer arrives and nights become shorter than 10 hours, wheat plants use this cue to initiate flowering.

   Under controlled conditions, wheat plants will flower when nights are longer than 10 hours if the dark period is interrupted by a brief period of light.

b) Conversely, some plants flower only when *nights are longer than* some *critical length.*

  ▸ *Plants requiring long nights to flower are called* short-day plants, *and they flower either in the spring or fall depending on other factors in the environment.*

  ▸ For example, *when nights are shorter than 12 hours, poinsettia plants will not flower, but when nights become longer than 12 hours, they flower.*

  ▸ *Again, under controlled conditions, flowering can be manipulated: in the case of short-day plants, interrupting the dark period with a burst of light that divides the dark period into two periods of less than 12 hours will keep the plant from flowering.*

c) Still other plants, such as corn are *day neutral* and their flowering is controlled by factors other than day or night length.

Figure 17.13 Effect of Photoperiod on Flowering in Long- and Short-day Plants

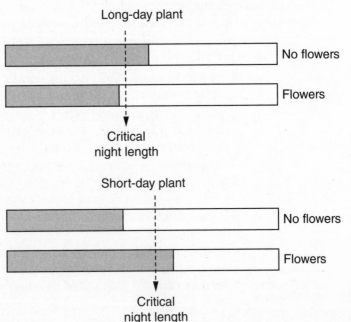

    ii. The red light and infrared light receptor, *phytochrome*, may be responsible, in part, for photoperiodic responses by interconversion of its two forms: P_{fr} and P_r.

        a) During the day, phytochrome is converted to P_{fr}, and at night phytochrome is converted to P_r.

        b) Monitoring the relative amounts of P_r and P_{fr}, as well as other stimuli, may contribute to a plant's responses to seasonal changes.

2. Exposure of plants living in temperate climates to a period of *cold temperature* is required for such processes as flowering, seed germination, and bud dormancy in some species.

    i. *Vernalization* is the response of plants to a period of cold temperature required in some species to *promote flowering*.

    ii. *Aging* of the *leaves* of deciduous trees involves both photoperiodism and exposure to low temperatures.

        a) Leaves transport all carbohydrate reserves to storage organs elsewhere in the plant.

        b) Chlorophyll synthesis stops, unmasking orange colors produced by *carotenoids*, and the production of red colored *anthocyanin* is stimulated.

E. **Plants can also sense the presence of *pathogens* (viruses, bacteria, and fungi), mainly through damage they cause to plant cells; and plants respond by producing compounds, called *phytoalexins* and *pathogenesis-related proteins*, that help protect the plant.**

PART VI:

EVOLUTION & DIVERSITY

ORIGIN OF LIFE

Chapter

18

I. Key Concepts

A. Many experiments have demonstrated that the three most important properties of living organisms could have arisen spontaneously—they are made of organic molecules, they must have a boundary that separates them from their environment, they must possess a genetic molecule.

B. The relative ages of fossils, and the rock layers they are found in, can be determined by studying the way the rock is layered into specific strata that were laid down on the Earth during specific time periods.

C. The absolute ages of fossils and rock layers can be measured by radioactive dating, and other molecular dating techniques.

D. Prokaryotes were the first living organisms and developed in an anaerobic environment.

E. Aerobic photosynthetic prokaryotes produced the O_2 in the atmosphere and the ozone layer surrounding the Earth that protects living organisms from DNA-damaging UV radiation from the sun.

F. Eukaryotes evolved from endosymbiotic relationships between different types of prokaryotes, which gave rise to present-day mitochondria and chloroplasts.

G. Multicelluar organisms probably evolved from colonial eukaryotes.

II. **Several key hypotheses have been tested regarding the origin of life on Earth.**

A. Even the simplest living organism must have the following *minimum requirements* to be a self-perpetuating entity subject to developing increasingly complex adaptations through natural selection.

1. The availability of organic nutrients, and/or the ability to make *organic molecules* from inorganic molecules

2. A *barrier* to delineate itself from the environment

3. A method of passing its characteristics on to offspring; i.e., a *genetic material* that specifies its own characteristics

B. The following *hypotheses, experiments,* and *observations* concerning *chemical evolution* suggest possible ways these requirements could have been satisfied.

1. *Organic compounds* can be produced from *inorganic compounds.*

   i. Alexander *Oparin* first hypothesized that atmospheric conditions on the early Earth—which were very different from current conditions—could have been favorable for the abiotic synthesis of organic compounds.

   a) Most organic compounds are synthesized by living organisms; *abiotic synthesis* is the synthesis of organic compounds in the absence of a living organism.

   b) Oparin hypothesized an *early Earth atmosphere* consisting of NH_3, H_2, H_2O, and methane (CH_4); there was *little*, if any, O_2 present on the early Earth, which is known to quickly degrade organic compounds.

   ii. Stanley *Miller*, Harold *Urey*, and other scientists have tested Oparin's hypothesis, demonstrating that *amino acids, ATP*, and *nucleotides* can be synthesized abiotically.

   iii. In addition, organic compounds have been found in *meteorites* that have regularly fallen to Earth from its formation to the present.

2. Organisms can live under *extreme conditions*, so, alternatively, the first living organisms could have arisen without contact with the atmosphere.

   i. Communities of organisms live in the oceans at great depths near *deep sea vents* where volcanic magma superheats the water creating abundant H_2S needed by chemoautotrophs.

   ii. Prokaryotes living in these areas are *chemoautotrophs* that do not need sunlight for energy, nor organic nutrients of any kind, and are the *base of food chains* that include invertebrates and vertebrates.

3. Organic compounds can spontaneously form spheres—*protobionts*, called *coacervates, microspheres,* and *liposomes*—that can maintain a unique internal environment compared with their surroundings.

4. *RNA* and other organic molecules are capable of *self-replication*, and both can act as *genotype* and *phenotype*.

   i. RNA molecules spontaneously fold into *specific shapes* (phenotypes) and can catalyze their own synthesis (*spontaneously reproduce*).

   ii. When a population of diverse, self-replicating RNA sequences is allowed to compete for substrates, only a few sequences remain after repeated rounds of synthesis, demonstrating that RNA molecules are subject to *selection* based on inherent (sequence-based) characteristics they pass on to progeny molecules.

   iii. *Ribozymes*—RNA molecules with *enzymatic activity*—exist in many organisms today.

   iv. Other organic molecules are capable of spontaneous self-replication, carrying their phenotype (how to self-replicate) on to progeny molecules.

Geologic evidence and fossil evidence chronicle the history of the Earth and its progression of living organisms.

A. **Millions of fossils of different types have been studied in detail.**

1. Most *fossils* are found in *sedimentary rock* layers.

2. Fossils of organisms include *hard body parts,* mineralized (petrified) bodies or *casts* of bodies, and *organic material* (including DNA) that has been *pressed* between rock layers, *frozen,* or *trapped* in other preservative coatings such as *amber* and *tar.*

3. *Trace fossils* include impressions left by organisms, such as footprints, holes produced by burrowing organisms, and so on—or products left by organisms, such as feces, nests, underground burrows, arrow heads, fire pits, and so on.

4. *Prokaryotic fossils* include large fossilized colonies of bacteria that form mats, called *stromatolites,* that are examined microscopically.

5. Several characteristics of a species make it more likely to be *present in* the *fossil record.*

    i. Species that existed for a *long* period of *time*

    ii. Species that had *abundant* members

    iii. Species that were distributed over a *large area*

    iv. Species with *hard body parts,* such as teeth, bones, and shells

B. *Radioactive dating* **can be used to estimate the age of the Earth, as well as the ages of fossils.**

1. The half-life of different radioisotopes is used to calculate the ages of different substances.

    i. *Isotopes* are atoms of the same element that have *different numbers* of *neutrons* in their nuclei.

        a) Two isotopes of carbon are carbon-12 and *carbon-14.*

b) Carbon-12 has 6 neutrons, and carbon-14 has 8 neutrons.

c) Carbon-14 is unstable—*radioactive*—due to the presence of extra neutrons in its nucleus.

d) Carbon-14 spontaneously *decays*—emits radioactive particles from its nucleus over time—converting it to carbon-12.

ii. The amount of time it takes half of any quantity of a specific isotope to decay is called its *half-life*, and differs for each isotope.

a) Carbon-14 has a half-life of *5715 years*; i.e., it takes 5,715 years for half of the carbon-14 in any sample to decay.

b) It takes another 5,715 years for half of the remaining carbon-14 to decay, and so on.

c) *Carbon-14* can be used to date fossils of *recent* origin (from about 60,000 years old to the present).

d) Other isotopes with much longer half-lives—such as *potassium-40* and *uranium-238*—can be used to date samples (such as fossils and rocks) that are much *older*.

Test Tip

If an application question on the test deals with radioactive dating, enough numerical information will be given regarding its half-life in order to answer the question using simple mathematics.

C. **The distribution and ages of fossils in the layers of the Earth's crust are used to determine the progression of living organisms that have inhabited the Earth.**

1. *Relative dating* of rock layers and fossils is possible because the lowest *stratum* of rock in a cross section of the Earth's crust is the oldest, with layers on top of it being of progressively younger ages.

2. The *absolute ages* of rocks and fossils are determined by *radioactive dating* and other molecular dating techniques.

3. The careful examination of large numbers of fossils and geologic data over more than 150 years—combined with DNA analysis and analysis of historical atmospheric composition—has resulted in an understanding of when key organisms first appeared on the Earth relative to geologic time periods.

 The key series of events in the history of life on Earth during the early Precambrian Era are listed in Table 18.1 and summarized in the next section.

Table 18.1 Major Events during the Precambrian Era

Million Years Ago	Event
4,600	Estimated origin of the Earth
3,500	Oldest prokaryotic fossils
2,500	Oxygen accumulating in atmosphere
1,700	Oldest eukaryotic fossils
700	Oldest animal fossils (multicellular)

A. *Prokaryotes* were the *first living organisms.*

  1. The *first prokaryotes* were *anaerobic.*

      i. There was not sufficient oxygen in the atmosphere of the early Earth to support aerobic life.

      ii. The first prokaryotes were *probably chemoautotrophs*—similar to some present-day prokaryotes such as the *archaeans*, also called *archaebacteria*—that live entirely on inorganic molecules, such as CO_2 and inorganic energy sources, such as H_2S.

  2. Later, *photoautotrophs* evolved.

      i. Early photoautotrophs were probably *similar to* present-day *cyanobacteria* that use sunlight as an energy source to split H_2O during photosynthesis to produce O_2 as a waste product.

ii. Photoautotrophs *produced* all of the O_2 currently present in the *Earth's atmosphere*.

a) Readily available O_2 was necessary for the development of *aerobic respiration*.

b) O_2 reacted with sunlight to produce the *ozone layer* around the Earth, which absorbs most of the sun's damaging *UV radiation*.

B. The *first eukaryotes* were formed by a *series of endosymbioses* each of which involved close, *intracellular, symbiotic relationships*.

1. Present-day *eukaryotic heterotrophs* (animals, fungi, and some protists) are derived from ancestral prokaryotic cells that took in an *aerobic prokaryote* that lived symbiotically within it and eventually evolved into present-day *mitochondria*.

2. Present-day *photosynthetic autotrophs* (plants and some protists) evolved from these successful eukaryotes when they took in a second endosymbiont—a *photoautotrophic prokaryote*—that lived symbiotically within them, eventually evolving into present-day *chloroplasts*.

Figure 18.1 The Origin of Eukaryotic Cells from Prokaryotic Cells

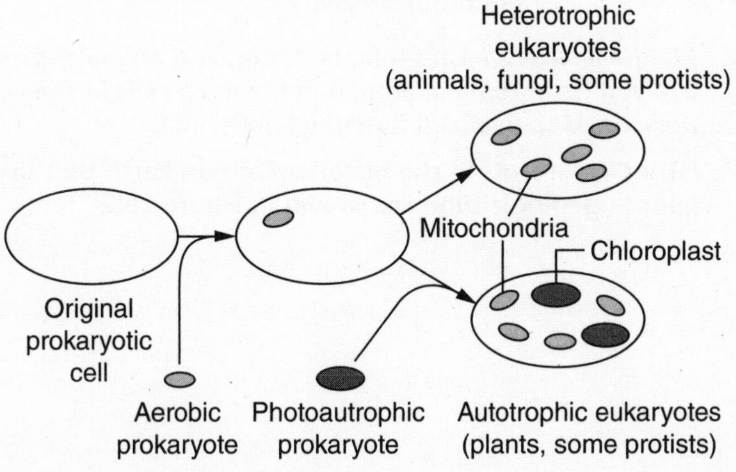

Heterotrophic eukaryotes (animals, fungi, some protists)

Original prokaryotic cell

Mitochondria

Chloroplast

Aerobic prokaryote

Photoautrophic prokaryote

Autotrophic eukaryotes (plants, some protists)

3. Strong *evidence* supporting the endosymbiotic origin of mitochondria and chloroplasts are their consistent structural, metabolic, genetic, and reproductive similarity to prokaryotes.

   i. The *size* of prokaryotes is similar to that of mitochondria and chloroplasts.

   ii. The *membrane structure* and *membrane proteins* of mitochondria and chloroplasts are similar to those of their proposed prokaryotic counterparts.

   iii. The *ribosomes* of mitochondria and chloroplasts are more similar to prokaryotic ribosomes than to those produced by the nucleus of a eukaryotic cell.

   iv. Mitochondria and chloroplasts have their *own DNA* that consists of *one circular chromosome* characteristic of prokaryotes, and they contain their *own ribosomes* and *tRNA* that are capable of transcribing and translating their own DNA without the help of the eukaryotic nucleus.

   v. The *ribosomal genes* of mitochondria and chloroplasts have sequences more similar to prokaryotic ribosomal genes than to those produced by eukaryotic nuclear DNA.

   vi. Mitochondria and chloroplasts *reproduce independently* of eukaryotic nuclei and in a manner *similar* to *binary fission* that is characteristic of prokaryotes.

C. *Multicellular organisms* (plants, fungi, and animals) probably evolved from *colonial organisms* in which cells in the colony developed specialized functions over time.

D. Other key events in the history of life on Earth that occurred later in geologic time are shown in Figure 18.2.

Figure 18.2 Geologic Time Scale and the History of Life on Earth

Geologic Time Scale		Millions of Years Ago
Era	**Period**	

Millions of Years Ago

0		2.5 first humans
Cenozoic	Quaternary / Tertiary	
100		65 end of the dinosaurs
Mesozoic	Cretaceous	144
200	Jurassic	
	Triassic	213 first dinosaurs,
	Permian	248 mammals, birds
300	Carboniferous / Pennsylvanian	286
	Mississippian	320
400	Devonian	360 first reptiles
Paleozoic	Silurian	408 first amphibians
	Ordovician	438
500		first land plants
	Cambrian	505 first fishes
600		590
Precambrian	Precambrian	
700		700 first invertebrates
4,600		

Be familiar with 1) the minimum requirements for the first living cell, 2) evidence regarding the origin of life, 3) major events during the Precambrian era, and 4) endosymbiosis and evidence for endosymbiosis.

EVIDENCE AND PATTERNS OF EVOLUTION

I. Key Concepts

A. Evidence of evolution from biogeography suggests that species and fossils in the same geographic area are similar due to common ancestry.

B. Continental drift—the transformative changes in the positions of the Earth's landmasses—must be taken into account when studying the biogeography of fossils.

C. Evidence of evolution from comparative anatomy reveals anatomical similarities between organisms—called *homologous structures*—that have a common hereditary origin.

D. Comparative embryology reveals additional anatomical homologies that are more evident when embryos of two species are compared as opposed to comparing adult forms of the species.

E. Comparison of species at the molecular level, such as comparison of the amino acid sequences of proteins or the nucleotide sequences of genes, reveals homologies between species that diverged from a common ancestor in the very distant past, as well as homologies between species that are very closely related.

F. Extinction of species is very common, and more than a dozen mass extinctions have occurred throughout geologic history.

G. Adaptive radiation is the rapid development of new species from a common ancestor and may occur after a significant genetic change in a member of a species, or after new habitat becomes available due to extinction of another (or many) species.

H. Punctuated equilibrium refers to the "stop-and-go" pattern of evolution in which a species is hypothesized to undergo most of its genetic/phenotypic changes during a short period of time as it is diverging from another species, and thereafter remains fairly unchanged for a much longer period of time.

II. *Evidence of evolution* **comes from many different sources including biogeography, comparative anatomy, comparative embryology, and comparative molecular biology.**

A. *Biogeography*—the study of the geographic distribution of both living species and fossils—suggested that species living in the same geographic region are more closely related to each other, and to fossilized ancestor species in the region, than they are to species living distant from them.

1. Species living in the *same geographic area* are generally *more physically similar* to each other than they are to species in a distant geographic area, even if the two areas have very similar climates and habitats. Following are some examples.

    i. Species of birds on an island near the coast of South America are more likely to be similar to birds on the South American coast than they are to birds on the African coast or on islands situated off the African coast.

    ii. Desert plants and animals are more similar to species on their own continent than they are to desert plants and animals on a different continent.

2. In addition, *living species* are more similar to *fossils* found in the *same geographic region*, as opposed to distant regions, for example:

    i. Fossils of extinct kangaroo species are present in Australia where kangaroos presently live, while fossils of kangaroos are absent from other regions of the world.

    ii. Fossils of animals resembling armadillos are found only in the Americas where armadillos currently live, while similar fossils are not found on any of the other continents.

3. A reasonable *inference* from these observations is that *species* living in the same region (and their regional fossils) are *similar* because they are related to each other and *share* a *common hereditary* history.

4. *Continental drift*—the movement of Earth's landmasses over the expanse of geologic time—has contributed to the distribution patterns of present-day organisms and their fossilized relatives.

    i. The *continental landmasses* are large pieces of the *Earth's crust* carrying one or two continents, *floating* on the *mantle* below them, and they have *moved* extensively throughout the Earth's history.

        a) At the end of the Paleozoic era (250 million years ago), all of the landmasses were joined together into one supercontinent, called *Pangaea*.

        b) By the middle of the Mesozoic era (135 MYA [million years ago]), the giant landmass was *beginning* to *separate*.

        c) By the end of the Mesozoic era (65 MYA), the present continents were mostly *separate* from each other, with *oceans* present *between* them.

    ii. This large change caused the *separation* of *dinosaur populations* living on the landmasses at that time, resulting in *closely related fossils* from that time period being now present on *widely separated* continents, such as South America and Africa, which were once joined.

    iii. Continental drift has also resulted in the *unique flora* and *fauna* of the *Australian* continent.

        a) *Australia separated* from Pangaea *before* the *diversification* of *placental mammals* that are, as a result, not native to Australia today.

        b) A different group of mammals—the *marsupials*—present in a few parts of the world at the time of separation, developed in isolation into the very diverse types of marsupials present today in Australia.

B. *Comparative anatomy* is the study of the similarities and differences between anatomical structures of living species or fossilized species.

   1. *Homologous structures* are anatomical features of two organisms that are *similar* in *structure* and *hereditary origin*, and suggest that the two organisms *share* a *common ancestor*, for example:

      i. The forelimbs of most vertebrates—whether the wings of birds or bats, the forelimbs of whales, the front legs of cats or dogs, or the arms of humans—all have the same basic arrangement of the same basic bones even though they vary in form and function.

      ii. The bones in the jaws of vertebrates differ in specific form and sometimes in function, but they all have a similar ancestral origin.

   2. Some *vestigial structures*—structures present in an organism that no longer have a function—are homologous to working structures found in related species and have a common ancestral origin, for example:

      i. Snakes and whales do not have legs, but still retain the pelvic bones of an ancestor common to snakes, whales, and other vertebrates with hind legs.

      ii. The tail bone in humans can be considered a vestigial structure derived from an ancestor common to humans and other vertebrates in which a similar bone is part of a functioning tail.

   3. *Analogous structures*, on the other hand, are features of organisms that have the *same function*, but a *different evolutionary origin*, for example:

      i. The wings of bats and the wings of bees are both used for flight, but are very different anatomically and are not derived from a recent common ancestor.

      ii. The eyes of vertebrates and the eyes of the invertebrate squids serve similar functions, but arose independently in each group of organisms.

Table 19.1 Comparison of Homologous, Analogous, and Vestigial Structures

Structures	Features	Examples
Homologous structures	Similar structures, similar origin	Arms of human, wings of bats, wings of birds
Analogous structures	Similar function, different origins	Wings of bats, wings of bees
Vestigial structures	Often homologous to functional structure of related organism	Pelvic bones of snakes, pelvic bones of dog

C. *Comparative embryology*—comparison of structures during embryonic development—highlights a set of homologies that are *not evident in* the *adult* bodies of related organisms, for example:

1. Mammals, birds, and reptiles all have the same four embryonic membranes—a chorion, amnion, yolk sac, and allantois—that have similar developmental origins, structures, and functions.

2. The digestive systems of vertebrate and echinoderm adults are very different, but both have deuterostome development, which demonstrates a closer evolutionary relationship than between echinoderms and other invertebrate groups with protostome development.

D. *Comparative molecular biology*—comparison of amino acid and DNA sequences of proteins and genes—allows for an even broader level of comparison between organisms as different as prokaryotes, plants, and humans.

1. A near *universal genetic code*, similar *biochemical pathways*—such as glycolysis—and similar *transcription* and *translation apparatuses* in all organisms suggests that all organisms share a common ancestor.

2. Comparisons of *protein* and *DNA sequences* are one of the most direct ways to examine *homologies* between organisms

at the deepest branches of evolutionary history, such as between prokaryotes and eukaryotes, or between the different branches of eukaryotes.

3. As a general rule, the *longer* two species have been *diverging* from one another, the *greater* the number of *differences* there will be between their sequences for a particular gene.

4. Certain *genes*—ones for fundamental life processes—are *highly conserved* among all species; for example, genes that code for *rRNA, tRNA, RNA polymerase,* and *DNA polymerase.*

5. *Mitochondrial DNA* is used to compare organisms, such as different populations of humans, that are *very closely related.*

6. DNA comparisons often confirm longstanding classification schemes, but have also lead to new understanding and reclassification of some species.

Test Tip

Be prepared to match a type of evidence with its category: biogeography, comparative anatomy, comparative embryology, or comparing a molecular aspect (protein or DNA sequence, or a fundamental process).

III. There are certain *patterns* that regularly occur throughout evolutionary history.

A. *Coevolution* occurs when two species have such a close relationship that they have evolved adaptations that facilitate the relationship, or counterbalance strengths or weaknesses, between two species, for example:

1. Some pollinators have very specific mouthparts adapted to reach the nectar of one particular species of flower, while the plant has evolved characteristics that match the pollinator's ability to recognize the flower (e.g., color, scent, etc.)

2. Symbiotic relationships, such as nitrogen-fixing bacteria that live in special nodules produced by plants, are some of the most extreme examples of coevolution.

3. Plants and their pathogens are constantly adapting to each other such that the plant develops an adaptation to fight the

pathogen, and the pathogen responds with an adaptation to overcome the defense.

4. Prey and predators may also coevolve in a similar way to the plant/pathogen interaction.

B. *Convergent evolution* **occurs when two species that are not closely related develop similar adaptations (sometimes these are analogous structures) in response to similar environmental pressures.**

1. Many aquatic organisms that are not closely related, such as dolphins (mammals) and fish have evolved adaptations— such as torpedo-shaped bodies, and smooth outer surfaces— that facilitate rapid movement through water.

2. Bird and flying insects both developed wings, but their wings have a very different structure and developmental basis.

C. **Mass extinctions are generally followed by major adaptive radiations.**

1. *Extinction* of a species is much more common than survival of a species: about 99% of all species that have ever lived on Earth are currently extinct.

2. A species may become extinct if its environment—including abiotic and biotic factors—changes more rapidly than the organism is able to adapt through evolution.

   i. An *adaptation* is a change in a characteristic of a species that occurs over time as individuals with the characteristic survive and produce more offspring than others without the characteristic (called an adaptation, because individuals with the characteristic are more "well adapted" to their environment).

   ii. *Abiotic changes* include temperature, sunlight, changing oxygen levels in aquatic ecosystems, and so forth.

   iii. *Biotic changes* may include introduction or development of a virulent pathogen, a competitive species or an efficient predator moving into another species' habitat, or habitat destruction caused by another species.

3. A *mass extinction* occurs when there is a significant *global change* that wipes out large numbers of species.

    i. During the *Permian extinction*, which occurred approximately 240 MYA (at the end of the Paleozoic era), approximately 90% of species present on the Earth at that time became extinct within a 5 MY period.

    ii. Some possible contributing factors include the formation of Pangaea, which reduced coastal areas and caused extreme temperature fluctuations on the interior of the giant landmass, and extensive volcanic activity that may have blocked out sunlight for an extended period.

    iii. During the *Cretaceous extinction* that occurred approximately 65 MYA (at the end of the Mesozoic era), about 50% of species, including almost all the *dinosaurs*, became extinct.

    iv. As well as extensive volcanic activity and a cooler climate, the effects of a comet or large asteroid hitting the Earth in the Gulf of Mexico may have been involved and could have almost immediately wiped out most species in North America due to an ensuing fire storm.

4. Adaptive radiations occur after mass extinctions and at other times when new *adaptive zones*—new areas or opportunities—open up.

    i. *Adaptive radiation* is the relatively rapid evolution of a large number of different species from a single common ancestor.

        a) Each species evolves different adaptations that help it survive by utilizing part of the environment in a different way from the other species.

        b) The larger the number of different habitats in the new area, the greater the possibility for different adaptations to evolve in response to the different environmental pressures or opportunities.

    ii. A number of *factors* may lead to adaptive radiation.

        a) If a species moves to a *new location* with new available niches, some members of the species may have characteristics that help them exploit a different niche better than other members.

b) If a species *gains* a completely *new characteristic* (through mutation), such as the ability to fly, new niches—new food sources, new hiding places, new ways to avoid predators, and so on—are then open to it due to its new characteristic; if different members have other characteristics that allow them to survive better in one niche or another, new species may develop.

c) If there is a *mass extinction*, new habitat that was formerly used by the extinct species, opens up; those species that have survived now have many new niches to explore and adapt to over time.

iii. A *major adaptive radiation*, called the *Cambrian explosion*, occurred approximately 580 MYA (at the end of the Precambrian era) and involved the rapid evolution of the *major animal phyla* currently known.

a) One possible reason for this major adaptive radiation may be that a mutation caused a developmental change that radically changed the animal body plan, increasing the morphological possibilities then available to these new animals.

b) Another possibility is that the evolution of hard body parts, such as shells and exoskeletons, altered predator–prey relationships, causing a biotic environmental pressure that affected may different species.

iv. Other significant adaptive radiations included the radiation of flowering plants after the development of effective dormancy and dispersal strategies (e.g., pollen and seeds), and the adaptive radiation of mammals after the mass extinction of dinosaurs.

Table 19.2 Major Events from 580 MYA to 57 MYA

Major Event	Time of Event
Cambrian explosion	580 MYA
Pangaea forms	250 MYA
Permian extinction	240 MYA
Separate continents	65 MYA
Cretaceous extinction	65 MYA
Radiation of mammals	65–57 MYA

D. *Punctuated equilibrium* is the proposal that evolution, instead of being a steady, gradual process, generally occurs in bursts, with rapid changes occurring early in the development of a species, followed by a much longer period of stasis when little change occurs.

Test Tip

The material in this chapter is mostly concept oriented, so it is worth taking the time to consider the examples presented in light of the concepts they illustrate.

NATURAL SELECTION, POPULATION GENETICS, AND SPECIATION

I. Key Concepts

A. Examining the fossil record, both Lamarck and Darwin agreed that species evolve over time, but each proposed a different mechanism.

B. Lamarck proposed the (incorrect) mechanism for evolution—called the *inheritance of acquired characteristics*— while Darwin proposed the mechanism for evolution called *natural selection*, which is supported by overwhelming experimental evidence.

C. Darwin's proposal of "descent with modification" by natural selection has two main parts that are broken down below for easy study.

D. Because the environment is constantly changing, and because natural selection is the interaction between organisms and the environment, natural selection can only cause adaptations that are beneficial under current environmental conditions.

E. A population is the smallest unit in which evolution can occur, and population genetics is the study of how a population's gene pool changes over time.

F. Microevolution occurs when the frequencies of alleles or genotypes in a population change and generally occurs for one of five main reasons—genetic drift, gene flow, nonrandom mating, mutation, and natural selection.

G. Natural selection is the only cause of changing allele frequencies that is likely to produce adaptations in a species—characteristics that help it adapt to the environment.

H. The different types of natural selection are stabilizing selection, directional selection, diversifying selection, and sexual selection.

I. New species are created when two former populations of a species are no longer able to mate and produce viable, fertile offspring, and can occur when species are physically separated (allopatric speciation) or when they continue to live in the same geographic area (sympatric speciation).

J. Reproductive isolation mechanisms develop in populations of a species that are developing into separate species, and include those that may occur before fertilization (prezygotic) or after fertilization (postzygotic).

II. Charles Darwin built on the ideas of other scientists to develop his theory of "descent with modification" by natural selection.

A. Jean-Baptiste *Lamarck* also proposed that species evolve (change over time), but proposed that this change occurred by a different mechanism than natural selection.

   1. From his study of *fossils*, Lamarck concluded that *species change over time*, developing new characteristics.

   2. He proposed that the way in which characteristics changed from generation to generation is by the *inheritance of acquired characteristics* that an organism develops during its life time; this proposal is also called *use and disuse*.

        i. His proposal was that if an organism uses a body part extensively, the body part will change, and that the change will then be passed on to its offspring.

        ii. Alternatively, if an organism does not use a body part, it will begin to deteriorate during the organism's life time, and, as a consequence, will not be passed on to its offspring.

   3. *Darwin* also recognized that species change over time, but proposed a *different mechanism* for how that change occurs, which he called natural selection.

B. *Darwin was influenced* **by the ideas proposed by a number of other scientific thinkers, as well as his own extensive observations of biogeography and of plant and animal breeding.**

1. Charles *Lyell* was a geologist who proposed that the *Earth* had been around for a *long* period of *time*, and held to the ideas of uniformitarianism and gradualism.

   i. *Uniformitarianism* is the recognition that the geologic processes—such as earthquakes, volcanic eruptions, erosion, and so on—that we observe occurring presently also occurred in the past.

   ii. *Gradualism* is the concept that these types of processes, occurring gradually over a long period of time, account for large-scale changes in the Earth's physical characteristics, such as the gradual uplifting of parts of the Earth's crust due to the additive effects of earthquakes that eventually produce mountain ranges.

   iii. These ideas lead Darwin, and others, to conclude that the *strata* (and their fossils) observable in exposed rock *represent distinct time periods* during the Earth's history.

2. Thomas *Malthus*—writing about the human population— proposed that, although humans have a reproductive capacity capable of producing *exponential population growth*, the population size remains fairly steady due to disease, wars, and limited resources.

   i. Darwin felt that this situation applied more generally to all species.

   ii. Darwin's theory of evolution incorporated this idea and further proposed that the availability of limited resources leads to competition between members of a species.

3. Darwin was familiar with *plant* and *animal breeding*, and recognized that great changes in the physical characteristics of many domesticated species were the result of *artificial selection* in which the selection of certain characteristics by breeders resulted in significant heritable changes over many generations.

4. In addition, Darwin's careful observation of *biogeography* during a 5-year ocean voyage around the world on the H. M. S. *Beagle* suggested that the patterns of living species and their fossils are the result of a similar selection process by the environment that—over vast amounts of time—have led to the diversity of species currently present on the Earth.

5. Darwin and Alfred *Wallace* both proposed that the mechanism of evolution was natural selection.

C. *Darwin's theory of evolution* by *natural selection* has two main parts that can be broken down into specific subparts for study purposes.

1. Although a species has the reproductive capacity for exponential growth, due to the limited availability of resources, competition occurs between members of a species resulting in some members producing more offspring than other members.

   i. Each species has the *capacity* for *exponential growth*.

   ii. *Resources* available to a species are *limited*.

   iii. This leads to *competition* among members of a species.

   iv. As a result, some members leave *more descendents* to future generations.

2. Much of the variation in characteristics among members of a species is inherited, so if a characteristic helps a member to survive and produce more offspring than other members subjected to the same environmental pressures, these "favorable" characteristics will be passed on to the member's offspring, increasing those traits in the species as a whole in future generations.

   i. Many of the differences in *characteristics* among members of a species are *inherited*.

   ii. Some characteristics help members to *compete better* for resources.

   iii. This leads to those members passing along these *specific characteristics* to their *offspring*, while other members have no, or fewer, offspring.

   iv. As a result, over *many generations*, the *characteristics* of the population will *change* so that most of them have characteristics that make them *more fit* to survive in the same environment.

D. *Darwin* **proposed that the** *mechanism* **by which** *evolution* **(changes in species' characteristics over time) occurs is through** *natural selection.*

1. *Natural selection* can be described as the collection of factors in a species' environment that "select" the "fitness" of a particular member's characteristics.

2. Natural selection results in *differential reproductive success*: the unequal genetic contribution of different members to future generations.

3. *Fitness* is a quantitative measure of differential reproductive success: how many fertile offspring a member of a species contributes to the next generation compared to other members.

4. Natural selection is *mediated by* the *environment*: the abiotic and biotic factors that all the members of the species must face.

5. The result of natural selection is a set of *adaptations*: characteristics that become prevalent in a species because they help the members who have them survive specific environmental pressures.

   i. Because aspects of a species' *environment change* over time, there is no one set of characteristics that will always lead to survival and reproductive success.

   ii. Since environmental conditions change, a characteristic developed through adaptation may not be adaptive under a different set of environmental conditions.

   iii. Therefore, *variability* is an *asset* of a species, because one set of characteristics might be favorable under one set of environmental conditions, and another set under a different set of conditions.

   a) The ultimate *source* of all *variability* is *mutation*: natural selection does not create variation, it just increases or decreases the number of individuals who have the trait in future generations.

   b) *Sexually reproducing* organisms create *additional variability* through *independent assortment* of chromosomes, *crossing over* during meiosis, and *random fertilization*. (See Chapter 12 for additional information on variation.)

6. Natural selection *acts on* the *phenotype* of an *organism*, but *affects* the *genetic makeup* of a *species*.

 III. ***Population genetics* is the study of how alleles are inherited from generation to generation within a population.**

A. A *population* is a group of individuals of the *same species* that share a gene pool, and it is the *smallest unit* in which evolution can occur.

1. A *gene pool* consists of all of the alleles for all of the genes for all of the members of a population.

    i. *Considering just one gene* with *two different alleles*, the frequency of the dominant allele (*A*) is usually represented by the letter *p*, and the frequency of the recessive allele (*a*) is usually represented by the letter *q*.

    ii. Since 100% of the alleles in this situation are either *A* or *a*, the sum of their frequencies is 1.

    $$p + q = 1$$

    a) For example, if 70% of the alleles in the population are *A*,

    $$p = 0.70$$

    b) This information can be used to calculate the frequency of the other allele, *a*.

    c) Since *p* + *q* = 1, and *p* is known, then:

    $$q = 1 - p$$
    $$q = 1 - 0.70$$
    $$q = 0.30$$

B. **If the frequencies of the two alleles *do not change* from generation to generation, a population is said to be in *Hardy-Weinberg equilibrium*.**

1. Hardy-Weinberg equilibrium occurs if the following *five conditions* are met, and describes the base situation in which a population is *not evolving*.

    i. The population is *large*.

    ii. There is *no migration* of individuals into or out of the population.

    iii. There is *no mutation* of either of the alleles.

    iv. *Random mating* occurs between members of the population.

    v. *Natural selection* is *not acting* on the allele, i.e., all genotypes are equally fit.

2. If all five conditions are met, the frequencies of the three possible genotypes of individuals in the population for the two alleles are given by the equation:

$$p^2 + 2pq + q^2 = 1$$

    i. Where p^2 is the frequency of the *AA* genotype

    ii. $2pq$ is the frequency of the *Aa* genotype

    iii. p^2 is the frequency of the *aa* genotype

    iv. For example, if the frequency of the *A* allele is 0.70, then $p = 0.70$, and the frequency of the *a* allele is 0.30 ($q = 1 - 0.70 = 0.30$), and the frequencies of the three genotypes are as follows.

        a) The frequency of $AA = p^2 = p \times p = (0.70 \times 0.70) = 0.49$.

        b) The frequency of $Aa = 2pq = 2 \times p \times q = (2 \times 0.70 \times 0.30) = 0.42$.

        c) The frequency of $aa = q^2 = q \times q = (0.30 \times 0.30) = 0.09$.

    v. The frequencies of all of the genotypes must add up to 1.

$$p^2 + 2pq + q^2 = 1$$

$$0.49 + 0.42 + 0.09 = 1$$

    vi. Allele and genotype frequencies can also be calculated if the frequency of *aa* (q^2) or *AA* (p^2) is given (see Table 20.1).

Table 20.1 Hardy-Weinberg Practice Problems

Symbol	Frequency of?	Example 1 If q^2 Is Given (*aa*)	Example 2 If p^2 Is Given (*AA*)
p	A	3) $1 - q = 1 - 0.20 = 0.80$	2) Square root of $0.25 = 0.50$
q	a	2) Square root of $0.04 = 0.20$	3) $1 - p = 1 - 0.50 = 0.50$
p^2	AA	4) $p^2 = p \times p = 0.80 \times 0.80 = 0.64$	1) **Given: the frequency of AA is 0.25***
$2pq$	Aa	5) $2 \times p \times q = 2 \times 0.8 \times 0.2 = 0.32$	4) $2 \times p \times q = 2 \times 0.50 \times 0.50 = 0.50$
q^2	aa	1) **Given: the frequency of *aa* is 0.04***	5) $q^2 = q \times q = 0.50 \times 0.50 = 0.25$

*Follow the calculations in the order given for each example.

Test Tip

It is unlikely, but if p^2 or q^2 is given on a test problem, it will be a perfect square to make your calculations easier. You are expected to know how to recognize perfect squares and to know how to add, subtract, multiply, and divide using decimals without a calculator.

C. *Microevolution* is the change in the frequencies of alleles or genotypes in a population from generation to generation and occurs if any of the five conditions of Hardy-Weinberg equilibrium are *not met*.

  1. The *smaller* a *population* is, the more likely it is to *exhibit random fluctuations* in allelic and genotypic frequencies called *genetic drift*.

      i. If a population is very large and an accident occurs in which a few of the members are killed—and their alleles are lost as a result—it will not change the frequency of alleles in the population very much, if at all.

ii. However, if the population is very small, say 50 individuals, then losing individuals and their associated alleles usually changes the genetic makeup of the population significantly.

iii. Genetic drift is a significant cause of genetic change (microevolution) of a species if only a few members of a population migrate to *found* a *new population*, such as birds who might be blown off course in a hurricane and end up in a new habitat.

iv. Genetic drift is also a cause of genetic change (microevolution) anytime a species is reduced to very small numbers due to *chance events*, such as hurricanes, earthquakes, fires, or habitat destruction.

2. *Gene flow* through immigration or emigration also causes allele frequencies to change (microevolution) as individuals carry all their alleles to the new population that they join.

3. *Nonrandom* mating causes changes in genotype frequencies, but not in overall allele frequencies (also microevolution).

   i. Nonrandom mating can occur when individuals in a population choose mates based on similar characteristics, such as individuals of the same size, color, scent, or other factor.

   ii. Nonrandom mating also occurs in species that tend to choose mates based on *proximity*, and often results in *inbreeding*.

   iii. Most nonrandom mating situations results in an *increase* in *homozygous* individuals within the population.

4. *Mutations* are constantly occurring in all organisms due to mistakes during DNA synthesis associated with cell division, and also by mutagenic substances in the environment that affect germ cells (see Chapter 15 for types of mutations).

   i. Mutations change the allele frequencies in a population (microevolution).

   ii. Mutations are also the only *source* of *new variation* within populations.

5. *Natural selection* is the only factor that causes changes in a population's genetic makeup that is likely to cause *adaptive evolution* in which a species is molded to better take advantage of its environment.

Natural selection can change a population in different ways.

A. *Stabilizing selection* occurs when individuals in a population that have phenotypes that are intermediate along a spectrum of possibilities have an adaptive advantage. Following are examples.

1. Birth weight in humans is affected by stabilizing selection, because low birth weight and high birth weight infants are less likely to survive than those of intermediate weight.

2. The number of eggs a bird lays is also affected by stabilizing selection, because producing too few offspring means leaving less offspring to the next generation, but producing too many requires additional care and feeding that may result in less healthy offspring.

B. *Directional selection* occurs when individuals in a population that have a phenotype at one end of a continuum have more of a chance of surviving than those who have intermediate phenotypes or those who have phenotypes at the other end of the continuum. Following are examples.

1. If large size becomes an advantage in a changing environment for a mammal, large size will be favored over small or intermediate sizes, causing a gradual shift in the species toward larger body size.

2. If flower color varies between members of a species, and pollinators prefer the more brightly colored ones, brighter colored flowers will have a selective advantage, be pollinated more often, and a change in the flower color of the species to the brighter color will occur over time.

C. *Diversifying selection* (also called *disruptive selection*) occurs when the intermediate phenotype for a trait has a selective *dis*advantage. Following are examples.

1. If insects have two different colorations that are both equally well camouflaged, but the intermediate color stands out against the background objects in the species' habitat, the two extreme phenotypes have a better chance of survival.

2. If, in a population of frogs, those that are larger and those that are smaller have greater fitness than frogs of intermediate size, then the species may evolve to have two distinct sizes of individuals.

Figure 20.1 Results of Stabilizing, Directional, and Diversifying Selection

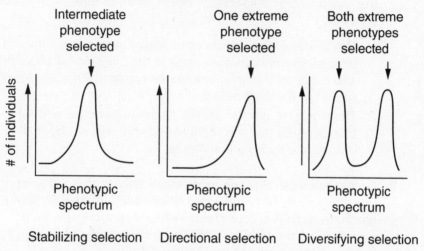

Intermediate phenotype selected	One extreme phenotype selected	Both extreme phenotypes selected

# of individuals

Phenotypic spectrum	Phenotypic spectrum	Phenotypic spectrum
Stabilizing selection	Directional selection	Diversifying selection

D. *Sexual selection* **is a special type of natural selection in which a phenotype that is particularly effective in gaining a mate is preferentially selected, such as the showy feathers of a peacock or a behavioral adaptation that produces a better display of a mating behavior.**

Microevolution creates *differences* within a population that *can lead to speciation*— the development of a new species from an existing one.

A. Two possible ways to *define* what constitutes a *species* are the morphological species concept and the biological species concept.

1. The *morphological species concept* compares similarities and differences between organisms as the basis for classification and is usually the only criteria that can be used to categorize species in the *fossil record*.

2. The *biological species concept* defines a species as a group of individuals that are capable of producing viable, fertile offspring in their natural habitat.

B. One species can diverge to produce two or more species under a variety of conditions, all of which involve *isolating mechanisms* that create changes that eventually prevent members of the two new species from mating to produce fertile offspring under normal conditions.

1. *Allopatric speciation* occurs when members of a population are separated by an impassable *geographic barrier* that physically isolates them for enough time for reproductive isolation mechanisms to develop.

   i. Allopatric speciation requires some type of physical separation that keeps two populations of a species from experiencing gene flow. Following are examples.

   a) A large lake may become divided into smaller ponds as an area of land rises and portions of the former lake dry out so that fish and other aquatic species no longer have contact with one another.

   b) A mountain range may gradually develop, dividing a species' habitat into two separate areas, so that one population of a species no longer has physical contact with another isolated population.

   ii. Eventually the populations must accumulate enough unique genetic changes so that, if the barrier is removed, individuals from the two populations are no longer able to sexually reproduce with one another.

2. *Sympatric speciation* occurs when populations of a species share the *same geographic area*, but become *reproductively isolated*—develop differences that keep the two populations from mating with one another or keep them from forming viable offspring or fertile offspring.

    i. *Prezygotic isolation mechanisms* act *before* a *zygote* is formed.

        a) *Habitat isolation* occurs when separated species prefer—and develop specialized adaptations that allow them to exploit—different habitats within the same potential home range, such as may develop when two populations of an insect species diverge to share different, distinct habitats located on the same tree.

        b) *Temporal isolation* occurs when separate species develop from populations that live or mate at different times of day or during different seasons.

        c) *Behavioral isolation* is when former members of a single species only prefer to mate with like members because they exhibit one particular type of behavior, such as when two populations of fireflies, which develop different light signal patterns for mating, evolve into two separate species.

        d) *Mechanical isolation* is when two former populations of a species cannot mate because they do not have the proper structures that allow mating to occur, such as when two different flower types have different structures that allow them to be pollinated only by different pollinators.

        e) *Gametic isolation* occurs if the sperm of one subpopulation are not able to fertilize the eggs of the members of another subpopulation of the same species, such as when flowering plants inhibit the growth of incompatible pollen that land on their stigmas, or when the sperm of one frog type is not recognized by receptor proteins on the eggs of another frog type.

    ii. *Postzygotic isolation* mechanisms act *after* a *zygote* is formed.

a) *Reduced hybrid viability* occurs when offspring between two separated species are produced, but are not viable (do not survive to sexual maturity).

b) *Reduced hybrid fertility* occurs when an offspring is produced by two separated species, and survives to adulthood, but is not able to mate either with like individuals or with either parent species, such as when the offspring of donkeys and horses produce mules that are sterile.

c) *Hybrid breakdown* occurs when the offspring of two separated species is viable and fertile, but, in the generations that follow, the resulting offspring are not viable.

Table 20.2 Summary of Types of Reproductive Isolating Mechanisms

Isolating Mechanism*	How It Happens
Prezygotic	*Act before a zygote is formed; the subpopulations...*
Habitat isolation	Begin to use different parts of a habitat
Temporal isolation	Begin to mate at different times
Behavioral isolation	Develop different mating behavior
Mechanical isolation	Develop different structures for the mating process
Gametic isolation	Develop gametes that do not recognize each other
Postzygotic	*Act after a zygote is formed; the subpopulations...*
Reduced hybrid viability	Produce offspring that have low survival rate
Reduced hybrid fertility	Produce offspring that have low fertility rate
Hybrid breakdown	Produce offspring whose offspring are feeble

*Each mechanism involves a different cause, but all have the same effect: the production of new species from a preexisting species because subpopulations can no longer mate and produce fertile, viable offspring.

CLASSIFICATION AND DIVERSITY

Chapter

21

I. Key Concepts

A. Carolus Linnaeus developed binomial nomenclature—the use of genus and species names to designate each organism—as well as the hierarchal taxonomic system using kingdom, phylum, class, order, family, genus, and species categories.

B. A domain is a classification category higher than a kingdom in which all eukaryotes belong to one domain—Eukarya—while prokaryotes are divided into two domains—Archaea and Bacteria.

C. A six-kingdom system of classification contains the kingdoms Archaebacteria, Eubacteria, Protista, Plantae, Fungi, and Animalia.

D. Phylogenetic trees and cladograms are diagrams showing evolutionary relationships between different groups of related organisms.

E. Viruses, viroids, and prions are subcellular, infectious entities that have some of the properties of living organisms.

F. The two major groups of prokaryotes—archaebacteria and eubacteria—differ in structure, biochemistry, and genetic sequences.

G. Protists are a diverse group of mostly unicellular eukaryotes.

H. Plants are derived from an autotrophic protist and developed evolutionary adaptations that allowed them to found terrestrial ecosystems.

I. Fungi are derived from a heterotrophic protist and most likely moved onto land along with plants in symbiotic relationships called *mycorrhizae*.

J. Animals are derived from a heterotrophic protist and are most closely related to fungi.

II. ***Taxonomy* is the naming and classification of organisms; *systematics* (also called *systematic taxonomy*) is a classification system based on *phylogenies*—evolutionary relationships between groups of organisms.**

A. Carolus *Linnaeus* developed the system of binomial nomenclature, as well as a hierarchical classification system from which modern taxonomy is derived.

1. *Binomial nomenclature* is a naming system that allows each species to have a unique scientific name.

   i. The *genus*—a more inclusive category than a species—is the first part of an organism's name.

   ii. The *species* name is the second part.

   iii. For example, the genus and species name of the American crow is *Corvus brachyrhyncos.*

      a) The genus name is capitalized, but the species name is not.

      b) By convention, a scientific name is italicized or underlined.

   iv. A scientific name may also show the degree of relatedness between two or more species, as shown in Table 21.1.

Table 21.1 Binomial Nomenclature

Common Name	Genus	Species	Relationship
American crow	*Corvus*	*brachyrhyncos*	The crow and the raven are more closely related than either is to the blue jay.
Raven	*Corvus*	*corvax*	
Blue jay	*Cyanocitta*	*cristata*	

Be prepared to determine, based on scientific names, the degree of relatedness between different species: species in the same genus are generally more closely related to one other than are species in different genera.

B. Linnaeus also developed a *hierarchical classification system* that includes seven different categories (or levels).

1. The highest level, the *kingdom*, is the most inclusive level and contains a large number of organisms that are more related to each other than to organisms in other kingdoms.

2. Each kingdom has a group of related *phyla*, and the organisms within each phylum are more related to each other than they are to the organisms in other phyla.

3. Each phylum contains a group of related *classes*, and so on.

   i. For example, all animals are classified in the same kingdom, Animalia, to which humans and all other animals belong.

   ii. The kingdom, Animalia, includes many different phyla, one of which is Chordata, to which all vertebrate and their close relatives belong.

   iii. Each phylum has many different classes, one of which is Mammalia, to which all vertebrates with hair belong, and so on.

Table 21.2 Hierarchical Classification System

Most Inclusive → → → → → → → → → → → → Least Inclusive						
Kingdom	Phylum	Class	Order	Family	Genus	Species
Animalia	Chordata	Mammalia	Primates	Hominidae	*Homo*	*sapiens*

2. Sometimes levels are divided into groupings that fall in between the levels, such as a "superclass" that falls between a phylum and a class, or a "subspecies" that is a group below the species level, and so on.

C. **Classification is an area of biology that undergoes steady changes as new fossils are found or as new ways to analyze the differences and similarities between organisms are developed—such as DNA sequence analysis.**

1. A *phylogenetic tree* is a diagram depicting the evolutionary relationships between groups of organisms, and is a working hypothesis.

Figure 21.1 A Phylogenetic Tree: Plant Evolution

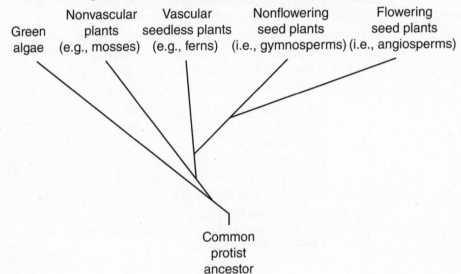

i. The types of homologies used to construct a phylogenetic tree can be morphological, embryological, or molecular.

ii. Many members of living and fossil groups are studied before a *phylogeny* is proposed.

iii. For some groups of organisms, there are competing phylogenetic hypotheses, because not enough data has been collected.

2. *Cladistics* is a branch of systematics that uses shared derived characteristics to construct *cladograms*.

Figure 21.2 A Cladogram: Chordate Evolution

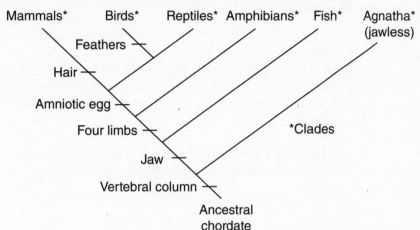

i. A *shared derived characteristic* is one that is shared by all members of a group, and not by members outside the group, as in the following example.

   a) A shared derived characteristic of mammals is hair.

   b) A vertebral column is a shared derived characteristic of all vertebrates.

ii. Any group that has a shared derived characteristic is called a *clade*.

   a) Mammals comprise a clade of organisms that have hair, but they are also part of the vertebrate clade (along with birds, reptiles, amphibians, and fish).

   b) Fish are members of the vertebrate clade, but not part of the mammalian clade.

iii. A shared derived characteristic is considered to have been present in a *common ancestor* of all the members of the clade, as illustrated in the following example.

   a) The common ancestor of all birds is assumed to have had feathers, because all birds do while other animals do not.

   b) The common ancestor of angiosperms is assumed to have had flowers: the defining feature—or shared derived characteristic—of all angiosperms.

D. A *domain* is a proposed level of classification higher than the kingdom.

    1. Prokaryotes are divided into two distinct groups called domains: *Archaea* and *Bacteria*.

    2. In the domain classification system, all eukaryotes are in a separate domain, called *Eukarya*, and are more closely related to those in the domain Archaea, than to those in the domain Bacteria.

Figure 21.3 Proposed Evolutionary Relationships Between Bacteria, Archaea, and Eukarya

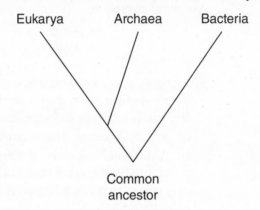

    3. In an alternative classification system, called the *six-kingdom system*, prokaryotes are split as in the domain system, and Eukarya is divided into four kingdoms: Protista, Fungi, Plantae, and Animalia.

Table 21.3 Comparison of the Three-Domain and the Six-Kingdom Systems of Classification

Prokaryotes (Fomerly Called *Monera*)		Eukaryotes			
Domain Archaea	Domain Bacteria	Domain Eukarya			
Kingdom Archaebacteria	*Kingdom Eubacteria*	*Kingdom Protista*	*Kingdom Fungi*	*Kingdom Plantae*	*Kingdom Animalia*
Unicellular		Both	Mostly multicellular		

III. **Viruses, viroids, and prions have some of the characteristics of living organisms, but are not made of cells.**

A. *Prions* are responsible for brain diseases in sheep (scrapie) and in cattle (mad cow disease).

1. Prions are proteins, which cannot self-replicate, but appear to infect mammalian brain cells.
2. They are misfolded proteins that enter brain cells, causing normal proteins to become misfolded.
3. This misfolding causes the proteins to clump, thereby destroying the cells.

B. *Viroids* are the smallest known unit that can self-replicate.

1. Smaller than viruses, viroids cause infectious diseases in plants.
2. They consist of a short, circularized, single-stranded RNA molecule with no surrounding protein.

C. *Viruses* are a diverse group of obligate, intracellular parasites that cause disease in cellular organisms.

1. Since viruses need to infect cells in order to reproduce, they most likely evolved after the origin of cells.
2. Viruses contain a nucleic acid molecule surrounded by a protein coat, and, sometimes, by an additional outer membrane covering.
   i. The protein coat surrounding a virus is called a *capsid*.
   ii. Some viruses have an outer membrane covering, called an *envelope*, that they obtain from the cells they infect.
      a) As this type of virus leaves an infected cell, it becomes enrobed by the cell's membrane.
      b) The membrane usually carries virus encoded proteins that help the new virus to recognize and infect other cells.

      iii. The *nucleic acid genome* of a virus can be either single-stranded or double-stranded DNA or RNA.

      iv. Some viruses may also carry a few of their own proteins from cell to cell within their capsid.

      v. Viruses do not contain ribosomes, tRNA, rRNA, amino acids, or any other component needed to make their own proteins: they use the host cell's infrastructure to carry out DNA and protein synthesis.

3. Viral replication depends on the type of nucleic acid the virus has.

      i. *DNA viruses* can enter a cell, shed their capsid, and either insert their genome into their host's DNA, or take over the host cell's transcription and translation machinery.

         a) DNA viruses cause the host cell to produce capsid proteins that are encoded by the viral DNA, as well as copies of the viral genome.

         b) Capsid proteins self-assemble to form protein coats that then encapsulate the new copies of viral DNA.

         c) The new viruses then leave the cell to infect more cells.

      ii. Some *RNA viruses*—called *retroviruses*—contain an enzyme, called *reverse transcriptase*, that reverses the transcription process by transcribing the virus's RNA into DNA.

         a) This copy of DNA can then integrate into the host's genome; viral DNA inserted into host DNA is called a *provirus*.

         b) Once integrated, it is transcribed and translated, causing production of capsid proteins and copies of its RNA that are used to make new viral particles.

         c) The new viruses leave the cell and infect other cells.

         d) *HIV* is a retrovirus that causes *AIDS*.

4. Viruses, called *bacteriophages*, infect bacteria.

      i. The bacteriophage, T4, alternates between a lysogenic and a lytic life cycle within bacteria.

a) In the *lysogenic cycle*, the phage inserts its DNA into the bacterial genome, where it waits until conditions are right for it switch to the lytic cycle.

b) In the *lytic cycle*, the phage reproduces by causing the bacteria to produce phage DNA and capsids; once assembled, they cause the bacterial cell to *lyse* (burst), releasing the many newly created phages.

 IV. *Prokaryotes* are a diverse, prolific group, and its members live in all types of environments.

A. **Prokaryotes have some similar features and others that vary from group to group.**

1. Similarities include the following.

    i. Most prokaryotes are smaller than eukaryotic cells— between the size of a mitochondrion and a nucleus.

    ii. Prokaryotes have no nucleus or organelles.

    iii. They have a single, circular chromosome, ribosomes, DNA polymerase, RNA polymerase, and most have a cell wall surrounding the plasma membrane.

    iv. Some bacteria have small, circular, extra-chromosomal DNA called *plasmids*.

2. Prokaryotes have different types of life styles.

    i. Many different types of *symbiotic* prokaryotes live on the outside and inside of many eukaryotes, including humans.

    ii. Other prokaryotes are *pathogens* of plants and animals and cause about half of the infectious diseases of humans, sometimes by producing toxins.

        a) Some prokaryotes produce toxins that they secrete, called *exotoxins*.

        b) Others produce *endotoxins* that are part of their outer covering.

    iii. Many prokaryotes are *saprobes* (decomposers) that live on dead organisms and organismal waste.

3. Some prokaryotes produce resistant spores called *endospores* that can remain dormant for long periods of time.
4. Different prokaryotes exhibit all four modes of nutrition.

Table 21.4 Modes of Nutrition

Mode of Nutrition	Description; Examples (Other Nonprokaryote Examples)
Photoautotrophy	Use light as an energy source and gain carbon from CO_2; cyanobacteria (also plants and some protists)
Chemoautotrophy	Use an inorganic energy source and gain carbon from CO_2; some archaebacteria
Photoheterotrophy	Use light as an energy source and gain carbon from organic sources; some prokaryotes
Chemoheterotrophy	Use an organic energy source and gain carbon from organic sources; most prokaryotes (also animals, fungi, and some protists)

5. Prokaryotes have different requirements for oxygen.
    i. *Obligate anaerobes* require an oxygen-free environment to live.
    ii. *Facultative anaerobes* can live with or without oxygen.
    iii. *Obligate aerobes* require oxygen to live.
6. Prokaryotes reproduce *asexually*, but they also have several methods of *genetic recombination*.
    i. *Transformation* occurs when a prokaryote takes up foreign DNA from its environment.
    ii. *Transduction* is when a virus transfers prokaryotic DNA from one cell to another.
    iii. *Conjugation* occurs when a plasmid is transferred from one prokaryote to another through a special tubelike structure called a *pilus* (pl. *pili*).

B. *Archaebacteria* **have some characteristics that are more similar to eukaryotes than to eubacteria ("true" bacteria).**

Table 21.5 Comparison of Archaebacteria and Eubacteria

Archaebacteria	Eubacteria
Several kinds of RNA polymerase	One kind of RNA polymerase
Initiator tRNA is methionine	Initiator tRNA is formyl-methionine
Some genes have introns	No introns
Not sensitive to some antibiotics	Sensitive to most antibiotics
Do not have peptidoglycan in cell wall	Have peptidoglycan in cell wall

1. Some archaebacteria live in extreme environments.
    i. *Methanogens* convert H_2 and CO_2 to methane gas (CH_4), and live in anaerobic environments, such as swamps, sewage, and the intestines of mammals.
    ii. *Extreme halophiles* live in high-salt environments, such as salt lakes.
    iii. *Thermoacidophiles* live in extremely hot, acidic environments, such as in hot springs or near deep sea vents in the ocean.
2. Other archaebacteria live in less extreme environments, such as in surface ocean water and in the soil.

C. *Eubacteria* **is a diverse group of prokaryotes distinguished by a number of physical and chemical characteristics.**

1. There are three basic shapes common in eubacteria: *bacilli* are rod shaped, *cocci* are spherical, and *spirilla* are spiral shaped.
2. *Gram-positive* eubacteria have a simple cell wall consisting of a thick layer of *peptidoglycan* (a molecule containing

short proteins and carbohydrates), while *gram-negative* eubacteria have a thinner cell wall with less peptidoglycan that is sandwiched between the plasma membrane and an additional lipid membrane to the exterior.

3. Eubacteria phyla are constantly undergoing revisions, but some major groups include the following.

    i. *Cyanobacteria* are photosynthetic.

        a) Some live in groups (*colonies*) that contain specialized cells—*heterocysts*—that produce nitrogen needed by the other cells in the group.

        b) Some are the photosynthetic partners in the symbioses known as *lichens* that grow on trees and rocks.

    ii. *Spirochetes* are a diverse group of heterotrophic spirilla.

    iii. *Gram-positive* bacteria (a group that also contains some gram-negative bacteria) are classified together because they have similar rRNA sequences and include bacteria found in the mouth and digestive tract of humans, bacteria used in yogurt production, and streptococci that cause strep throat.

    iv. *Proteobacteria* has three main subgroups.

        a) *Enteric bacteria* include salmonella that causes food poisoning, and other species that live in the human digestive tract, including *Escherichia coli*, which makes vitamin K.

        b) *Purple bacteria* (photoautotrophs and photoheterotrophs) carry out a type of photosynthesis that splits molecules such as H_2S—instead of H_2O—releasing sulfur gas instead of oxygen.

        c) *Chemoautotrophic proteobacteria* include the nitrogen fixing bacteria that live as symbionts in plant root nodules.

V. **Kingdom Protista includes the most diverse group of eukaryotes, most of which are unicellular.**

A. Most protists have mitochondria, and some have chloroplasts, both of which were derived by *endosymbiosis*. (See Chapter 18 for additional information on endosymbiosis.)

1. Mitochondria are absent in a few groups of protists.
2. Mitochondria and chloroplasts are derived from separate endosymbioses.
3. Different endosymbioses may be responsible for the distinct types of chloroplasts present in red, brown, and green algae.

B. Protist classification is constantly changing as new molecular data becomes available, but one possible classification scheme is shown in Table 21.6.

C. Historically, "animal-like" protists are called *protozoa*, and "plant-like" protists are called *algae*.

Table 21.6 Characteristics of the Major Groups of Protists

Group/Phyla	Characteristics	Examples
Archaezoa	**Lack mitochondria**	
Diplomonads	Mostly parasitic	*Giardia* (human parasite)
Trichomonads	Anaerobic, symbiotic	Termite symbiont
Euglenozoa	**Have flagella**	
Euglenoids	Autotrophic or mixotrophic	Euglena
Kinetoplastids	Kinetoplast organelle	Sleeping sickness pathogen
Alveolata	**Have alveoli (organelle)**	
Dinoflagellates	Mixotrophic or parasitic	Phytoplankton; red tides
Apicomplexans	Apical organelles	Animal parasites (malaria)
Ciliates	Have cilia and two nuclei	*Paramecium; Stentor*

(continued)

Table 21.6 (*continued*)

Group/Phyla	Characteristics	Examples
Amoeboids	***Have pseudopodia***	
Rhizopods	Thick pseudopodia	Amoeboid dysentery
Actinopods	Needlelike pseudopodia	Plankton
Foraminiferans	Needlelike pseudopodia	Plankton
Myxomycota	Have multinucleate form	Plasmodial slime molds
Acrasiomycota	Have multicellular form	Cellular slime molds
Stramenopila	***Flagella are branched***	
Bacillariophyta	Silica shells	Diatoms
Chrysophyta	Carotenes and xanthophylls	Golden algae
Phaeophyta	Large, multicellular algae	Brown algae (kelp)
Oomycota	No chloroplasts, large egg	Water molds; plant parasites
Rhodophyta	Phycobilins (pigments)	Red algae
Chlorophyta	Plantlike chloroplasts	Green algae, and photosynthetic partner in lichen symbiosis

D. Different groups of protists have unique physical or dietary features.

1. Some protists, including some Euglenoids and Dinoflagellates, are *mixotrophs*: a unique form of nutrition in which the organism can alternate between autotrophic and heterotrophic nutrition.

2. A *kinetoplast* is a special type of organelle that contains extranuclear DNA and is characteristic of one group of Euglenozoa: the Kinetoplastids.

3. An *alveolus* (pl. *alveoli*) is a small membrane-bound organelle that may function in water balance and is characteristic of the Alveolata.

4. An apical collection of organelles functions in many Apicomplexans during host cell penetration.

5. *Pseudopodia* are thick or thin projections of plasma membrane-bound cytoplasm that function in motility and feeding in many single-celled amoeba-like protists.

6. *Carotenes* and *xanthophylls* are accessory photosynthetic pigments characteristic of the, mostly unicellular, golden algae.

7. Another group of accessory pigments used in photosynthesis, called *phycobilins*, are characteristic of red algae.

E. **Red, brown, and green algae include seaweeds, and many have plantlike characteristics.**

1. *Brown algae* are the largest protists, are all multicelluar, have chloroplasts, and some have an alternation of generations life cycle.

2. *Red algae* are mostly multicellular, have chloroplasts different from those of brown algae, and life cycles are diverse (but many have alternation of generations).

3. *Green algae* include unicellular, colonial, and multicellular (seaweed) types, have chloroplasts similar to plant chloroplasts, and are the protists most closely related to plants.

F. **Each of the multicellular groups of eukaryotes—fungi, plants, and animals—most likely descended from different protist ancestors.**

 VI. ***Fungi*** **are eukaryotic heterotrophs with mitochondria; they have extracellular digestion, absorbing nutrients from dead organisms, wastes, or host organisms.**

A. **Many fungi share similar structural features.**

1. The cell walls of fungi contain *chitin*—a polymer of glucose.

2. The body of a fungus, called a *mycelium* (pl. *mycelia*), is composed of many interwoven, threadlike, *hyphae* (sing. *hypha*).

   i. Most fungi have multicellular hyphae in which the cells are separated by walls, called *septa* (sing. *septum*).

ii. *Coenocytic* fungi have hyphae that are not separated into cells by septa, but instead have a continuous stream of cytoplasm containing many nuclei.

iii. The cells of some fungal mycelia are *dikaryotic* (contain two nuclei), because some types of sexual reproduction in fungi involve *plasmogamy* (the fusion of the cytoplasm of two cells) without *karyogamy* (the fusion of the cells' two nuclei).

3. Some parasitic fungi have hyphae specialized for feeding called *haustoria*.

B. **The major groups of fungi, called *divisions* (instead of phyla), are distinguished mainly by their type of sexual reproduction, as shown in Table 21.7.**

Table 21.7 Characteristics of the Major Divisions of Fungi

Division	Characteristics	Examples
Chytridiomycota (chytrids)	Most ancient group; unicellular or coenocytic	Many saprobes and parasites
Zygomycota (zygomycetes)	Zygosporangia for sexual reproduction; coenocytic	Black bread mold (*Rhizopus stolonifer*), some mycorrhizae
Ascomycota (sac fungi)	Ascospores for sexual reproduction and conidia for asexual reproduction	Unicellular yeasts, cup fungi, morels, *Penicillium*, common fungal partners in lichen symbiosis, some mycorrhizae
Basidiomycota (club fungi)	Basidiospores for sexual reproduction	Unicellular yeasts, mushrooms, puffballs, rusts, shelf fungi

VII. *Plants* **are multicelluar eukaryotes; almost all plants are photoautotrophs with chloroplasts that carry out photosynthesis, with cell walls containing cellulose, and with embryos that are protected and nourished within the parent body.**

A. Plants were some of the first organisms to colonize land and, therefore, exhibit specific adaptations for living in a relatively dry environment.

1. The epidermis of the plant shoot is covered by a waxy *cuticle,* which protects the plant from drying out; *stomata* in the leaves and stems allow for gas exchange with the environment.

2. Plants produce reproductive *spores* covered by a hard, durable coat that allows them to be dispersed in the air without drying out and to remain dormant until environmental conditions are right for germination and growth.

3. Roots and vascular tissue allow the plant to obtain water and transport it, as well as nutrients, throughout the plant.

   i. Most plant roots form symbiotic relationships with fungi, called *mycorrhizae,* which increase their surface area for water absorption.

   ii. Most plants also have *xylem* for transporting water and minerals from the soil to the rest of the plant, and *phloem* for transporting the products of photosynthesis from the leaves to the rest of the plant.

   iii. In addition, xylem, especially when it is strengthened by *lignin,* supports the plant body so it can become taller to gather sufficient sunlight.

4. Some plants have also developed seeds and pollen.

   i. *Pollen* allows for protection and dormancy of sperm during dispersal through the air.

   ii. *Seeds* allow for dormancy, longer-range dispersal of offspring, and provide embryos with nourishment while they germinate.

5. *Flowers*, and the *fruits* that develop from them, are an additional adaptation providing for extended protection of seeds during their production and development, and aid in dispersal of pollen and seeds.

B. **Evolution favored plants with a sturdy, long-lived diploid form—the *sporophyte*—in preference to the haploid form— the *gametophyte*.**

1. In bryophytes, the gametophyte is the dominant form of the organism.
2. In seedless and seeded vascular plants, the sporophyte is the dominant form.

C. **All plants are *monophyletic*—that is, they are derived from a common ancestor.**

1. The closest relatives of plants are *charophytes*, a type of green algae.
2. The adaptations previously mentioned developed over time in some groups of plants.
3. The evolutionary relationships between the existing plant phyla (also called *divisions*) are shown in the phylogenetic tree in Figure 21.1.
4. The major characteristics of each plant phylum are listed in Table 21.8.

Table 21.8 Characteristics of the Major Phyla of Plants

Group/Phyla	Characteristics	Examples
Nonvascular plants	*No true vascular tissue, no seeds, gametophyte is dominant*	
Bryophyta	Soft, mat-like appearance	Mosses
Hepatophyta	Gemmae for asexual reproduction	Liverworts
Anthocerophyta	Gametophyte is phallic shaped	Hornworts

(continued)

Table 21.8 (*continued*)

Group/Phyla	Characteristics	Examples
Seedless vascular plants	*Vascular tissue, no seeds, sporophyte is dominant*	
Lycophyta	Most are extinct trees	Club mosses, many epiphytes*
Sphenophyta	Most are extinct trees	Horsetails, *Equisetum*
Pterophyta	Frond leaves, spores located in sori	Ferns
Nonflowering seed plants	*Vascular tissue, seeds, pollen, sporophyte is dominant*	
(Gymnosperms)	(plants with "naked seeds")	
Gnetophyta	Three genera, not closely related	*Welwitschia, Gnetum, Ephedra*
Cycadophyta	Resemble palms	Cycads
Ginkgophyta	Fan-shaped deciduous leaves	Ginkgo
Coniferophyta	Cone-bearing trees and shrubs	Pines, spruces, yews, firs
Flowering seed plants	*Vascular tissue, seeds, pollen, sporophyte is dominant*	
(Angiosperms)	(flowering plants)	
Anthophyta	Flowers, fruit	Herbaceous plants, trees, shrubs
Monocots	One cotyledon, parallel veins	Corn, grasses, oat, rye, lily
Dicots	Two cotyledons, net-veined leaf	Oak, pea, daisy, rose, okra

*epiphytes—nonphotosynthetic, nonparasitic plants that live on other plants

VIII. **Kingdom *Animalia* contains multicellular, heterotrophic eukaryotes that are most closely related to kingdom Fungi.**

A. Differences in body type—which have their bases in development—are the major criteria used to classify animals into phyla.

1. *Tissue types* are determined by embryonic germ layers in animals.

   i. Some animals do not have true tissues.

   ii. Others are *diploblastic,* having two tissue layers: ectoderm (outer) and endoderm (inner).

   iii. Most are triploblastic, having three tissue layers: *ectoderm, mesoderm* (middle), and *endoderm.*

2. *Body symmetry* can be either radial or bilateral.

   i. Animals with *radial symmetry* have a circular arrangement of body parts.

   ii. Animals with *bilateral symmetry* have dorsal (back) and ventral (front) surfaces, anterior (head) and posterior (tail) ends, and two sets of lateral (side) body parts that are generally mirror images.

   iii. *Cephalization,* the formation of a head with major sense organs, is closely associated with bilateral symmetry.

3. The arrangement of *body cavities* among animal groups varies. (See "Development" in Chapter 16 for further descriptions of developmental differences in animals.)

   i. *Acoelomates* have a solid body plan without a coelom cavity.

   ii. *Pseudocoelomates* have a coelom partially lined with mesoderm.

   iii. *Coelomates* have a coelom fully lined with mesoderm tissue.

4. In addition, coelomates can exhibit either protostome or deuterostome development.

   i. In *protostomes* ("first mouth"), the mouth is formed from the blastopore and the anus is formed from the other opening, and determinate, spiral cleavage is common.

ii. In *deuterostomes* ("second mouth"), the opposite mouth/anus arrangement occurs, and cleavage is often indeterminate and radial. (See "Development" in Chapter 16 for further information on these differences.)

B. **Characteristics of the major animal phyla are listed in Table 21.9.**

Table 21.9 Characteristics of the Major Phyla of Animals

Group/Phyla	Characteristics	Examples
Parazoa	*No true tissues, no symmetry*	
Porifera	Sessile[1] adult, no nerves or muscles, choanocytes: cells for filter feeding[2]	Sponges
Eumetazoa	*True tissues*	
Radiata	*Two tissue layers, radial symmetry, gastrovascular cavity[3]*	
Cnidaria	Sessile (polyp) and motile (medusa)	Jelly, hydra, coral
Ctenophora	Small, motility by ciliated combs	Comb jelly
Bilateria	*Bilateral symmetry*	
Acoelomates	*No coelom*	
Platyhelminthes	Flat body, free-living or parasitic	Planaria, tapeworm
Pseudocoelomates	*Coelom partly lined with mesoderm*	
Rotifera	Many are smaller than protists, some reproduce by parthenogenesis[4]	Rotifers
Nematoda	Round slender worms	Hookworm, pinworm
Coelomates	*Coelom fully lined with mesoderm*	

(continued)

Table 21.9 (*continued*)

Group/Phyla	Characteristics	Examples
Protostomes	*Mouth forms from blastopore*	
Nemertea	Anterior proboscis for feeding	Proboscis worms
Lophophorates	Lophophore for filter feeding	Bryozoans, brachiopods
Mollusca	Muscular foot, mantle, visceral mass	Snail, squid, oyster
Annelida	Segmented body	Earthworm
Arthropoda	Jointed appendages, exoskeleton	Lobster, insects, spiders
Deuterostomes	*Anus forms from blastopore*	
Echinodermata	Adult has radial symmetry	Sea star, sea urchin
Chordata	Embryonic notochord, dorsal nerve cord, postanal tail, pharyngeal slits	Close relatives of vertebrates, and vertebrates; e.g., shark, amphibian, fish, reptile, bird, mammal, hagfish

[1] *sessile*—not able to move from place to place
[2] *filter feeding*—filter feeders have structures for straining food from water
[3] *gastrovascular cavity*—digestive cavity with one opening
[4] *partenogenesis*—a type of asexual reproduction in which unfertilized eggs develop into offspring

    1. The circulatory systems of animals may be open or closed.
        i. In an *open circulatory system*, the circulating fluid—often called *hemolymph*—is pumped through vessels to tissues where it leaves the vessels and directly bathes the tissues, and then is returned to the vessels.

       ii. In a *closed circulatory system* the circulating fluid, called *blood*, is confined to vessels, and is in contact with the tissues through capillaries instead of leaving the circulatory system in the tissues.

         a) Most mollusks and arthropods (for example, crustaceans, insects, and spiders) have open circulatory systems.

         b) Some mollusks (such as squids and octopuses), earthworms, proboscis worms, and chordates have closed circulatory systems.

  2. Animals also differ in the general type of digestive system they have.

       i. Some animals, such as cnidarians and flatworms, have a *gastrovascular cavity* with one opening that acts as both mouth and anus.

       ii. Protostomes and deuterostomes generally have a *complete digestive tract* with a separate mouth and anus.

B. All *vertebrates* (and a few related groups) belong to the phylum Chordata, and have four distinctive characteristics that are always present during embryonic development. (Note: All animals that are not vertebrates are called *invertebrates*.)

  1. All chordate embryos have a stiff, flexible rod running longitudinally through the body—called a *notochord*—that is replaced in the adult by the vertebral column in vertebrates, a subgroup of chordates.

  2. The *dorsal hollow nerve cord* develops into the brain and spinal cord in most vertebrates.

  3. *Pharyngeal slits (and pouches)* develop into the gills of fish and amphibians, and into other structures in other groups of vertebrates, such as certain jaw and auditory structures.

  4. A *postanal tail* (one posterior to the anus) develops into a muscular tail in most vertebrates.

  5. The evolutionary relationships among chordates are shown in the cladogram in Figure 21.2, and the major characteristics of vertebrate groups are shown in Table 21.10.

Table 21.10 Characteristics of the Major Vertebrate Classes

Superclass/Class	Characteristics	Examples
Agnatha	**Vertebrates without jaws**	
Myxini	Mouth has short tentacles	Hagfish
Cephalaspidomorphi	Mouth has adhesive sucker	Lamprey
Gnathostomata	**Vertebrates with jaws**	
Chondrichthyes	Aquatic, cartilaginous skeleton	Sharks, skates, rays
Osteichthyes	Aquatic, bony skeleton, two-chambered heart	Fish
Amphibia	Four limbs, has metamorphosis from aquatic to terrestrial form, three-chambered heart	Frogs, salamanders, newts, etc.
Reptilia	Four limbs, amniotic egg, lungs, scales, mostly terrestrial, three-chambered heart	Snakes, turtles, lizards, dinosaurs, alligators
Aves	Four limbs, amniotic egg, lungs, feathers, hollow bones, toothless, four-chambered heart	Birds: e.g., blue jay, lark, penguin, ostrich, eagle
Mammalia	Four limbs, amniotic development, lungs, hair, mammary glands, four-chambered heart	Platypus, kangaroo, bat, human, whale, mouse

C. **There are three main types of mammals that differ in the details of their reproduction.**

1. *Monotremes* are egg-laying mammals, and include platypuses and spiny anteaters.

2. *Marsupials*, such as kangaroos and wombats, give birth to young before they are fully mature and the young develop further in an external pouch.
3. In *placental mammals* (also called *eutherians*) the young complete development in the uterus.

D. Humans belong to the mammalian order, *Primates*, which has two suborders.

1. The *prosimians* include lemurs and tarsiers.
2. The *anthropoids* include monkeys, gibbons, orangutans, gorillas, chimpanzees, humans, and their fossilized relatives.

SPECIAL SKILLS FOR
EXPERIMENT-BASED
QUESTIONS

I. **The questions on the SAT E/M Biology Subject Test vary in the amount of time required to complete them.**

A. How long a question takes to answer depends on a number of factors.

1. One factor is *how familiar you are with the material*: the more you know, the less time you will spend on a question.

2. Another factor is *how the question is structured*: questions that require more reading and/or more analysis will take longer to complete.

B. In general, there are three question lengths in approximately equal numbers on the test: questions that take less than 15 seconds, those that take less than 1 minute, and those that take a little longer than 1 minute.

1. Fact recall, matching, definitions, locating a data point on a graph, locating a structure on a diagram, and so forth take the shortest amount of time.

   i. You have 60 minutes to answer 80 questions, so these questions will only take up a total about 5 minutes if you are well prepared for them.

   ii. This will allow you to spend more time on the questions that take longer.

2. Another third of the questions generally take less than 60 seconds to answer.

    i. Story problems in genetics, considering complex examples, considering true and false statements about a given situation, comparing complex processes (such as mitosis and meiosis, or photosynthesis and cellular respiration) are examples.

    ii. Most of these questions are single questions (as opposed to question sets).

    iii. These questions will take about 15 to 20 minutes of your total time to answer if you are well prepared for them.

3. The final third of the questions require the most time because they involve the most reading as well as analysis of a large, complex data set.

    i. You need to be well prepared for the test so you can answer the questions that take the least amount of time in approximately 20 to 25 minutes.

    ii. That will leave you with about 35 to 40 minutes to (calmly) read and answer the longer question sets.

    iii. There are about 6 to 7 sets of these questions with between 2 and 5 questions per set.

    iv. The question sets usually fall at the end of the first core of 60 questions (which everyone answers), and at the end of either the E or M subtest (which consists of 20 questions). (Remember, you only take either the E subtest, or the M subtest.)

    v. The *order of the question types* is as follows:

        a) *Shorter questions* (matching and single questions)

        b) *Three to four longer question sets*

        c) *Shorter questions* (as you start the E or M section)

        d) *Two to three longer question sets* (at the end of the E or M section)

    vi. This location is of advantage to you, because most of the questions that generally take the shortest amount of time come first, allowing you to move rapidly through them without long pauses to read extensive material.

vii. The rest of the information in this chapter is designed to help you develop the best skills and strategies for approaching the longer question sets with confidence.

II. Calculators are not allowed on the SAT Biology E/M Subject Test.

A. Be proficient with basic operations (addition, subtraction, multiplication, and division) involving whole numbers, fractions, and decimals.

B. Be proficient with exponents and square roots of perfect squares.

III. Be proficient with basic algebraic concepts.

A. Be proficient in rearranging equations and solving equations with one variable, such as in the following example.

$p + q = 1$, solve for p when q is 0.1 (answer: $p = 0.9$)

B. Be able to perform substitution, such as in the following example.

What is $2pq$ when p is 0.2 and q is 0.8? (answer: $2pq = 0.32$)

IV. Be proficient at reading and interpreting graphs and data sets.

A. Be proficient in identifying independent and dependent variables in experiments and on graphs.

1. An *independent variable* is the variable in an experiment that is manipulated (changed) by the experimenter, and on which a second variable usually depends.

2. The *dependent variable* is the variable that is measured in an

experiment as the independent variable is changed; i.e., it is dependent on the independent variable.

3. By convention, the independent variable is usually plotted along the *x-axis*, and the dependent variable is usually plotted along the *y-axis*.

B. Be proficient in reading data from a chart or graph.

1. Use a straight edge to locate the point on a graph corresponding to an *x* (or *y*) value.

2. Then use the straight edge to locate the corresponding *y* (or *x*) value.

3. For example, in the graph in Figure 22.1, the *x* value of 20 degrees corresponds to a *y* value of approximately 26 mol/min.

Figure 22.1 Independent and Dependent Variables

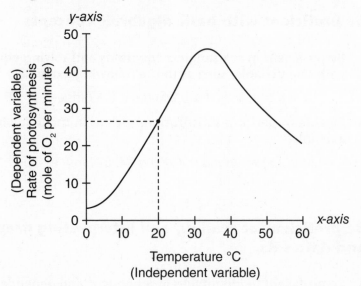

C. Be proficient in matching graphs with different types of relationships between the two variables, as illustrated in Figure 22.2.

Figure 22.2 Graphical Representations of Various Relationships Between Variables

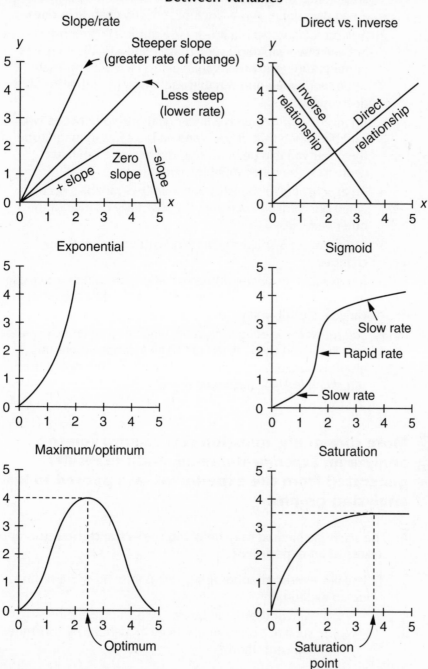

1. The steeper the *slope* of a line, the greater the rate of change; also, notice the graphical difference between a positive slope, a negative slope, and a slope of zero (no change in rate).

2. A *direct relationship* is a linear (straight line) relationship between two variables, such that, if one variable increases in magnitude, the other variable also increases by a set value (and when one variable decreases, the other variable decreases).

3. An *inverse relationship* is a linear relationship between two variables, such that, if one variable increases in magnitude, the other variable decreases (and when one variable decreases, the other variable increases).

4. An *exponential relationship* between two variables occurs when one variable increases exponentially relative to the other variable.

5. A *sigmoid* (or S-shaped) curve indicates a series of rate changes.

6. A *maximum* (or *optimum*) occurs when one variable increases for a time, levels off, and then decreases, while the other variable steadily increases.

7. *Saturation* (or *leveling off*) occurs when one variable increases for a time and then "levels off." The location where the graph is horizontal (or near horizontal) is often called the *saturation level*, or *saturation point*.

 More commonly, question sets require you to analyze an *experimental setup*, and the results generated from the experiment, as opposed to just analyzing graphs.

A. The *scientific method* may help you understand the setup and results of an experiment.

1. Usually, a researcher has a *hypothesis* in mind while setting up an experiment.

   i. A hypothesis can be in the form of a *question*, such as "Is enzyme activity influenced by substrate concentration?"

   ii. A hypothesis can also be stated in an "*if, then*" format, such as "If enzyme activity is influenced by substrate concentration, and an enzyme's activity is measured at different substrate concentrations, then the rate of enzyme activity will change when different concentrations of substrate are tested."

2. An experimental setup usually involves *changing an independent variable*, and measuring the change in a dependent variable.

   i. For example, the different substrate concentrations at which an enzyme reaction occurs could be an independent variable, and the amount of product formed at the different concentrations could be the dependent variable measured.

   ii. All *other variables* that may also affect enzyme activity—such as pH, enzyme concentration, and temperature—*should be held constant* during the experiment so that any change in the dependent variable is the result of changing only the independent variable.

   iii. The *dependent variable* is usually *measured* (sometimes indirectly); for example, the amount of product produced during a given time period (such as production of a gaseous product or a product that changes the color of a pH indicator per minute) can be reported as the rate of the chemical reaction.

3. *A control* is generally included in an experiment to define *a reference point* (or *baseline*) for comparing changes.

   i. The result of the control is generally known in advance.

   ii. For example, an enzyme reaction without any substrate is expected to show no enzyme activity, and therefore acts as a *negative control*.

4. The *results* of an experiment are usually *specific data* and may be in the form of *a table, a chart, a graph, or a written or pictorial description.*

5. *Analyzing results* involves *comparing the data obtained* under the different experimental conditions or between control and experimental conditions.

   i. You may be required to *recognize various patterns in the data*, such as those shown in Figure 22.2, or similar patterns shown in data tables or pictures.

   ii. Results answer questions presented in the original hypothesis (which is often unstated, as opposed to being directly stated, in the test material).

6. *Drawing conclusions* requires the highest level of reasoning skills.

   i. You may be asked to choose a statement that is a *reasonable conclusion* for one particular result, or for the entire set of data presented.

     a) Determine *which part of the data* needs to be considered for the particular question and focus your attention on it.

     b) Or, determine if *all the data* needs to be considered to draw the conclusion.

   ii. Alternatively, you may be asked to choose *a conclusion that cannot be drawn* from the experimental results.

     a) In this type of question, all the other answer choices will be conclusions that could be drawn from the data.

     b) The best way to keep a clear record of your thoughts regarding the answer choices is to place a "Y" for yes next to those choices (in the test booklet) that are conclusions.

     c) Or (and this is true of any negatively worded question) mark the answer choices with a "T" for true or an "F" for false.

     d) Negatively worded questions may take the form, "Which of the following is not a conclusion that can be drawn from the data?"

     e) Or it may say, "All of the following conclusions can be drawn from the data, EXCEPT . . . "

VI. **What is the best way to approach the analytical question sets?**

A. **The analytical question sets take more time to read and answer than single, stand-alone questions.**

1. Answer the shorter questions at the beginning of the test first; don't rush through the shorter questions, but move as quickly and carefully through them as you can.

2. When you come to the question sets, it is not uncommon to panic when you see how much material you have to read; you wonder how you will ever be able to absorb all the material and apply it rapidly enough.

3. *There are three good reasons you should not panic.*

   i. You have paced yourself well during the shorter questions, and have plenty of time left over to devote to the longer question sets.

   ii. It takes less time to effectively read the longer question sets than you might think at first glance.

   iii. You may not need to examine all parts of the material in detail.

4. So, don't panic, breathe deeply, and approach these question sets with confidence.

B. **The best strategy for efficiently answering question sets is to** *focus on one question set at a time.*

1. *First,* briefly read all material provided for a question set, including the questions (this will tell you scope and depth of your task).

   i. Glance over the material first to gather the following information.

   a) What are the different parts of the material? Say to yourself (for example), "There is an explanation of an experimental design, a chart with the data results, and a graph."

   b) Note the number of questions. Say to yourself (for example), "There are three questions I must answer."

      ii. Then, very quickly read all the words and numbers in both the material and the question.
- a) Do this rapidly.
- b) Do it only to get an idea of all the information available to you.
- c) Do not concentrate on understanding every detail yet.

2. *Next,* read the first question carefully, including all the answer choices.

      i. Read the answer choices critically, and cross out any that are clearly incorrect.

      ii. Determine which part of the material you need to focus on. (Experimental setup questions often come first, followed by data questions, followed by conclusion questions.)

      iii. Now focus on (and read carefully) the parts of the material you need to answer that question.

      iv. If you need to, refer back to the data while eliminating the rest of the wrong answer choices, or to confirm the correct answer choice you're considering.

3. *Finally,* fill in the oval on the scoring sheet for the first question, and then repeat the steps for the rest of the questions in the set.

      i. Avoid the temptation to start on the next set of questions until you have answered all the questions in a set.

      ii. As a last resort—if you have eliminated at least one wrong answer choice—it is better to guess at an answer before moving on to a new question set, because it will take more time to get back into the question once you leave the question set.

      iii. If you have time for a final review *after* you have completed the *entire* test, then go back and reattempt *any* test question you are not sure about.

iv. Circling the number of *any* test question you may want to recheck as you work your way through the entire test is the best way to quickly find those questions if you have time for a final review of your test.

C. **Taking as many practice tests as possible will allow you to become familiar with the types of questions on the test, to learn how to pace yourself effectively, and to develop the necessary analytical skills to handle all the test questions as efficiently and successfully as possible.**

INDEX

Notes

Notes

Notes

Notes

Notes

Notes

Notes

Notes